For Professor George F. Kennan,
with respectful greetings and
good wishes,
Andrkley

Belgrade, 1961.

Daring Diplomacy

DARING DIPLOMACY

The Case of the First American Ultimatum

ANDOR KLAY

THE UNIVERSITY OF MINNESOTA PRESS
MINNEAPOLIS

PRINTED AT THE NORTH CENTRAL PUBLISHING COMPANY, ST. PAUL

Library of Congress Catalog Card Number: 57-7809

PUBLISHED IN GREAT BRITAIN, INDIA, AND PAKISTAN BY THE OXFORD UNIVERSITY PRESS, LONDON, BOMBAY, AND KARACHI

AUTHOR'S NOTE

THIS book, the first on the subject, represents an attempt to render a full account of a singular incident in American diplomatic history, one which led to the dispatching of the first American ultimatum.

The events traced herein through official records, little-known documents, and unpublished sources took place in the formative years of our Foreign Service. Transoceanic cables were nonexistent. Most diplomatic and consular officers were predisposed to take no initiative in any important respect for fear of compromising their government. They spent a good deal of their time penning elaborate descriptions of situations that had changed completely by the time the reports reached their destinations. In contrast, the present chronicle highlights the enterprise and courage of certain American representatives abroad who made grave decisions without the benefit of past precedent, and took firm and swift action without instructions from their superiors in Washington.

Although this book rests on research material ordinarily associated with scholarly endeavor, it has not been cast in that orthodox format over which so grimly presides, like the sacred bird of ancient Egypt whose name it brings to mind, the great "Ibid." Not one "passim," "loc. cit.," "supra," or as little as a coy "cf." was allowed to intrude. Analyses of legal issues, diplomatic techniques, and historical ramifications were not pursued beyond a point where the book's primary purposes no longer demanded them and where the interest of the nonspecialist could be expected to recede or terminate. For the use of the specialist, a list of sources was placed at the end of the book together with a guide to official collections of basic documentation. Details of certain movements, and characterizations of certain attitudes, when given without attribution to specific sources, were drawn from or closely based on miscellaneous contemporary correspondence, personal memorandums, and other records, with only a modicum of reconstructed local color added. Records not specifically identified in the book because of their relative unimportance are extant in private collections made accessible to me, or in my own collection.

Shorter or longer detours taken from the main route of the fact-finding excursion were intended to illuminate the subject in its broader context and bring to light certain data not previously published or not easily obtainable elsewhere. Occasional spontaneous "asides" in the main text or in footnotes were inspired by the example of Plutarch who, interrupting himself in his Life of Pericles to pass on some gossip from here and there, remarks with a smile visible over the vast distance of eighteen centuries that "these things coming into my memory as I am writing this story, it would be unnatural for me to omit them." By the same token, it may be mentioned here that the passive hero of this book was born, as I was, in Hungary; fought, like some of my forebears, in the Hungarian uprising of 1848–49; became, like myself, a naturalized citizen of the United States; and owed his life to Americans who had, as I have, the honor to be in the service of the United States government.

A hundred years ago, on the floor of the House of Representatives during a debate of the case herein presented, it was declared that "the spot on which a person entitled to the protection of our Government stands, whether at home or abroad, is as inviolable as the sanctuary of the gods." In that spirit, this book is dedicated to everyone everywhere who is persecuted because he wants to be free.

⌄ ACKNOWLEDGMENTS

I WISH to recognize obligations of a personal kind by expressing here my grateful thanks to the Honorable Robert N. Wilkin, United States judge (retired) for the Northern District of Ohio, for help in locating Martin Koszta's long lost original Declaration of Intention; to the Honorable Lionel K. Legge, associate justice of the Supreme Court of the state of South Carolina, for assistance in the research on Duncan N. Ingraham's personal history; to Ambassador Christian M. Ravndal, Robert M. McKisson, Leslie C. Tihany, and other officers of the Department of State and the Foreign Service, for their stimulating interest and occasional help; to the Honorable John A. Blatnik, member of Congress from Minnesota, for his discussion of the Koszta case on the floor of the House of Representatives on the basis of my articles in the *American Foreign Service Journal* and *Coronet Magazine*; to Jeanne Sinnen, editor on the staff of the University of Minnesota Press, for highly valuable assistance; to Mrs. Joseph Dach of Washington, D.C., for helpful suggestions; and especially to my wife, for constant help through the evenings and weekends during which, because of my full-time employment of a different nature, both the research and the writing had to be done.

A. K.

Washington, D.C.

CONTENTS

ILLUSTRATIONS

DARING DIPLOMACY

Prologue

PROLOGUE

THE town is softly silhouetted against the blue-gray sky of twilight. A few fading sunrays still quiver on the multicolored flags which dangle from masts of vessels anchored at this free port, but the cypress-studded cemeteries beyond the bay are already obscured. The heavy blanket of salty air is occasionally punctured by the nasal tenor of a Moslem cantor wailing on the balcony of a slender minaret at the foot of Mount Pagus. Swift little caïques dart to and fro like so many waterbugs as sailors return to ships and native traders withdraw to shore.

Throughout the inner city a movement resembling a multiple change of guard is in progress. Daytime crowds yield the town to hordes of the night which now invade it through narrow alleys and winding back streets. A bizarre panorama of costumes is seen: rich silken gowns, ragged beggar raiment, sober European dresses, fancy turbans and fezzes, African tunics, embroidered Albanian dolmans and Egyptian capes, Greek breeches looking like pantalooned petticoats or petticoated pantaloons — all merging into a cacophony of attires.

As the stroller slowly makes his way on the battered, dung-littered flagstones, he is jostled by an Armenian cobbler carrying a long-handled last on his shoulder, or elbowed by a swaggering Turkish corporal who uses his saber as a walking stick, or perhaps

3

prodded from behind by a nanny goat which, with heavy udders, slim ankles, and sluggist gait, resembles some elderly odalisque. The foot-traveler had better hug the wall of the nearest dilapidated house to let pass a phlegmatic camel laden with huge bundles or carrying a saddle-bench which sags under the bulk of an over-nourished local dignitary. Boisterous dervishes and quarrelsome vendors gabble and gesticulate; two porters throw dice in front of a grimy little tavern as a third one watches, bemusedly picking his nose; half-naked children and mangy stray dogs are underfoot; flies swarm overhead; the stench of rotting fish, seaweed, and tar is nearly suffocating. And yet, the arabesqued arches of the Bazaar in the twilight, and the scampering native women with dark eyes glittering over nose-veils, exude an atmosphere that transports the visitor into the midst of the magic Thousand-and-One Nights.

This is Smyrna in the mid-nineteenth century, incorrigible old roué among towns of antiquity, member of the so-called Homeric League of cities claiming Homer's nativity, destroyed by neighboring Lydia in the sixth century before the birth of Christ, rebuilt on its old site according to plans prepared by Iskander whom we call Alexander the Great, leveled by earthquake early in the Christian era, rebuilt once again under the Roman emperor Marcus Aurelius, seized by Turkish pirates, ruled by the Knights of St. John, ravaged by Tartars, swept by plague and fire, indomitably emerging again and again as a perennial threshold between East and West.

Each day at this early evening hour traffic converges on streets leading to popular cafés and houses of well-earned ill repute. Many a fugitive from civil or military law, soldier of fortune, *agent provocateur*, and professional assassin floats in with the human tide which inundates the thoroughfares.

From a small coffeehouse at water's edge a buzz of conversation filters to the outside through ragged patches of a curtain of smoke. Part of the café juts out over the bay, supported by spikes driven into the ground, forming an open balcony surrounded by railing. Low chairs and small oval-shaped tables serve the convenience of guests who wish to enjoy the tepid evening breeze and a broad view of the harbor. Such a guest is now sitting out here alone: a youngish

4

man of massive build, with a short brown beard, dressed in a suit neither oriental nor quite occidental in design.

Smoking a nargileh and taking an occasional sip from a small cup as he gazes out to sea, he is unaware of the surreptitious approach of three men slowly moving toward him from behind. Suddenly they hurl themselves at him: one is at his throat, another grabs his arms, the third lifts him up. He can utter no more than a muffled sound before he is thrown into the water directly below. The attackers jump in after him.

The victim's outcries as he struggles desperately to keep his head above water cannot pierce the din outside the café. No one is nearby on the balcony to prevent the abduction. Passers-by in the narrow side street dare not interefere; too many corpses have been washed ashore lately, some of them probably those of bystanders with a sudden impulse to mix in other people's shady business.

A small skiff with four men in it is rapidly approaching the spot. In a moment, the splashing, panting prey is knocked unconscious with an oar; he is dragged up into the boat which sways violently and almost capsizes in the process, and now the oarsmen pull away, steering toward a huge ship anchored at a short distance.

In a few minutes no sign or sound of the disturbance remains on the scene. The moon presides in silent dignity over stars above and jabbering waves below.

The events of this evening, and their consequences during weeks and months to follow, came to cause portly ambassadors and suave foreign ministers to lose their composure, admirals and generals to utter oaths worthy of the best traditions of the services, legislators to point with pride or view with alarm, savants of international law to pore over large pages of small print in thick volumes stacked high, and crusading editors to write blazing philippics.

On this evening of July 22, 1853, somebody, a nobody named Martin Koszta, native of Hungary, fugitive from Austria, resident of America, and visitor in Turkey, made a fortuitous entry from a café at Smyrna into the hall of history as a significant figure in mankind's march toward freedom.

Backstage

BACKSTAGE I

EVERY window in Europe was rattling in the gale of newly awakened national consciousness that swept across the old continent as the first half of the nineteenth century was drawing to a close.

Institutions considered unshakable came crashing down, governments toppled, thrones were shattered. Streets were full of frightened police, piazzas were teeming with singing mobs under flags of every color, shots swished through the air from balconies and barricades, infernal machines exploded in public buildings, roofs were set on fire, screams sounded from alleyways, volleys were fired into crowds.

Revolutions broke out from the Baltic to the Mediterranean, from France to the Russian frontier. The whole elaborate edifice built on the ashes of Waterloo sank to the ground in Europe's most widespread convulsion between the Napoleonic era and the First World War.

An erudite and arrogant dogmatist named Marx, assisted by the utopistically inclined son of a prosperous millowner named Engels, was inciting the "proletariat" of all countries to unite and overthrow the social order. His theories had as yet little concrete influence on men and none on events. Far clearer and more effective than the grim cabala of dialectical materialism was one or

9

another of the brief, emotional slogans that hovered over the turmoil, representing ideals rooted in the innermost yearnings of man through the ages. Beautiful dreams fired the imagination of the man in the street in his pursuit of a new order of things.

One leading motif was sounded by a Frenchman of brilliant pen and piercing voice as he addressed a crowd with the fervor of some ancient prophet: "You will put in the place of armed men and infantry and cavalry and cannon a little box which you will call a balloting box, and from that box will proceed an assembly which will act as a soul to all of you, a sovereign and popular council which will decide, will judge, will settle all of your disputes!" [1]

Men firmly believed or desperately hoped that the millennium was within their reach. They well knew that others before them had at times so believed or hoped, only to be tragically disappointed, but — "men fight and lose the battle, and the thing they fought for comes about in spite of their defeat, and . . . it turns out to be not what they meant, and other men have to fight for what they meant under another name." [2]

Long had the common man of Europe subsisted on a diet of hopes, with seeds of revolt as his principal nourishment. Now, sights fixed on the achievements of the American and French revolutions, he did not fail to observe the omens since the Corsican's banishment to Saint Helena in 1815 — and the omens were many:

First Congress of German Confederation; revolt of South American colonies (1816) . . . Argentina's independence established (1817) . . . Karlsbad Resolutions for the suppression of revolutionary propaganda in Germany (1819) . . . Ferdinand VII of Spain forced to accept Constitution (1820) . . . Greek revolution; Italian revolution in Piedmont suppressed; Colombia declares independence; John VI of Portugal accepts Constitution; Santa Anna proclaims Mexican Republic (1821) . . . Monroe Doctrine announced (1823) . . . Greek independence recognized (1829) . . . July Revolution in France; flight of Charles X; Belgian uprising against Dutch supremacy; Polish revolt (1830) . . . Polish revolt crushed; uprisings in Papal States (1831) . . . Abolition of slavery in the British Empire (1833) . . . King Miguel of Portugal expelled by Constitutionalists (1834) . . . Queen Christina of Spain concedes Constitution (1836) . . . Papineau's Canadian rebellion; introduction of full parliamentary government in Canada (1837) . . .

But even these developments had been only overtures to subsequently staged grand operas. The climactic year, 1848, was highlighted by a torrent of events ideally suited for the rapidly developing art of designing banner headlines:

INSURRECTION IN SICILY (January 12) . . . SICILIAN KING GRANTS CONSTITUTION (February 10) . . . CONSTITUTION GRANTED IN TUSCANY (February 17) . . . LOUIS PHILIPPE FALLS, SECOND FRENCH REPUBLIC PROCLAIMED (February 24) . . . REVOLUTION IN LUXEMBOURG (February 28) . . . SARDINIAN KING GRANTS PEOPLE'S CHARTER (March 5) . . . POPE PIUS IX GRANTS POPULAR REFORMS (March 11) . . . REVOLUTION IN VIENNA, METTERNICH OVERTHROWN (March 13) . . . REVOLUTION IN BUDAPEST (March 15) . . . MILAN RISES AGAINST AUSTRIAN TROOPS (March 18) . . . REVOLUTION IN BERLIN (March 18) . . . BAVARIAN KING ABDICATES (March 19) . . . MILAN AND VENICE LIBERATED (March 22) . . . PRUSSIAN KING PROMISES CONSTITUTIONAL REGIME (March 23) . . . CROATIAN NATIONAL COMMITTEE FORMED (March 25) . . . AUSTRIAN EMPEROR FLEES FROM VIENNA (May 17) . . . UPRISINGS IN BOHEMIA, MORAVIA, DALMATIA (April 8–20) . . . INSURRECTIONS IN TRANSYLVANIA AND POLAND (April 15–25) . . . IMPERIAL ARTILLERY BOMBARDS PRAGUE TO CRUSH REVOLT (June 17) . . . INSURRECTION IN PARIS (June 23) . . . UPRISING IN VIENNA (October 6) . . . VIENNA BOMBARDED TO END REVOLT (October 31) . . . COUP IN PRUSSIA (November 9) . . . POPE FLEES TO PROVINCES (November 24) . . . FERDINAND OF AUSTRIA ABDICATES, FRANCIS JOSEPH I BECOMES EMPEROR (December 2) . . .

All this and more within that one year, involving the destinies of two hundred and sixty million people — one fourth of this number in the Habsburg Monarchy and the German Confederation, another fourth in Russia, thirty-six million in France, twenty-eight million in Great Britain, the rest in the smaller states.

11

DARING DIPLOMACY

A certain "Mr. and Mrs. Smith" landed in March 1848 at New-haven, England. The gentleman, wearing an ill-fitting jacket bor-rowed from the shipmaster, was made further unrecognizable by a week-old beard and a pair of large blue goggles. He and his wife were met at the pier by a small group of awkwardly bowing and scraping citizens headed by the local teacher who happened to be a genuine Mr. Smith.

A few weeks later another couple arrived on English soil, a certain "Herr und Frau Meyer." The gentleman had been des-cribed as "immobility personified, the Chinese principle in its highest expression, the Status Quo incarnate," in whose belief democracy "could only change daylight into darkest night." [3]

Was it any wonder that to many the world seemed to be coming to an end? Surely nothing less than the end of a world could have transformed Louis Philippe of France into "Mr. Smith," and made the name Meyer suitable for adoption by Prince Clemens Lothar von Metternich-Winneburg, formerly master of Austria and chief arbiter of Europe.

Across the Atlantic, people viewed the European scene through spyglasses that registered no colors other than black and white. To them, all monarchs appeared to be repulsive composites of Beelze-bub and Nero, all rebels the Archangel Gabriel and Robin Hood combined. This peculiarity was due not only to distortion caused by extreme physical distance but also to wishful thinking gener-ated by remembrance either direct or only a step removed. A person born on the same day as the American nation was no more than seventy-two if alive in 1848, and among New Yorkers in their sixties in the latter year were many who had been present as boys in the crowd which heard George Washington deliver his first inaugural address. Albert Gallatin, member of the Pennsylvania Constitutional Convention in 1789, and secretary of the treasury under Jefferson, was still alive to read press reports about the democratic revolutions of 1848 and to mourn the collapse of the last of them a year later.

Citizens of the youthful United States were moved to particular admiration by a small East European nation's struggle for freedom. The very word Hungary "made the world's dead spirit leap again . . ." [4] The Hungarian equivalent of the Marseillaise reverberated far and wide, and stirred the souls of men wherever it was heard even without the throbbing rhymes of its original language:

> "Rise, Magyar, your country calls,
>   The time has come: now — or never!
> Shall we be slaves or shall we be free?
>   This is the question; make your choice!
> By the God of Magyars we swear —
>   We swear to remain slaves no longer!" [5]

These words of a young literary genius named Petőfi — destined to die at twenty-six in the revolution partly of his making — served as battle cries for a people rising to liberate itself. In a smoke-filled room of the Café Pilvax at Budapest, he and a group of other Prometheans compiled a list of "Twelve Points of Freedom," printed it within the hour in open defiance of censorship authorities, distributed the copies in the streets and soon had the population of the capital in a rebellious frenzy. They demanded:

1. Freedom of the press. 2. Ministerial responsibility. 3. Annual sessions of parliament, with a national assembly elected by universal suffrage. 4. Personal and religious freedom, and equality before the law. 5. Formation of a national guard. 6. Equitable sharing of taxation. 7. Suppression of feudal privileges. 8. A jury system based on equal representation. 9. Creation of a national bank. 10. Formation of a national army, sworn to protect the ancient Hungarian Constitution and not subject to service abroad. 11. Amnesty for political prisoners. 12. Union of Hungary and Hungarian Transylvania.

How could Americans, seeming to hear echoes of the Boston Tea Party, of American independence, of inalienable rights, have failed to be moved? Far away from the scene of action but not yet farther from their own self-liberation than the frontiers of living memory, how could they have not sympathized with the Hungarians who were bracing themselves for apparent re-enactments of Bunker Hill, Valley Forge, and Yorktown? "The fact that possibly

13

the great majority of Americans have suffered from maladjustment, lack of success, or even actual oppression and tyranny, whether in the lands of the Old World or the older settlements of our own, has caused them to develop a remarkable feeling of sympathy for the 'under-dog' of any sort, economic, political, social. Lying deep in our sub-consciousness, this usually comes to the surface as emotion, and has appeared many times. In international relations it has colored our feelings with regard, among others, to Greeks, Hungarians, Irish, Cubans, and the natives of India, not always intelligently or wisely or with knowledge of the facts. It has colored our attitude toward criminals and politicians. It is a trait which domestic statesmen do, and foreign ones ought to, reckon with. It is an instinctive reaction, not a reasoned proposition, and derives straight from the life history of millions of individuals. At any moment it may appear against a foreign nation thought guilty of oppression, against politicians who attack a rival too ruthlessly, against the money power or others considered too privileged." [6]

On their part, the Magyars had followed the growth of American freedom with profound interest. They felt that nothing less than the Promised Land was being built on the free soil of the New World. A noted Hungarian traveler, Sándor Bölöni Farkas, who visited the United States in 1831 and became the first of his people to be received by an American president (Andrew Jackson), declared in a book he wrote about his experiences here that "America is a happy fatherland where everyone is equally born into freedom and independence . . . This is the road for us to take, the road to liberty, independence, salvation." János Balogh, a leader of the Hungarian Diet of 1832–36, drilled his young son on a special political catechism which included questions and answers such as these: "Who was the greatest man?" "George Washington." "Which is the best government?" "A republic." "What art thou?" "I am a democrat." Lajos Kossuth, leader of the 1848–49 revolution, frequently alluded in his speeches and articles to Washington's noble character, Franklin's sagacity, Jefferson's principles. He used American examples to illustrate the practical functions of a democratic system of government. He had taught himself English in prison from a copy of the King James Bible, some of Shakespeare's plays, and an antiquated dictionary, with results that were to earn him during his American tour in 1851–52 the admiration of such virtuosos of the language as Emerson, Greeley, Webster, Longfellow.

Improvised Hungarian troops were already battling the formidable professional armies of the Habsburg emperor when the Magyar leaders drafted a Declaration of Independence on the pattern of its American namesake: ". . . In maintenance of our inalienable rights we feel ourselves duty bound to make known the motives and reasons that have prompted us to make our decision, in order that the civilized world may learn that we have not taken this step out of overweening confidence in our wisdom, nor out of revolutionary excitement, but that it is an act of the last necessity adopted to preserve from utter destruction a nation persecuted to the limit of a most enduring patience . . ."

The premise was followed by an itemized indictment based on the grievances of thirteen million aspirants for freedom, in a manner strikingly reminiscent of the list of charges preferred by the American founding fathers against George III.

The entire military might of the Austrian court proved inadequate for the task of squelching the Magyar revolt which continued stubbornly even after the collapse of similar efforts elsewhere in Europe. Emperor Ferdinand V was compelled to abdicate and his young successor, Francis Joseph I, turned for assistance to Nicholas I of Russia who was worried about the effect Hungarian successes were likely to exert on the peoples of his Polish dominion. In case of ultimate triumph, the revolution was certain to spread to Austria's Galician provinces, and thence to Poland, Moldavia, and Wallachia, whose peoples were only waiting for the propitious moment in which to rise.

The tsar was ready to furnish aid. He proclaimed: "The insurrection in Hungary has of late made so much progress that Russia cannot possibly remain inactive . . . It was but natural that the two Cabinets should understand one another on this point of common interest, and our troops have consequently advanced into Galicia to cooperate with Austria against the Hungarian rebellion." [7]

Fresh, well-equipped Cossack divisions poured into Hungary through the Carpathian passes. Fewer than 150,000 battle-weary Hungarians faced nearly a half-million Russians and Austrians. Prince Windischgraetz, the Austrian commander-in-chief, called for *Unbedingte Unterwerfung* (unconditional surrender).

American eyes dimmed upon reading the "Overseas Intelligence" columns in the press.

A former congressman from Illinois drew up a resolution for presentation to a large public meeting at Springfield. Its text, enthusiastically adopted without change, read: "RESOLVED, That in their present glorious struggle for liberty the Hungarians command our highest admiration and have our warmest sympathy; That they have our most ardent prayers for their speedy triumph and final success; That the Government of the United States should acknowledge the independence of Hungary as a nation of free men at the very earliest moment consistent with our amicable relations with the government against which they are contending; That in the opinion of this meeting, the immediate acknowledgment of the independence of Hungary by our Government is due from American free men to their struggling brethren in the general cause of republican liberty and not violative of the just rights of any nation or people." [8]

The author of the draft, Abraham Lincoln, was as conscious as Kossuth himself of the indivisibility of that liberty which the Hungarian leader defined as "the unity of the principles of freedom." According to Kossuth, "wherever it is broken, there is always danger for free principles everywhere in the world . . . Those who strive for freedom are brothers, wherever they be."

In the Congress of the United States, an increasing number of legislators clamored for effective action to help the Hungarians. Influential Senator Henry Stuart Foote presented a motion calling for a severance of diplomatic relations with Austria.[9] President Taylor invested an able diplomat, Ambrose Dudley Mann of Virginia, "with power to declare our willingness promptly to recognize [Hungary's] independence in the event of her ability to sustain it." The chief executive justified his extraordinary action on the grounds of "the feelings of the nation" which were "strongly enlisted in the cause and by the sufferings of a brave people who had made a gallant . . . effort to be free . . ." [10]

To indicate the intensity of the feelings cited by the president, one example may suffice. Dr. Francis Bowen, noted scholar, philosopher, proprietor of the *North American Review*, and author of occasional articles in it critical of the Hungarians, failed to receive an appointment to the McLean professorship of history at Harvard College because, in the opinion of Henry Wilson, president of the Massachusetts Senate, a man who was not sympathetic to the Hungarian cause was unfit to teach history.[11]

Outnumbered, outgunned, isolated, but still fighting, the Magyar forces went to their doom in a blaze of tragic glory. Acts of frenzied heroism, with results similar to those of the epic charge of the British Light Brigade at Balaclava a few years later, were routine occurrences during the final days. On August 13, 1849, Prince Pashkiewitch, generalissimo of the armies of the tsar, theatrically but accurately reported to his sovereign: "Hungary lies prostrate at your Majesty's feet!"

A contemporary, Austria's greatest dramatic poet Grillparzer, had written in one of his tragedies: "This is the curse of Habsburg's noble house: / Half-way to halt and doubtfully to aim / At half a deed, with half-considered means." However, as far as the aftermath of the Hungarian revolution was concerned, he could not have been more wrong: nothing was "half-way" or "doubtful" about Habsburg "deeds" or "means" in that respect.

Thirteen commanding generals of the Hungarian armies in the field were summarily hanged by the Austrians, even though the tsar himself had requested clemency for "these intrepid soldiers." Among them was a cousin of Queen Victoria of England, General Count Carl von Leiningen-Westerburg, who, refusing to appeal to the queen for intercession with the Austrian emperor, said: "It is good to live long, but it is far better to live forever."

Hungary's first prime minister was shot, although he was so ill as a result of an unsuccessful attempt at suicide that he had to be carried on a stretcher to the place of execution.

Thousands of officers and men were hanged, shot, imprisoned, or forced to serve in specially supervised regiments of the imperial armies.

The country, divided into control zones under martial law, was governed in absolutist fashion by authoritarian bureaucrats with the aid of military disciplinarians and a network of secret agents. Governor-President Kossuth and most of his closest associates fled abroad in the hope that the struggle might yet be renewed and finally won. Kossuth clung to that hope and worked for it with almost superhuman energy through the rest of his long life which ended only on the very threshold of the present century, at the age of ninety-two, in Italy.*

Friends of freedom throughout the world mourned the fate of the Hungarians, and Americans were particularly dejected. Daniel Webster, in a speech made on November 7, 1849, declared: "We have all had our sympathies much enlisted in the Hungarian effort for liberty. We have all wept at its failure. We thought we saw a more rational hope of establishing free government in Hungary than in any other part of Europe . . ." [13] Appointed secretary of state a few months later, Webster became embroiled in a series of sharp conflicts with the Austrians and repeatedly came to grips with the emperor's chargé d'affaires at Washington, the Chevalier

* On at least one occasion his dreams seemed on the verge of realization only to be frustrated in the last moment. On May 5, 1859, Napoleon III of France and Kossuth discussed terms on which the emperor was to extend the war then being waged by France and Piedmont against Austria to Hungary in order to liberate that country. The principal condition stipulated by Napoleon was the assured neutrality of England, and Kossuth undertook to secure that neutrality. On July 3, 1859, at another interview with Napoleon, he showed letters signed by Viscount Palmerston, Lord John Russell, and others of his admirers in the newly installed Liberal cabinet, guaranteeing English neutrality in case of an extension of the war to Hungary. Thereupon the emperor, satisfied, made a pact with the Hungarian leader. A week later, however, in a sudden reversal which stunned his allies and enemies alike, Napoleon made an armistice with the Austrians at Villafranca, at a personal meeting with Francis Joseph I. His unexpected decision to do so came after his announcement of a great victory for him and his ally in the battle of Solferino. In that battle, one of the greatest military engagements of the nineteenth century, nearly 300,000

18

Part of the Western section of Smyrna (destroyed by fire in 1922), with
a well-known boardinghouse — perhaps the one Koszta stayed at — in
the right foreground (from L. Boissonnas,
L'Image de Grèce, Genève, *1919*)

"The Bridge of the Caravans" at Smyrna *(from L. Boissonnas,*
L'Image de Grèce, *Genève, 1919)*

Hülsemann, a pugnacious gentleman whose name will frequently recur in our narrative.

Among former officers of the Hungarian revolutionary army who, like Kossuth himself, found their first asylum in Turkey, there was a former captain of infantry named Martin Koszta (approximate pronunciation *Costah*).

Among officers of America's armed forces who had watched the struggle of the Magyars with the comprehension of professionals and the buoyancy of free men, there was a naval captain from South Carolina named Duncan Nathaniel Ingraham.

The chance meeting of these two a few years later at Smyrna culminated in the dispatch of an American ultimatum, with a time limit of only a few hours, portending a possible armed clash between the young republic and the ancient empire.

The personal background and character of these men, the peculiarities of the place where they met, and the dynamics of the times in which they lived were so unusually appropriate to the drama as to appear almost contrived.

Their meeting and its consequences were to form an important chapter in the history of American consular protection. The results of the encounter came to exert an influence on the development of modern American naturalization processes, and loomed large behind the eventual enactment of a statute which spelled out anew one of the indispensable rights of man as a being born free.

---

soldiers participated; over 20,000 fell, and several times as many were wounded. Losses of the Austrians under the supreme field command of their militarily inexperienced emperor were considerably heavier than those of the French-Italian allies, but both sides were equally shaken by the physical and moral impact of the carnage. On a personal tour of the battlefield, the gory sight of devastation brought upon the French ruler an attack of nausea followed by recurring fainting spells. Under the effect of the shock he decided to make peace without even consulting his ally. The resultant dramatic upset dashed many a grandiose plan, including that of Kossuth who, in view of Napoleon's earlier enthusiastic utterances about Hungary's forthcoming liberation, could never understand the emperor's change of heart. The text of the secret correspondence between the monarchs in regard to the armistice remained unknown until 1923 when an Italian historian, Senator Francesco Salata, had an opportunity to study the documents at the Imperial Archives at Vienna — thrown open by the republican government — and published them in Rome.[12]

˄ BACKSTAGE II

T H E first members of the Koszta family to migrate from their native Greece to Hungarian Transylvania arrived there perhaps as early as the twelfth century, in an era of close Hungarian-Byzantine contacts, or in the thirteenth, after the Mongolian invasion of the country, when devastated regions were repopulated by invited masses of foreigners, including many Greeks. Although the family soon conformed to Hungarian phonetics by altering the spelling of the original surname — from Kosta to Koszta — their Hungarian peasant neighbors preferred to call them *Görög* ("Greek"). The epithet is parenthetically supplied with the family name in available genealogical records of several generations of Kosztas.[14] These records show that on June 17, 1701, the Kosztas were awarded a royal patent of nobility for meritorious, if now unknown, services to the Crown. The diploma conferred upon them the privilege of calling themselves "Koszta de Belényes," using as predicate the name of the village in which they were then living — and in which Martin Koszta was born in 1819.

American and English newspapers of a century ago referred to Martin Koszta as a man who at an unusually early age rose to the position of judge. Cited were statements of the man's personal friends, Hungarian exiles in England and in the United States, who were said to have a good knowledge of his background. The information was incorrect, due to an erroneous translation of a peculiar Hungarian idiom. *Biró* in Hungarian means "judge" in English, but *kisbiró*, in literal translation "small judge," what Koszta in fact had been in his native village while still in his teens, was merely a town crier, the kind that still existed in the 1920s when this writer was a boy in a Hungarian village about the size of Koszta's birthplace.

The *kisbiró*, wearing a uniform somewhat similar to that of the dashing Hungarian Hussars, and carrying a small drum, would make stops at natural strategic points of the village such as a little hill in front of the church or a wooden bridge over the brook. Beating his drum till a sizable group of peasant folk assembled, he announced the latest ordinances issued by the village authorities, together with sundry news of regional interest. The announcements, read from crumpled pieces of paper if the crier knew how to read, and diligently memorized beforehand if he did not, often included such tidbits as the dates on which the village bull was available for breeding purposes, or the exact number of poultry claimed by Mrs. Kovács to have been stolen from her back yard by wandering gipsies.

The *kisbiró* was not an arm of the law, although perhaps a finger of it as an instrumentality of public enlightenment. He served at a modest salary payable in daily installments of edibles and yearly issues of clothing. The fact that the functions of this "small judge" had nothing in common with those of a member of the judiciary need cast no reflection on the good name of the particular *kisbiró* called Martin Koszta who became a town crier because his family was poor. The landed property granted the Kosztas together with the patent of nobility by His Apostolic Majesty Leopold I more than a century before had somehow slipped out of their hands. As to the circumstances of the loss, the chronicler knoweth not; but it is noteworthy that countless similar losses on the part of both high and low Hungarian nobility of the period were known to have been closely connected with such popular causes as wine, women, and song.

When the War for Liberty broke out in 1848, Koszta, like all able-bodied Hungarians ranging from the adolescent to the senescent, volunteered or was drafted for service in Kossuth's army. That he proved a good soldier is evidenced by his rise within a few months from enlisted man to captain in the Fifty-Fifth Infantry Battalion. The commander of that formation, Colonel Dániel Ihász, eventually became one of Koszta's companions among the exiles headed by Kossuth himself at Viddin, Bulgaria, in the late summer of 1849. Exile records show that in the fall of that year, when the Hungarian group was transferred to Sumla, Turkey, Koszta acted as commander of one of the mounted units leading the melancholy procession of homeless heroes of a lost cause to their next asylum, and that in the following year when they moved on to the final Turkish station of their peregrinations, to the town of Kutahya, both Koszta and his erstwhile commanding officer were still together in the colony.

After the collapse of the Central and Eastern European revolutions, the Turkish government found itself under increasing pressure from Austria and Russia to force the extradition of the exiles then on Ottoman soil. The emperor of Austria demanded the extradition of the Hungarian "Kossuth dogs," and the tsar that of the "Polish brutes." The vigorous squeeze play kept the chancelleries busy for years. The Turkish Porte again and again declined to comply with the demands, arguing that no specific treaties existed between the three high parties concerning extradition obligations and procedures. This position was maintained all the more firmly because the friendship of England and France, at a time when foretokens of the Crimean War were already discernible, was of great importance to the sultan — and the exiles had the strong sympathies of the British and the French. Sir George Stratford-Canning, ambassador of the Court of Saint James at Constantinople, had informed the Turks that Great Britain would look with great displeasure on Turkish acceptance of demands for the extradition of the exiles. On September 3, 1849, he reported to his chief, Lord Palmerston, that "on grounds of humanity not unmixed with consideration as affecting the Porte's character and future policy, I have not hesitated to advise a decided resistance to the demand of extradition," and on December 17 added: "I admire the courageous firmness with which the Sultan and his Government have determined to make a stand in the cause of humanity, and of the rights of honor and dignity, against a demand alike objectionable in substance and in form."

Turkish steadfastness was enthusiastically applauded throughout the Western world. Illustrative of the general anti-Austrian popular feeling at the time is especially one of numerous incidents, which occurred in London in the fall of 1850, when Baron Julius Haynau, marshal of the empire, arrived there on an unofficial visit. His sanguinary misrule as military dictator of Lombardy had earned him the sobriquet "the Hyena of Brescia," inspired both by his deeds and by the convenient play on words: Haynau — Hyena. Because of his Bloody Assizes on the Magyars after the debacle of 1849, he was also widely referred to simply as "the Hangman." The Viennese cabinet and the high command hesitated to recall him from Hungary despite his pathological cruelties, since he happened to be an illegitimate son of the elector of Hesse, William IX; but finally the emperor himself stepped in when demonstrations broke out against Haynau even in Austria itself. It was soon after the euphemistically phrased announcement of his removal and his receipt of several of the highest decorations within the Crown's gift that the marshal decided to make a tour of a Continent well aware of his long record of brutal excesses.

Almost at once after his arrival in London, Haynau paid what he called "a visit of inspection" to the plants of Barclay, Perkins & Company. A clue to the reason for his interest in the firm lies in the fact that Messrs. Barclay and Perkins operated England's best known brewery. The marshal, a lifelong admirer of beer and ale, had decided to import British ale into Austria for the pleasure of himself and of his truly limited circle of friends. Accompanied by an aide, he marched into the plant.

"When it became known that he was present, nearly all the laborers and draymen ran out with brooms and dirt, shouting, 'Down with the Austrian butcher,' and uttering other alarming epithets. The Marshal was soon covered with dirt, and perceiving some of the men about to attack him, he ran into the street to Bankside, chased by a mob and belabored with all sorts of weapons. He finally took refuge in a public house where he was rescued by the police." [15]

Haynau left England hurriedly after this humiliating experience at the hands of pro-Kossuth Englishmen, which two years later served as Austria's main reason for refusing to send a military representative to the funeral of the Duke of Wellington. Traveling to Belgium, the marshal was saved with great difficulty from mob violence at Brussels, and retreated to Vienna in a rage. Soon he was to read colorful accounts in the Western press about the thunderous ovations accorded Kossuth in England, just before the Hungarian's voyage to America, and to suffer the first of a series of apoplectic attacks, the last of which in the spring of 1853 was to cause his death.

But to return to the precarious situation of the exiles in Turkey:

Although the courts of Austria and Russia finally relaxed their diplomatic pressure on Turkey because weightier issues were bringing an armed showdown with the sultan closer with each passing month, expulsion continued to threaten the patriots. A chance shift in Turkish cabinets or policies, conducive to an unfavorable change in the official attitude toward the exiles, remained an ever-present possibility.

One ingenious way of securing permanent relief from all dangers of extradition or summary expulsion lay in a religious conversion reminiscent of the Marranos conversions in medieval Spain.* Although Kossuth, a devout Lutheran, emphatically declined an invitation to become a Moslem, and many, including Koszta, followed his example, a great number of others were willing to embrace Islam. They learned the rudiments of the faith in the Hungarian language, memorized a set of its most important tenets in Turkish, marched to the nearest mosque, and declared before the

---

* Fourteenth- and fifteenth-century Jews in Spain sought refuge in baptism when huge pogroms were in progress, but covertly remained true to their religion. Even some of those among them who rose to high dignity in the Church secretly continued to practice their original faith. To cope with the problem, the Inquisition was introduced.

Imam in the prescribed manner that "Allah is great and Moham-med is His Prophet." The conversion made them immune from further molestation by their political enemies because members of the "True Faith" could never be extradited to "infidels."

Those who left their ancestral religion for the sake of expediency were not necessarily opportunists, cowards, or renegades in the ordinary sense of the word. These hardheaded, tough-skinned, battle-scarred soldiers, religious in their own unorthodox ways, appeared to attribute little importance to the formality of con-version. The act was regarded by them as a tactical one born of patriotic necessity. Without the personal security it offered, they could not ensure their self-preservation, the prerequisite without which they could not fight another day — and not one among them doubted for a moment that such a day would come.

Some of the exiles recorded in their diaries the names of numer-ous converts.[16] One of the first neophytes was a legendary hero not only of Hungary but of several other countries as well: General Josef Bem, who had been one of the principal field commanders of the Hungarian revolutionary army.* This military genius — dwarflike in appearance, idolized by his soldiers, speaking a curi-ous mixture of Polish, French, and German, and using Hungarian for cussing purposes only — inspired many an exile to follow his example when he embraced the Moslem religion. Together with him, numerous high-ranking officers whose names had often ap-peared in the Western press in connection with heroic military action became converts. Among these were such eventual officers of the Turkish army as General Kmety, alias Kiamil Pasha; Gen-eral Stein, later Ferhad Pasha; and Colonel Bangya, later Mehmed

* An outstanding leader of Davoust's corps in Napoleon's expedition to Russia, this Pole received the Chevalier's Cross of the Legion of Honor from the emperor himself; commanded the Polish artillery in the insurrection of 1830; escaped to France, became a professor of physics in Paris, left teaching to lead an insurrectionist group in Portugal; later fought in the Austrian revolt, then joined the Hungarians, received from Kossuth the command of the army of Transylvania and repeatedly outmaneuvered the best Austrian strategists. He suffered wounds in every campaign he fought. Upon his conversion he took the name Murad Tefshik Amurat, to which the rank of pasha was attached when he became a member of the sultan's general staff. He was governor of Aleppo, Turkey, when death ended his storybook career.

Emir Bey.* Martin Koszta, however, remained a Protestant to the end.

Further traces of the young Magyar are disclosed by available records of the events of February 15, 1850. On the morning of that day, Kossuth and scores of his former officers and men moved to a new locality designated by the Porte as their next place of settlement *pro tem.* This group included several former generals of note, among them Mészáros, ex-minister of war; Koszta's former commanding officer, Colonel Ihász; and Captain Koszta himself. The memoirs of one of this group, published some fifteen years after his death, contain one of the scant references to be found anywhere about Koszta in that period, stating that at the new settlement "Koszta devoted his time to studies of mathematics and military science and acquired a knowledge of French. He was a young man of honesty and firm character, about 25–26 years of age." When the diarist left the emigration for England, he gave the captain "my Hungarian fur coat, my hunting bag, my tea kettle, the jacket of my Magyar national costume, et cetera, as parting gifts." [17]

In May 1850, Koszta himself was able to leave Turkey. He traveled to Southampton with a few Hungarians and a large number of Poles. A few entries in exile diaries indicate that he had tried to persuade several others, especially Colonel Ihász, to join him, but that the colonel declined, citing Kossuth's daily need of his services as a sort of handyman. A few months later, when in accordance with a congressional resolution the American frigate *Mississippi* was sent to bring Kossuth and his closest companions to the United States as the nation's guests, Ihász was among those who boarded the ship as members of the governor's entourage. But when Kossuth and his associates stepped ashore at New York on December 4, 1851, amid the deafening cheers of crowds estimated at more than one hundred thousand Manhattanites, Martin Koszta

---

* Among other converts, nearly three hundred, eight women are also listed. Each of these women had served in the revolutionary army as an enlisted man. The true sex of two was discovered after they received wounds in battle and had to be thoroughly examined by army physicians; but the rest successfully masqueraded as men even in the emigration until the day when, to the astonishment of their comrades, they appeared in ladies' garbs at a mufti's office to apply for acceptance into the Islamic fold.

was already a resident there, having arrived some months earlier.

The former captain's next verifiable move can safely be called the most important he ever made.

On July 31, 1852, he appeared at the Court of Common Pleas for the City and County of New York.

With hand raised in solemn oath and eyes fixed on a flag of thirty-one stars and thirteen stripes, he declared his intention to become a citizen of the United States of America.

He signed a slip of paper about the size of a dollar bill.

Another year was barely over when that slip of paper saved his life.

BACKSTAGE III

WHEN Koszta strode out of the old Court House, he had reason to be confident that the difficult initial period he had gone through in the big city was at an end. His existence in America was now legally acknowledged; he now had a stake in the country; he now had a future.

On his arrival in the New World about a year before, he had found himself in the predicament of countless others before and after him who spoke no English and did not know where to turn. Powerful American Hungarian organizations of later decades were as yet no more than tentative intentions discussed over wine-filled glasses in dark saloons in the Bowery. Individual employers of Hungarian birth willing to use whatever services could be rendered by men of no definite trade or profession, no qualifications other than being an ex-compatriot, and no experience except in, say, town-crying and soldiering, were nowhere in sight until after the Civil War.

Koszta had few personal friends within reach. Most of the immigrants he had known in the old days had moved to New Jersey, Pennsylvania, Ohio, Illinois, Iowa. True, he could have joined one or another group of these new American pioneers. For instance, several of his acquaintances, led by former government commissioner Count László Ujházy, had succeeded in obtaining loans suffi-

Backstage

cient to rent a tract of land in Decatur County, Iowa, near the Missouri border. With much enthusiasm they laid grounds for a chain of model farms, naming the settlement New Buda in honor of ancient Buda, seat of Magyar kings through the centuries. But Koszta had declined an invitation to join them. As a matter of fact, subsequent events justified his decision. Ujházy and his enterprising partners soon found the Iowa climate unsuitable for themselves as well as for their planned produce, had to give up the costly experiment after some two years of efforts, and moved on to Texas to face new uncertainties and ultimate failure. But Koszta's main reason for not joining them probably lay in his ambition to become a well-assimilated American as soon as possible — and the road to the fulfillment of that ambition assuredly did not lead through the ethnic isolation of a minority settlement. Determined to make his own way in an American environment, he had drifted away from his acquaintances of revolutionary times and from friends made in Turkish exile. He had ceased to cultivate contacts even with the highest ranking man he knew well: Colonel Asbóth, former aide-de-camp to Kossuth, who himself aspired to full assimilation and eventually accomplished it in a spectacular manner.*

Lonely, tongue-tied, penniless, Koszta's prospects were dim at first. But a young and physically powerful man like him had little reason to worry about his next meal as long as he was willing to set aside Old World sensitivities, preconceived attitudes, premature social ambitions. And Koszta was willing.

* He was a prominent "Forty-Eighter," as Hungarian, German, Austrian, and other erstwhile fighters for freedom proudly called themselves in the United States. He learned English quickly, worked until the outbreak of the Civil War as draftsman and surveyor, and was partly responsible for the planning of New York's Central Park and Washington Heights. In the Civil War he became chief of staff to General Frémont in the Union Army, gained fame for heroism in several battles, and rose to the rank of major general. After the war, he was appointed America's first minister to Argentina.

"Forty-Eighters" of this caliber included such men as the German Carl Schurz who went on to become general, minister to Spain, senator, secretary of interior; another German, Henry Villard (born Heinrich Hilgard), who became head of the company that built the Northern Pacific Railroad and eventually president of the firm from which today's General Electric Company evolved; still another, Louis Prang, who founded the color-postcard and Christmas card industry. The Hungarian Ágoston Haraszthy established the Cali-

29

He went to work as a stevedore at the port of New York, later as a carpenter's apprentice, and finally as a night watchman at the Lower Manhattan lumber yard of a German "Forty-Eighter" named August Ritter.[20]

Sitting in a shack night after night like a human watchdog, with no more actual guard duty than what mere physical presence accomplishes, he had a wealth of time in which to pore over dictionaries and grammars, creaky springboards to better types of work and a concurrent rise on the social and financial scale. But the peculiarities of his unique non-Germanic, non-Latin, non-Slavic native tongue make it hard for a Hungarian to befriend, let alone master, the English language. His very equipment for speech, in a physical sense, seems reluctant to respond to it. Just to pronounce "the" as it should be pronounced is a feat almost impossible for a Hungarian to accomplish in one lifetime. And there are numberless other problems: to force the lips to avoid making a "v" out of a "w" when the Magyar alphabet refuses to recognize the existence of a "w"; to cease rolling the "r" and thus sacrifice one of the most virile of Hungarian sounds; to place emphasis on different syllables according to the demands of illogical rules that bewilder a man who grew up putting emphasis on the first syllable at all times; to have to ask silly questions like "how do you do?" which is not a question but only a noise calling for

fornia wine industry; another Hungarian, Julius Stahel, became a major general, recipient of the Congressional Medal of Honor, and consul general in Japan, China, and Russia.

From a virtually endless series of individual examples of "Forty-Eighter" careers, a startling political fact and a provocative military reflection emerges. It was the "Forty-Eighter" mass that swung the German vote in the West to the new Republican party and in 1860 gave the final push needed by Lincoln to carry Illinois. "The election of Lincoln and, as it turned out, the fate of the Union, was thus determined not by native Americans but by voters who knew least of American history and institutions." [18] Moreover, there were no fewer than half a million foreign-born volunteers in the Union Army, including an estimated 20 percent of all Hungarian immigrants, the highest ratio of all nationality groups.[19] If this huge block is subtracted from the total number of the Union Army's members, and the remainder is compared with the strength of the Confederate forces, it becomes apparent that the ultimate results of the War between the States might have been very different had foreign-born volunteers not participated.

reciprocation in kind . . . And so it goes, an infinite series of puzzlements for one reared in the comfort and security of a language built, like the Magyar, upon a rock of consistency in syntax and pronunciation.

And yet Koszta's progress must have been satisfactory because in the summer of 1852 Herr Ritter promoted him to the position of clerk.

Some of Ritter's business associates took an interest in the quiet, handsome former officer of the famed Hungarian revolutionary army. It seemed to them that here was a "gentleman" of brains and diligence who was willing to work hard and undoubtedly had a future. Recalling that Koszta had mentioned knowing a number of enterprising Italians, Greeks, Englishmen, and others in the sultan's domains, someone suggested one day that Koszta be sent to Turkey for a few weeks to reconnoiter the export-import field. It was soon decided to finance a round trip for him on a cooperative basis.

Plans were laid and in September 1852 Koszta boarded an American merchant vessel, the *Mimosa,* bound for Smyrna.

In retrospect, the ship's name has a certain symbolic significance. The flower Mimosa was well known on the Continent by its Latin sobriquet, *noli-me-tangere* ("do not touch me"), a name resembling the motto embroidered on flags of American revolutionary times. That motto, under a design showing a coiled rattlesnake, read: "Don't tread on me." * From the actuarial viewpoint, the Hungarian passenger of the *Mimosa* was distinctly accident-prone; he was likely not only to be "touched" but even "treaded on."

The ex-captain traveled lightly, carrying but one suitcase with him.

---

* The symbol originated from Benjamin Franklin's suggestion in his Pennsylvania Gazette that a cargo of rattlesnakes be sent to London parks in retaliation for British injustices. It was embroidered on the first flag of an American naval squadron which appeared on the masthead of the *Alfred*, flagship of Esek Hopkins, commander in chief of the American Navy, in December 1775. It was hoisted there by no smaller a future hero of that Navy than John Paul Jones, then serving as a lieutenant on the vessel.

He was armed: his weapon was a slip of paper, carefully folded within an envelope and desposited at the bottom of the suitcase.

A few days after his arrival at Smyrna, Herr Ritter's commercial sleuth journeyed to Constantinople and did not return to the Aegean seaport until February 1853.

During his stay at the Turkish capital he took steps to ensure his personal safety in the country where not long previously he had been in danger of expulsion, but where his status was strikingly different at this time. His American naturalization was now under way. He could produce, if need be, a legalized copy of his original "first paper." He felt that he was entitled to protection not only from American representatives in Turkey but also from the Turkish authorities; he knew from past examples that the Turks could issue him, through the good offices of the American consul at Smyrna or of the American minister at Constantinople, a so-called *Tezkereh*, an internal pass affording conditional protection and certain privileges to the bearer as a visiting foreigner.

Calling on the United States consul at Symrna, Koszta inquired — as the consul had occasion to recall months later in his letter of July 5, 1853, to the secretary of state — if that official "could, in virtue of the said declaration [of intention to become a citizen] give him the protection of this Consulate as a 'citizen of the United States,' during his stay here."

The consul was acquainted with the policy of the State Department, according to which "a foreigner who has merely declared his intention to become an American citizen without having carried that intention into effect, is not an American citizen." [21] He told Koszta that "as he had not fulfilled the requirements of the law of naturalization, I could not consider him an American citizen, but that I would grant him my unofficial influence in case he might have any difficulties with the authorities, and advised him to leave this country as soon as possible, as it would be imprudent for him to stay here without the protection of some Consulate."

However, the Turks had their own views of these matters, as

was shown by the fact — cited by American Minister Marsh in a report to the secretary on July 7, 1853 — that a *Tezkereh* issued to Koszta at Smyrna, and another one given him at the Turkish capital, described the Hungarian-Austrian-American legal hybrid "as an American citizen or *protégé*, and thus his claim to American protection had been distinctly allowed, and recognized by the American authorities at Turkey..."The Turks gave Koszta recognition on the grounds of their own interpretation of what a declaration of intention was worth, and the Americans had no choice but to extend the courtesy of recognition to the Turkish documents without challenging the terminology used in those documents.

The contrariety sprang from a peculiar situation which had often disturbed Western representatives in Turkey. As the American minister explained, "by established usage which has been recognized in Turkey for centuries, all Franks [Westerners] having no native protection may put themselves under the patronage of any Christian nationality represented at the Porte which consents to receive them, and when so received they are treated in all respects as the subjects of the protecting power. This is every day's practice; and for a long period there has not been a Legation at Constantinople, or a Frank Consulate in Turkey, which has not had foreign non-naturalized Franks under its full protection and jurisdiction. In some cases the *protégés* have been counted by hundreds and even thousands."

The minister added an observation of particular relevance as regarded Koszta: "Austria herself has numerous *protégés* owing her allegiance neither by birth or naturalization, and the practice is too well established here to admit of its legality being questioned."

Koszta was entitled to consider himself something of an expert with respect to these perplexing practices. At the time of his own exile in Turkey, persons of different nationalities had paid almost daily visits to "Frank" consulates, requesting or demanding letters of protection on grounds varying from the doubtful to the preposterous. Many had succeeded in obtaining such letters, and in turn received a privileged status on Turkish soil. The documents were loosely described not only by their possessors but often by Turkish officials themselves as "passports," "guaranty certificates," "nationality credentials," creating the erroneous impression that the bearers had been vested with the citizenship of the sponsoring authorities. Anomalies bloomed in and out of season in this bureaucratic no-man's land, and oft-promised weedings were put off year after year. The laxity prevalent on all sides was due at least in part to humanitarian considerations.

According to announced American policy, the Department of State had "authority to grant passports only to citizens of the United States." [22] But the principle left large areas of practical problems in obscurity. A so-called first paper, duly issued and recorded by a court of justice, was a thing peculiarly American and no one abroad knew for certain just how far its meaning and validity might extend. Doubt in this respect existed even at home. While it was agreed that the document could not clothe its possessor with full citizenship, the belief persisted that benefits or privileges difficult to define but nonetheless real were inherent in it along the broad lines of citizenship. Granted that the bearer was not yet a citizen; but he was no longer quite a foreigner. To specify what he was from viewpoints of municipal law and of the law of nations, no agent abroad was prepared to do, in the absence of conclusive test cases. At the time, not even general instructions were at the disposal of our consuls; the first issue of "General instructions to the consuls and commercial agents of the United States, prepared under the direction of the Department of State" did not appear until 1855.

Attitudes of policy-making officials fluctuated among uncertainty, caution, and contradiction. Conflicts often appeared in the publicly expressed views of the Department of State regarding cases of the type mentioned. For example, no less recently than around the time of Koszta's departure for Turkey, Secretary Everett had declared that those who had "first papers" appeared to be entitled to "some recognition" and should be given by American agents abroad "all the aid we can properly give them."

But his statement ended with the sobering observation that "no just offense could be taken by the United States" if the certificates should prove "of little value to the holders," and that "it will be for the European authorities to pay such respect to the document as they think proper." [23] Our officers at posts abroad who from time to time had the exasperating duty to deal with "declarants" were expected to decide for themselves how much "aid" could be "properly" given. Their decision had to rest mostly on instinct, and their action on personal responsibility.

Koszta was not likely to be much concerned at the time with diplomatic and legal technicalities connected with his "first paper." He had the document, he was proud of it, and he attributed certain powers to it. Its certified copy, augmented by the Turkish passes obtained at Smyrna and at Constantinople, accompanied him like a bodyguard as he busily traveled around on business for some three months.

Whatever the extent to which his endeavors in behalf of Herr Ritter and his other sponsors were successful, it appears that certain matters not of a business nature were at least partly responsible for the prolongation of his stay. Diaries of Italian and Hungarian exiles, acquaintances of Koszta at Symrna, contain more than one brief, spicy allusion to his romantic interest in at least two women in town. One was the daughter of an Italian restaurant owner named Cristo ; the other, a young French divorcée called Madame Vigny.

In days of great and urgent need soon to follow, both ladies showed strong devotion to the man, each in her own way and both with an energy worthy of the lively temperament of their respective nationalities.

Koszta took temporary residence at a boardinghouse patronized by westerners.

On the evening of June 19, he happened to be absent from the hostel when a man subsequently identified as one Jovicich appeared there. It was not unusual for outsiders to walk in from the street for a cup or two of coffee. The stranger soon engaged in conversation one of the permanent boarders, an Armenian named Baldukian, assistant to a local veterinary surgeon and frequent next-chair neighbor of Koszta at the communal dinner table. Jovicich launched a skillful interrogation of Baldukian about the American Hungarian and his local contacts.

The next evening, when Koszta stayed in, Jovicich failed to return. But on the evening after that, on June 21, accompanied by an Italian later identified as one Luca, he came back for more coffee — and more information.

These two were strong-arm hirelings of the Austrian consul general at Smyrna.

Two years previously, in the spring of 1851, they had abducted late one night a Hungarian exile as he left the always-open Church of the Capuchins. A few weeks afterward his bullet-ridden body was found in a dark alley of the Trieste waterfront.[24]

It was on Wednesday, June 22, while sitting at dusk on the terrace of Cristo's café where the proprietor's comely daughter was due to join him, that Martin Koszta was kidnapped by a gang of hooligans headed by Jovicich, and carried aboard the Austrian brig Hussar then at anchor in Smyrna bay.

The Play

THE EMERGENCY

June 22-23, 1853

CRISTO'S daughter Lisa gaily breezed into her father's waterfront café to keep an early-evening date with the young Hungarian from America.

Guests were huddled in flocks, talking and gesturing agitatedly. Some of them, noticing her entry, called to her in alarm:

"The Hungarian has been kidnapped! . . . Koszta is gone! . . . He is a prisoner!"

The assault had taken place only a few minutes earlier, but Cristo's customers already knew that the Austrian consul general was the mastermind behind it. Eyewitnesses, now present in the café, had had a glimpse of Jovicich, Luca, Andrea "the Slav," and one Filipucci, all four long known to agents and clients of the exile grapevine telegraph as hirelings of the Austrians and participants in previous plots against former subjects of the emperor.

Cristo decided that the first thing to do was to mobilize Koszta's known friends among Hungarian and Italian exiles. He volunteered to go to the establishment of one of his competitors where Hungarians usually gathered. In turn, Lisa hurried to the boardinghouse where her friend had stayed, to inform some of the lodgers known to her.

Through channels of her own, Madame Vigny also received the

disturbing news within the hour. Forthwith, she visited the bishop of Smyrna who, she happened to know, was a cousin of the Austrian consul general, Peter Ritter von Weckbecker.

While no record of the interview is available, subsequent developments suggest that the bishop believed his cousin guilty. He made repeated attempts during the following two days to bring the official to reason. But Herr von Weckbecker angrily disclaimed the slightest knowledge of the abduction. The prelate finally decided to appeal to public opinion. He issued a brief but strongly worded statement to the local press, "openly voicing his disapproval" of the abduction.[25]

The exiles plunged themselves into feverish activity. In a private room of Cristo's café, Italian exile leaders composed appeals to Western missions, Turkish officials, and prominent private individuals at Smyrna. Both Lisa and Madame Vigny, natural rivals turned natural allies, were present, as were a few Italian-speaking Hungarians whose compatriots were holding a simultaneous caucus of their own at one of their regular haunts in the inner city.

Most of the inflamed Hungarians demanded an armed attack upon the *Hussar* and another upon the Austrian consulate. Only after a series of speeches by their more moderate elders did they settle for less spectacular and more judicious action. At the suggestion of ex-Captain Virágh, doorman at Smyrna's largest occidental nightclub called the Crescent, it was decided to make a search of Koszta's quarters in an effort to locate certain "protective documents" the captive had mentioned to his friends as being in his possession.

It was also decided to approach the American consul at Smyrna, a gentleman of controversial repute named Edward S. Offley.

Few officers of the American Foreign Service had ever had to confront their duties in a milieu psychologically less advantageous than that which surrounded the lonely bachelor sitting at the American consul's desk at Smyrna.

Born in Turkey of an American father and a mother of uncertain national origin, Offley was listed in the register of the Department of State with this remark after his name: "An American citizen born abroad." His initial recommendation for the post came from William H. Stiles, American minister to Vienna, who had met Offley in 1847 during a chance stay at Smyrna. In a letter to Secretary of State Buchanan, he described the man as "a gentleman of character and intelligence . . . of the most courteous manners," adding that "I do not know that I ever met with an individual with whom upon so short acquaintance I was better pleased." Stiles mentioned that Offley's father, a native of Philadelphia, was one of the first American merchants to settle at Smyrna and held the office of United States consul there for many years; upon his death his son David succeeded to the office and held it during the rest of his life.* When David died, his brother Edward took temporary charge of the office.²⁶ †

In those days, "the Government was . . . unable for the most part to select from among its citizens in the various foreign ports persons whose circumstances enabled them to hold the office of Consul and to discharge the duties in an efficient and satisfactory manner for the slender and uncertain emoluments derived from fees. A large majority of the persons appointed desired the office of Consul for their own personal benefit. When an American citizen undertook to establish himself abroad in some commercial occupation in a port where the United States was not represented by a consular officer, it was usual for him to seek the prestige with the consequent aid to his business enterprises which his appointment as Consul would afford. With the help of influential friends, whose solicitations it was not easy to resist, he was generally able to bring about his appointment. It was not unnatural that in many cases men so appointed should have regarded the office primarily as an aid in building up a profitable business often at the

---

* David Offley is confused with Edward in most of those historical and international legal reference works which make at least brief mention of the incident at Smyrna.

† The history of the American consular service shows only one similar case of succession, that of the Sprague family in which three generations represented the United States at Gibraltar for more than a century. Horatio Sprague was consul there from 1832 to 1848; his son, Horatio Jones Sprague, born at Gibraltar, held the same position from 1848 to 1891; and the latter's son, Richard Louis Sprague, from 1891 until his death at Gibraltar in 1934.

41

expense of other merchants in the port over whom the office of Consul gave them undue advantage."[27]

Offley had neither business enterprises nor family fortune; but he did have a natural priority for succession and the warm recommendation of Minister Stiles.

Numerous American residents of Smyrna joined Stiles in urging Edward Offley's appointment. A memorandum to President Polk, dated November 10, 1847, and signed by several of Offley's local supporters, is on record, praising him. Many others, however, objected to him, either at the very outset or later, on a variety of grounds, some palpably false. A number of his opponents took a prejudiced view of him as a virtual foreigner who had spent relatively little time in the United States. Others resented his nongregarious nature, an obstacle to requests for special favors. In 1851, three years after his appointment, a campaign was organized against him under the leadership of J. B. Paterson, a partner in the firm of Atkinson & Company at Smyrna. Paterson and his followers were determined to have Offley replaced with some American businessman of their choice, very probably Mr. Paterson himself. They petitioned the secretary of state to remove "this man who is not an American," whose knowledge of English was "imperfect," whose health was "bad."[28] Not one of these allegations was true. They accused him of incompetence; the principal proof offered was that he had taken depositions in a case of litigation at Smyrna in a manner so inept that the court found the documents entirely unusable. The truth of this matter was that Offley who, besides good English, spoke several languages fluently, did his best to elicit coherent testimony from illiterate witnesses of diverse nationalities, and that the court merely found that the witnesses did not know enough of the case to render acceptable testimony.

The anti-Offley group mobilized everyone within reach who had had contact, no matter how cursory, with the consul and was inclined or could be persuaded to judge him unfavorably. Typical of some of the testimonials submitted to the Department of State about Offley is an affidavit obtained and forwarded by a local missionary, in which it was asserted that the consul was "very much of a Greek in his manners and appearance, who spoke English quite imperfectly . . . He is understood to be Greek in his religion insofar as he cares for religion at all . . ." [29] As a matter of fact, he happened to be a Quaker, the only member of the Society of Friends in or near Smyrna Province at the time.

As the campaign broadened and gained momentum, merchants, missionaries, and travelers harassed the Department of State like gadflies. Even British Consul Brant joined in the drive, resentful of Offley's absences from the Sunday evening parties of local Western representatives and viewing such absences as unmistakable signs of arrogance, negligence, or both.

But the consul's immediate superior, Minister Marsh, resident at Constantinople, repeatedly refused to give his blessings to the anti-Offley forces. He found no reason to be dissatisfied with Offley as consul. While Marsh had no desire to antagonize the important American merchants of Smyrna, he was loath to lend any support to the guerrilla warfare carried on against a man whose deportment and efficiency in office were satisfactory.

Offley's friends among the Americans, British, and French at Smyrna did not remain silent in the face of the concerted attacks upon the official. The Department was besieged from both sides.

The anti-Offley group prevailed upon influential businessmen at Boston to petition the secretary of state for Offley's replacement, arguing that American trade relations with the Near East were suffering because of the man's incompetence, and urging that an American businessman be appointed in his place. Petitions to this effect were sent to the president himself as well as the secretary, signed by scores of executives of large business enterprises at Boston at the behest of their representatives and clients at Smyrna.

On the other hand, respected citizens of Philadelphia stressed in their own appeals to the Department the Offley family's excellent reputation in the City of Brotherly Love, emphasized their full confidence in Edward Offley whose father and brother had been known and esteemed by them, and demanded official support for the maligned consul at faraway Smyrna.

By the end of 1851 Secretary of State Webster had his fill of the maneuverings which eddied and swirled around Offley. Webster informed the consul of the various charges raised against him, and asked for a definitive reply to them.

In his answer, Offley ably refuted the accusations point by point. Betraying an understandable sensitivity about his birth abroad and the brevity of the time he had spent in the country represented by him, the consul concluded his account by stating that "I know I have done and always will do as much for my country as those who have had the good fortune to be constant residents . . ." [30]

To the great chagrin of the anti-Offley brigade, the secretary of state found the reply satisfactory — and the Department ceased to engage in further correspondence concerning its representative's fitness to serve at Smyrna or anywhere else.

It was against this background about a year later that Consul Offley suddenly found himself burdened with the irksome matter involving Martin Koszta. To those who had long tried and failed to bring about his removal, a new and promising opportunity seemed to beckon. As Paterson put it later, "the fat is now in the fire, and while wishing to rescue the poor young devil [Koszta], we hope to exorcise the old one [Offley] . . ."

It was about ten o'clock in the evening when the search of Koszta's room was begun. At about the same time an English-speaking emissary of the exiles arrived at the American consulate and alternately begged, requested, and demanded to be led before "his Excellency Mister Offley" to inform him about "a terrible crime committed against an American." On gaining admittance into the consul's study, he gave a fervid report about the disturbing events of the evening, and announced that perhaps within the hour certain documents, possibly including an American passport, would be brought to the consul for examination.

Offley was sufficiently impressed to take preliminary steps at once. As he wrote later, "I immediately applied to the Governor of this city, informing him of the occurrence, stating that if the refugee who had been arrested was really the holder of an American passport, I claimed him from the Turkish authorities."

Hardly was the note dispatched to the pasha when another

44

emissary arrived at the consulate. He brought no American passport, he said; none had turned up among Koszta's effects; possibly Koszta had been misunderstood in respect to such a passport. But something else had been found at his quarters, something perhaps just as important. Offley recorded this second visit and the discovery in these words: "Some hours after, at about midnight, a person called on me and handed me a document which he stated had been taken from the trunk of the person that had been arrested. This document is a copy of a declaration made in the Court of Common Pleas for the city and county of New York, on the 31st day of July 1852, by Martin Koszta, an Austrian subject, wherein he declares on oath that it is his intention to become a citizen of the United States."

What the consul held in his hand was a certified copy of the original, bearing the following endorsement: "Clerk's Office, Court of Common Pleas for the city and county of New York: I certify that the foregoing is a true copy of an original declaration of intention remaining of record in my office. In witness whereof, I have hereunto signed my name and affixed the seal of said Court this 31st day of July 1852. GEORGE W. RIBLET, Clerk."

The declaration itself read as follows:

"State of New York. In the Court of Common Pleas, for the City and County of New York.

"I, Martin Costa [Koszta's name was variously spelled in the documents of the case], do declare on oath that it is bona fide my intention to become a Citizen of the United States, and to renounce forever, all allegiance and fidelity to any foreign Prince, Potentate, State or Sovereignty whatever, and particularly to the Emperor of Austria, of whom I am a subject.

"Signed 31 day July 1852. — MARTIN COSTA. — GEORGE W. RIBLET, Clerk." *

* The whereabouts of the original of this controversial document remained unknown until the research for this book led to its discovery in stacks of old records of the Court of Common Pleas for the City and County of New York. That court, together with the Superior Court of the City of New York, was abolished in 1896, and the records of both were transferred to the Supreme Court of the state of New York for storage. A picture of the original document, not previously published, is included on the next page.

According to the document, as the consul could plainly see, Koszta had abrogated his previous allegiance. Also, he had declared his intention to become an American. To what extent did this change his physiognomy in the eyes of the law, American, Austrian, and international?

Upon the answers to these questions hung the life of the prisoner of the *Hussar.*

STATE OF NEW-YORK.

In the Court of Common Pleas, for the City and County of New-York.

I, *Martin Costa*

do declare on oath, that it is bona fide my intention to become a Citizen of the United States, and to renounce forever, all allegiance and fidelity to any foreign Prince, Potentate, State or Sovereignty whatever, and particularly to the *Emperor of Austria* of whom I am a subject.

Sworn this 31 day July 1852 *Martin Costa*

Geo. M. Kibler CLERK.

Martin Koszta's "first paper"

Dawn is breaking over Smyrna.

Offley is asleep, yet to face the first full day of what is to be the most turbulent episode of his career.

Asleep too is Ali Pasha, governor of Smyrna, who had already retired for the night when the American consul's note arrived at his residence.

But the exiles at Cristo's café are wide awake despite the exhausting deliberations of the evening and night, fortified by innumerable cupfuls of the best Italian coffee of the house — "on the house."

It is about four o'clock in the morning when the final draft of an appeal to the American, French, British, and Dutch consulates is complete in florid Italian and lithesome French. A revised and enlarged version, now also finished, is to be delivered to influential

American and British residents at Smyrna. Copies in sufficient number are soon available, thanks to fast-writing sometime teachers and state officials among the exiles.

Several men are selected from among those who possess pistols, to act as special messengers. They are instructed to walk slowly, avoid side streets whenever possible, and upon reaching their respective destinations, slip the enveloped copies under the doors.

The appeal begins in these words: "Most honored Mr. Consul: A deplorable event, an act of armed aggression perpetrated yesterday against the person of a Hungarian exile, in violation of every human and divine law, has impelled us, the undersigned, to submit this joint appeal to you . . ."

A description of the abduction in colorful terms is followed by references to past assistance received from Western representatives. Urgent intervention is requested. In conclusion, "in the name of God, and of humanity thus brutally trampled underfoot, the undersigned, representing the exile population of Smyrna, raise their voices and cry aloud to have the representatives of the uncivilized governments of Europe make amends for this nefarious act, and to find some way of obtaining guarantees for the honor and safety of the exile group in these troubled times." [24]

The exiles had decided not to spell out the names of Austria and Russia as "the uncivilized governments of Europe." A few considered the omission prudent, and the others felt that the exact meaning of the allusion would be obvious to everyone concerned.

Four men are quickly elected to sign the copies: Antinori, former member of the Chamber of Deputies at Rome, now ornithologist; Fumagalli, former colonel in the Garibaldi Division at Rome, now language teacher; Gottra, former colonel in the Engineer Corps at Venice, now civil engineer; Storari, former major in the artillery at Rome, now diamond cutter.

When the long session is ended and the exiles, together with Cristo and Koszta's two lady-friends, walk out of the café into the early morning mist, the first rays of the rising sun are just spreading over the waterfront; a hot, humid day is in prospect.

A member of the group suddenly calls something to the attention of his still arguing comrades. A naval vessel is approaching the international port.

In a moment, the ship is close enough to be recognized from ashore.

It is American.

In a new flurry of excitement the exiles return to the café for still another conference. Here is a godsent opportunity to make a new approach in behalf of their unfortunate friend.

The group files back into Cristo's place. The women get busy brewing more coffee.

Discussions are resumed in the conference room of the improvised Foreign Office of the Homeless.

THE COMMANDER

June 23, 1853

THE sloop of war *U.S.S. St. Louis*, Duncan Nathaniel Ingraham commanding, dropped her sails and came to port in Smyrna Bay.

The officer of the watch briskly walked up the narrow staircase leading to the bridge and made a brief report to the commander.

Ingraham, after a glance around deck, withdrew to his cabin to await his breakfast. It was soon brought in by a colored valet who limped because of a deformed leg, bore for some less obvious reason the nickname Brandywine, and was a member of a family of slaves owned by the Ingrahams back home at Charleston, South Carolina.

Five days before their arrival at Smyrna the officers and men of the *St. Louis* celebrated their captain's birthday which, although he was a veteran of the War of 1812, was only fiftieth. He had served in that war as a midshipman, first on the frigate *Congress* and later abroad the *Madison*, participating in naval action at the age of a present-day grammar school child; he was not yet ten at the time. In those early days of the Republic, when ships were wood and sailors were iron, midshipmen received their education at sea.* A large part of that education consisted of long, tedious

* The Naval Academy at Annapolis was not established as such until 1850. In its early, limited form, called the Naval School, it was opened in 1845.

49

periods of voyage, sometimes lasting a half year or more without any interruption and with accommodations hardly better than those available to contemporary inmates of prisons. Ingraham's own first cruise, on the *Congress*, took nine months. Junior officers of ships lived "in an inside cabin devoid of light and air, where twelve to fourteen men ate and slept in a space which today would be considered insufficient for two persons. In those days the art of putting up vegetables and fruits of tin was, of course, undreamed of, so that on long cruises all hands were reduced to the dreary monotony of salt beef, salt pork, hard bread, and occasional issues of rice, with the result that that dread disease of all sailors, the scurvy, often ravaged the crews of our men-o'-war . . ."[31]

The South Carolinian's love of the sea and talent for seamanship appeared hereditary. One of his grandfathers had been a sea captain in the Surinam trade. His father had served under John Paul Jones on the *Bon Homme Richard,* had taken part in the celebrated action against the *Serapis* in 1779, and could inculcate in his boy through personal experience the meaning of the stirring outburst of defiance: "I have not yet begun to fight!" Duncan's uncle Joseph had lost his life at sea as a navigator of another renowned vessel, the *Pickering.*

The family was connected by ties of blood or marriage with many of the most prominent Americans and Englishmen of the times. The first American ancestor of the Ingrahams was a leader of the Scotch-Jacobite insurrection who fled from England in 1715 and settled down in Massachusetts. A grandfather of the commander, George Abbott Hall, first collector of the port of Charleston, South Carolina, was an intimate friend of George Washington. Also related to the Ingrahams had been Governor Gibbes of colonial South Carolina; Vice Chancellor Mathewes of the colony; Captain Frederick Marryat, the famed British author of thrilling sea stories; Admiral Sir Edward Belcher, writer and world traveler; and many other celebrities. The commander's wife, whom he married in 1827, had similarly distinguished ancestry; she was a granddaughter of Henry Laurens, president of the Second Continental Congress, as well as of John Rutledge,

*Martin Koszta
(engraving from the
portrait painted at
Smyrna in 1853)*

*Commander Duncan
Nathaniel Ingraham,
U.S.N. (from a portrait,
1854)*

Karl Freiherr von Bruck,
Austrian minister to
Turkey (lithograph, 1855)

George P. Marsh,
American minister to
Turkey (portrait
by George P. A. Healy
at Dartmouth College)

governor of South Carolina and while a justice of the United States Supreme Court, President Washington's appointee to succeed John Hay as chief justice.* An uncle, Johns Laurens, was Washington's aide and secretary at Valley Forge. A more detailed drawing of the American branches of the family on either side would silhouette the nation's historical face at infancy, adolescence, and young manhood.

Duncan Ingraham became a lieutenant in the Navy in 1825 and a commander in 1838, the year in which that rank was first introduced. Before the Mexican War, he was in charge of the brig *Somers*; during that war, he served on Commodore Conner's staff as flag captain, participating in the capture of Tampico. In 1850, he was appointed commanding officer of the Philadelphia Navy Yard, and after two monotonous years of shore duty received command of the *St. Louis*.

The first few months of his new assignment were uneventful, except for a curious episode which he set down in a letter to his family: † "In command of the U.S. Ship St. Louis, I was sent to [Leoni——?] and [Tripoli?]. After leaving Ferris Island about 12 hours, I encountered a most terrible Gale which lasted about 40 hours. When the Gale had abated, I changed my course for [Nepite——?], giving orders when the ship had run a certain number of miles, to call me. About 4 o'clock A M, I dreamed I saw the Harbor and all the shipping, by six ten A M the ship had run on shore. I at once jumped up, went on deck and saw by the color of the water I was very near land. I at once hauled off shore and [sounded ?] in [202 ?] other water. The vessel would have been on shore in 15 minutes. She had run near the [Char——?] Canal." [32]

The ship commanded by this "delicate looking man of intelligence and culture," who "bore the reputation of being a brave and good officer," [33] was of the class known in the old Navy as a ship sloop. In the British and continental navies such ships were usually

---

* The Senate refused to confirm the nomination, apparently because of Rutledge's opposition to Jay's Treaty.

† The letter, undated, undecipherable in part, was copied by the author from the original showed him by a granddaughter of the commander, the late Mrs. George Ingraham Hutchinson.

51

termed corvettes and corresponded to modern light cruisers; they were called full-rigged ships, in contradistinction to the brig-rigged variety. By the contemporary system of measurement the *St. Louis,* launched in 1828, registered 700 tons, equivalent to 431 present-day tons, and was rated as an eighteen-gun ship although it usually carried twenty guns. In view of the important role these guns were destined to play at Smyrna, it should be mentioned that they were four eight-inchers and sixteen thirty-two pound-ers.

With a complement of one hundred and ninety officers and men, the *St. Louis* had made her first cruise in 1829 under the command of Captain Sloat, who on July 7, 1846, as fleet commander, planted the first American flag on the shores of California. The vessel was one of three units of a squadron assigned to Caleb Cushing, Amer-ica's first minister to China — and an eventual participant in the diplomatic action resulting from Ingraham's adventure at Smyrna — when he made his journey to the mysterious realm of the Emper-or Tao Kwang in 1843. And now, ten years after that trip to the Far East, the *St. Louis* made her first appearance at the colorful Middle Eastern port on an assignment of reconnaissance.

There was much to be reconnoitering about in that zone during those particular weeks and months. Ominous movements were being made, preparatory to the Crimean War which was to come as the ostensible outgrowth of a dispute between France and Rus-sia about the custody of holy places in Palestine. In June 1853, when the *St. Louis* moved to Middle Eastern waters, units of the British and French fleets dropped anchor off the Dardanelles; the overture of war was being rehearsed, and the curtain readied to go up, as the *St. Louis* arrived at Smyrna Bay.

Brandywine limped into the commander's cabin, carrying a tray weighted with a breakfast presumably worthy of a southern gentle-man's palate. He also brought the unexpected news that a delega-tion from ashore had just reached the ship, only a few of whose dozen or more members spoke English. They requested an urgent interview with "his Excellency the American captain" in what they said was "a matter of life and death" involving "an American citizen."

Hats and caps of various European and Middle Eastern styles were snappily removed by the visitors as Ingraham appeared on deck to face the group of Smyrniotes.

Present in the delegation were the Italian signers of the appeal composed on the previous night, of whom Fumagalli, the language teacher, was the only one with a good knowledge of English. Also included in the group were several Hungarians, among them ex-Captain Virágh, who was able to express himself in English with a fluency best described as desperate. A few Greek exiles completed the roster.

Excitedly interrupting each other at every turn, the spokesmen gave Ingraham an overly detailed and not overly coherent account of the events of the previous evening. Coming finally to the point, they asked: would the American captain intervene on Martin Koszta's behalf? The man is an American citizen, or national, or protégé, one of the three; whatever he is, he is certainly no Austrian, nor does he owe any allegiance to the Turks, and his native land is under illegal foreign rule. If a former exile who became an American can be kidnaped with impunity and shipped back to the dominions of the tyrant against whom he had fought for the very freedoms the Americans are upholding, what is to be the fate of thousands of his confreres? What is to become of those who are still without protection, without citizenship, without a permanent home? Would the imperial Austrian fleet remain unchallenged in its disregard for international law, and be allowed to practice outright piracy on Turkish waters?

What, asked the delegates, did "his Excellency" propose to do to save the life of Martin Koszta?

After a few moments of scrutinizing the eager faces of the awkward, stuttering, outlandish, but earnest men before him, Ingraham gave his reply.

He said that he needed a little time to acquaint himself more closely with the case; that he would be glad to contact appropriate authorities on shore for the purpose of obtaining full information and official advice; and that he would then see what could be done. If steps were warranted, they would be taken.

Eyes glittering, brows perspiring, the delegates shook hands with the commander one by one, clicking their heels and muttering their thanks, then climbed into their rowboats amid excited chatter about prospects and hopes.

The commander returned to his cabin and drafted a brief note, addressing it to "The American Consul at Smyrna" whose name he did not know.

He was about to call for his servant when Brandywine limped in unsummoned and reported that another delegation had arrived, this time one of Americans and Englishmen instead of "furriners."

Eyebrows at half-mast, Ingraham once again went up on deck.

The group which now awaited him was headed by Joseph Langdon of Boston, resident at Smyrna, one of the recipients of the exile appeal. In his company were a number of American and British businessmen, likewise Smyrna residents for years: Messrs. Blackler, Browning, Paterson, Wolff, Burrows, d'Andria, McRaith, Mathon, and Whittall.*

Hardly had Langdon begun to explain that he and his companions desired to intercede for a man named Koszta when the commander begged to interrupt. Stating that he had just talked with an exile delegation about the same matter, he repeated what he had told the previous callers. The situation, he said, obviously necessitated a thorough investigation, if only to determine whether the victim had any just claim on the United States or not. Such an investigation, however, was for the American consul at Smyrna to conduct, and he, Ingraham, was just about to send a note to that gentleman requesting him to come aboard. He assured the visitors that he would be pleased to inform them of subsequent developments.

Langdon replied that he and his associates came to the commander in preference to going to the consul because, to be perfectly frank, they had reason to doubt the consul's ability to cope with the delicate matter at hand. Paterson broke in to add gruffly that

* Descendants of several of these persons are still living at Smyrna.

the doubt could be extended to any other matter as well, as far as the consul's abilities were concerned.

Ingraham chose not to react to these remarks. He merely reiterated his assurances, shook hands all around, thanked the gentlemen for visiting him, and retired to his cabin.

He now sat down to write into the captain's journal a brief account of events up to the moment. Meanwhile, his note to the consul went on its way.

About a half hour later the officer of the day appeared in his chief's cabin, bringing the compliments of the American consul at Smyrna, Mr. Edward S. Offley, who had just stepped aboard.

Ingraham hurried upstairs.

"How do you do, Mr. Consul?"

"How do you do, Commander?"

Trivial formality signaled the beginning of a harmonious but hazardous association between two men of different callings and temperaments. Vacuous niceties marked the commencement of a series of actions to save one life now and make many others more secure in the future.

By midday of June 23, when Ingraham and Offley sat down together in the commander's cabin, the incident's details and early sequel were already known throughout Smyrna. Before the first twenty-four hours following Koszta's abduction were over, excitement reached a point seldom surpassed even in this town of explosive tempers and strange surprises.

The leading newspaper of the Western community raised the question in its issue for the day: "Is it permissible for armed boatmen, without legal warrant, without attendance of any official whatever, to appear in a public place and seize a man by force? . . . We need not stress the consequences of this sort of action. The question is of the utmost interest to the European colonies in the Levant, and we hope it will be decided in such a way as to guarantee the safety of everyone." [34]

The public was already too impatient to listen to rhetorical questions or declamatory expressions of hope.

One protest meeting followed another in various parts of the town.

Local newsmen recorded some of the outcries of fervid exile orators: "Snatch Koszta from the Austrian butchers! . . . Seize the Austrian ship! . . . Attack the Austrian Consulate! . . . Down with all tyrants! . . ."

An Italian speaker, shaking his fists, screamed in rage: "On fire with the Austrian Consulate! We need hostages . . . let's take the Consul of the Emperor!"

More than a hundred well-armed Greeks within the city, former members of the famed kilt-wearing *Evzone* formations, who looked upon "Kosta" as one of their own in view of his remote Greek ancestry, declared themselves ready to launch attacks on any target in order to force the man's release.

The mood of the crowds grew ugly. A few temperate leaders tried to calm the enraged masses and cajole them into acceptance of a temporary policy of watchful waiting. These sober heads emphasized that action was in the making; that matters were being handled by the American consul who had repeatedly helped exiles in the past; that even American armed force was now present, on the *St. Louis,* under the command of a high-ranking and experienced officer said to be sympathetic to exiles.

Smyrna was in a ferment.

"The pious and devoted female sex, moved to tears by the imprisonment of Koszta and despairing of obtaining justice from human sources, had recourse to the Holy Virgin as a haven of salvation . . . A young girl, Carolina Palomiri, made an offering of double work for two days to save up four piasters for a Mass to be offered for Koszta . . . Mrs. d'Andria gave special gifts to the poor three times during the week . . . Mrs. Mainetti gave alms of two hundred piasters . . ." [24]

Not in any way pious but just as determined womanfolk, practitioners of a profession reputedly the oldest in the world, were mobilized by the proprietress of Koszta's boardinghouse, an agile madame in the specialized sense of that gentle form of address. Disreputable though these women may have been by conventional standards of morality, they had their own code of sporting ethics. They decided to go on a Lysistratean strike against the Austrians; "being full of indignation, they vowed vengeance against the Austrian officers and refused to have anything to do with them." [35] This bizarre blackout promised to spoil almost completely the shore leave of the emperor's seamen.

Well-informed residents had special information about the kidnaping through sources of their own. They knew that Herr von Weckbecker had paid an unexpected visit to Ali Pasha, governor of Smyrna, shortly after Koszta's capture. Two local newspapermen saw him arrive at the *Konak* (the governor's palace), and later that same evening they were told by members of the governor's staff that the purpose of the Austrian's visit was to warn about a dangerous Austrian criminal who had allegedly arrived in town. Weckbecker wanted to know if the governor had any official objection to the man's arrest by special agents of the consulate. He explained that such a move would rid Smyrna of a highly undesirable alien without involving the Turkish police and without stirring up unpleasant debates over issues of extradition. The governor replied that he had not been aware of such a man's presence in the city; that the control of both criminals and foreigners was initially a police function not requiring his personal attention; that in view of the consul general's interest in the case, he would inform him of possible developments, but that the consul general might find it both practical and advisable to place at the disposal of the local police whatever information he had about the criminal. Weckbecker backtracked, saying that he did not yet know the man's exact whereabouts. He added that he would remain in touch with the governor, and departed in a morose mood.

There was another intriguing circumstance known to "insiders." [24]

At the approximate hour of Koszta's capture, a group of six or seven Austrian naval officers in full uniform appeared at "Captain Paolo's," an Italian restaurant with a sidewalk café not far from the so-called Bridge of Caravans. Taking seats on the canopied veranda, and ignoring the hostile murmur of some of the guests, they ordered coffee and beer and quietly chatted among themselves. After a while, exiles sitting nearby noticed that a man in mufti arrived, took a seat at some distance from the Austrians, summoned a waiter, and said something to him in a low tone of voice. The waiter proceeded to the table of the officers, whispered something to them, whereupon they rose, tossed a few bills on the table, and departed in haste. One of the exiles later learned from the waiter — in return for a reasonable *bakshish* — that the man in mufti had only wanted to know "if the officers would accept a round of drinks from an admirer of the valiant Austrian Navy." The waiter himself expressed surprise at the discourteous reaction of the officers.

The exiles wondered if the offer of drinks was not a prearranged code designed to inform the officers that Koszta's kidnaping had taken place on schedule and necessitated their return to the *Hussar*.

THE CONFRONTATION

June 23, 1853

"HONORABLE Gentlemen, the bells of the Church of the Capuchins and also the bells of the Church of the Franciscans are ringing at this noon hour as I take pen in my hand. If the unfortunate Martin Koszta is still alive on the *Hussar*, which who knows, he can hear the sound of these bells. Permit me to tell why the bells ring at noon each day in all Catholic churches everywhere in this world. They ring to commemorate the defeat of the Turkish invaders at Nándorfejérvár [present-day Belgrade] in 1456, when the Hungarian general János Hunyadi beat them. His Holiness the Pope Callixtus III, representing West which was saved by Hunyadi from East, ordered the commemoration for all time. Honorable Gentlemen, will those who now represent West save the life of a successor to Hunyadi's soldiers? Please answer in your hearts!" [36]

In the commander's cabin aboard the *St. Louis*, Offley sums up the situation for Ingraham in a manner characteristic of a man steeped in bureaucratic regulations.

He explains that Koszta had filed a declaration of intention popularly known as the "first paper," but that he had received no American passport. The man had obtained one *Tezkereh* from

59

the Turks at Smyrna and another at Constantinople. Whatever nationality or citizenship may be his under municipal or international law, he is not an American as far as the consulate at Smyrna is concerned, unless and until more than the documentation now available can support the claims proffered by his friends. It is impossible at this time and place to assess all factors bearing on his present status and on certain difficult problems relating to his past allegiance. No final determination of his case can be made by the consulate, not even by the legation at Constantinople which would soon receive a full report from the Smyrna office. The matter is certain to be transferred by the American minister to the Department of State for decision, and several weeks are bound to pass before the receipt of instructions from Washington. The Turks are likely to wash their hands of the whole business, at least until they see which way the Western winds are blowing, and one cannot blame them under the circumstances. The commander is no doubt familiar with more than one late unpleasantness between American and Austrian diplomats, since the European and American press had widely reported them. Clashes arising from the memorable Hungarian revolution had repeatedly threatened during the past few years an outright suspension of relations. Koszta's predicament has now created a situation which is not only disconcerting but, in the context of the larger picture, downright dangerous.

Ingraham's reply is typical of the naval officer, the self-reliant man of action.

He admits, to begin with, that he knows little about the technicalities involved. He does recall recent American-Austrian altercations referred to by the consul, but they are of little official concern to him. As a matter of personal interest, he had followed the Kossuth revolution and its aftermath rather closely. But all this seems to him irrelevant at the moment. The fact is that a man has been outrageously kidnaped. His life is in danger. The danger undoubtedly increases as the hours go by. It may be that the Austrians will move quickly, long before officials in Washington can decide what course to take. Something will have to be done very soon. While Mr. Offley's hands are, of course, tied, his own are relatively free because of certain singular advantages inherent in his position. As a naval officer in command of a vessel, extraordinary authority is vested in him by the ancient laws of the high seas. He can take emergency action. He is willing to apply measures likely to prevent the Austrians from forestalling diplomatic intervention. If Koszta's immediate release cannot be brought about, at least a *status quo* may be established and enforced until the governments involved can settle matters between themselves. Time must be gained for whatever cumbrous procedures may be required under protocol for a definitive solution.

He proposes that Offley and he visit the commanding officer of the *Hussar*. He, Ingraham, will make an attempt to deal with his Austrian opposite number as one naval person with another, without directly involving Offley in any way beyond his mere physical presence. Such presence, however, would be highly desirable, partly to enable the consul to prepare a subsequent eyewitness report for his superiors, and partly to lend silent but assuredly effective civil authority to the naval approach. The gambit can do no harm and may do some good. They may even be able to talk with Koszta himself.

Offley agrees at once to accompany Ingraham to the *Hussar*.

Commander Ingraham and Consul Offley proceeded to the Austrian ship on one of the lifeboats of the *St. Louis*. "We asked the Officer of the Watch if the Captain were on board; he replied that he had gone ashore to see the [Austrian] Consul. We then informed the officer that we had come to see the man who had been seized the day previous and who was confined on board the brig. He replied that no such person was there."

The American move seemed to have been anticipated.

The two men promptly proceeded to the Austrian consulate. They were admitted to the study of Peter Ritter von Weckbecker, His Imperial Majesty's consul general at Smyrna. The consuls exchanged curt, formal greetings; Offley introduced Ingraham and — as described in his subsequent report to the Department — "we requested him to allow us to interrogate Koszta in regard to his nationality. He answered that as he had given him up to the commander of the brig, he could not interfere in the matter."

In other words, Weckbecker did not deny that the man was in Austrian hands. But he had decided to give the Americans — to use their vernacular — the run-around. He was soon made to realize the futility of attempting to carry such tactics too far. The visitors told him plainly that "we had just come from aboard the brig, and that the Officer of the Watch had told us the commander was at the Consulate and that no such person [Koszta] had been sent on board of their vessel."

It was obvious to them that "an understanding had taken place between the Consul and the commander of the brig in order that we might not be allowed to see Koszta," and they were determined not to be thwarted. "We firmly insisted on seeing [Koszta] . . . After many objections he agreed to send for the commander of the brig."

Weckbecker did not have to send farther than another room. A score of exiles had seen Captain August von Schwarz of the *Hussar* arrive, together with an aide, at the Austrian consulate about an hour earlier. These exiles had lined up across the street well before noon, waiting in grim silence, keeping a virtual death-watch. When the consul general noticed them through the windows of his study, he ordered the building surrounded by Croatian sharpshooters of the imperial marines, with long bayonets fixed on their rifles.[24] The man who had ordered the kidnaping of a person from soil of foreign sovereignty was naturally unconcerned about the fact that the sidewalks around the consulate were not his emperor's property.

The commanding officer of the Austrian brig appeared in Weckbecker's office. "We asked him if he were willing to allow us to go on board and see Koszta, to which the commander acceded . . . We went on board with him and with the [Austrian] Consul."

The excitement in the streets and out at the harbor had received further stimulus from the visible comings and goings of Americans and Austrians. Upon leaving the Austrian consulate, the mixed quartet of officials found the streets lined with sullen spectators all the way from the building to the waterfront.

On the deck of the *Hussar*, the captive was led before the Americans.

He looked ill, fatigued, miserable, yet defiant; his beard was unkempt, his dress torn, and he wore chains on his wrists and ankles so that he was more dragged than led by his two armed guards.

Commander Ingraham immediately demanded the removal of the chains. Captain von Schwarz complied without argument. Ingraham and Offley then shook hands with the prisoner.

"He appeared confused by the ill treatment of the previous day. We interrogated him on what grounds his friends claimed for him American protection, and if he had an American passport; he replied that he had not any, and that he had nothing but the declaration already mentioned, which he had shown me on his arrival in this city."

Koszta had no opportunity on this occasion to describe to his visitors the ordeals he had undergone since his abduction. Some details, however, can be cited here from a report eventually published over his name: "Loaded with chains . . . I was closely tied to a pillar, although my arms and legs were likewise tied. In that position, and with my dress wet with the sea water, I remained eight hours, when my moral strength yielding to my physical sufferings, I fainted. The next thing I knew was that my arms had been untied by the physician of the *Hussar*, and medical attendance was administered to me. I continued to be tied to the pillar until 9 A.M. of the 23rd of June. About that time I was seized by four men and carried — not being able to walk myself — into the saloon of the vessel, where twelve officers and soldiers, attended by the Austrian Chancellor [of the consulate] were assembled to interrogate me. The Chancellor then addressed me several questions, among which were the following:

"Q.: Why are you here?

"A.: I do not know.

"Q.: Think for what reason you are here.

"A.: I know of no other reason than because you have appointed assassins to seize and carry me.

"Q.: By what authority did we do that?

"A.: I do not know.

"Q.: But where were you born, and what countryman are you?

"A.: My native land is Hungary. Perhaps you think that that fact gives you a right on me; but you have no such right, as I have abjured allegiance to Austria and declared my intention of becoming an American citizen, and I actually am under American protection.

"While this interrogatory was being made, an officer came from the deck and whispered a few words to the Commander [von Schwarz]. He soon came again and called the Commander into the adjoining cabin, where they spoke for some time. Subsequently the Commander went on deck, and on his return to the saloon he said in soft language, till then unknown to me, that I seemed to be a gentleman, and invited me to sit. This compliment was in consequence of seeing off the Smyrna harbor the U.S. sloop-of-war. The interrogatory continued some time longer, and it was then presented to me for my signature. After reading it I signed it and was returned to the hold, where I found a mattress and a chair. Shortly after, Captain Ingraham, accompanied by Mr. Offley, visited me . . ."[37]

And now he had spoken with the Americans who, after the brief interview with him, left the brig "without having expressed," recorded Offley, "any opinion on the matter."

THE INTERLUDES

June 23 (cont'd), 24-25, 1853

AROUND six o'clock, when the commander was still closeted with the consul in the latter's study, Attaché Griffith reported that according to a message from Hungarian exiles, Andrea the Slav, one of Koszta's identified abductors, had been found stabbed to death near the Bridge of the Caravans. A cousin of the victim, a beachcomber with a long police record, confessed to the crime, saying that there had been a personal feud between him and Andrea. Under strenuous interrogation he admitted that he had expected to find a great deal of money on the victim, and found none; he said that Andrea was supposed to have been paid on the previous evening for "some special work done."

A further report, of an exceedingly serious nature, was received at the American consulate later in the evening, some time after Ingraham had returned from there to his ship. It was brought by two attractive women who were greatly agitated and almost hysterically demanded to see the consul at once. One was Madame Vigny; the other, Cristo's daughter Lisa.

On admittance into Offley's study they poured out a story about a bloody lynching they had just witnessed, one which momentarily shocked them out of their exclusive preoccupation with the fate of their Hungarian paramour.

They said they had been on their way from Cristo's café to Madame Vigny's flat when they heard echoes of some kind of uproar from the general direction of "Captain Paolo's." Hurrying to the scene, they found a pandemonium of mob violence broken loose. The fury of the crowds had fallen on two Austrian naval officers who had shortly before appeared at the restaurant. They were attacked with sticks, chairs, knives, stilettos. One of them was stabbed to death; his body was picked up by a group of men and carried toward the wharves amid derisive chants; a few Turkish policemen standing nearby seemed paralyzed with fear. The other Austrian was felled by blows with a chair, suffered many wounds but was able to rise; a few courageous natives succeeded in getting him out of the raging crowd and when last seen, were helping him reach his ship.

Consul Offley instructed Griffith to escort the ladies home — and hurried to the office of the governor of Smyrna.

The director of Ali Pasha's chancery requested the American consul to wait a few minutes until the momentarily expected departure of the Austrian consul general who had come to see His Excellency a while ago and was still in conference with the governor.

Had Offley been able to enter the conference room, he would have witnessed the gradual degeneration of a high-toned discussion into a fierce dispute climaxed by an exchange of insults, in which the reserved Herr von Weckbecker utterly lost his self-control, and the dignified governor, a relative of Sultan Abdul Mejid himself, tottered on the verge of apoplexy. The consul general bellowed demands for "satisfaction . . . retaliation . . . damages . . . guarantees . . . revenge . . ." and the like, for the death of the unfortunate twenty-two-year-old naval cadet Baron Hackelberg. The governor, who had at first expressed his official as well as personal sympathy, was thrown into a tantrum when Weckbecker, raging, denounced the entire Turkish government and cast aspersions on His Sublime Majesty, the sultan. The pasha finally "escorted, in fact, pushed" the Austrian to the door and roared:

"You committed the first outrage! Now you handle the second one!" [38]

The emperor's representative, choking with fury, never even noticed his American colleague in the anteroom as he stormed out of the building.

Offley saw enough to think it expeditious to put off his intended conference with the governor. His Excellency was certain to be far too indisposed to discuss anything with anyone for at least the rest of the day.

The next day being Friday — the Sunday of the Moslems, — Consul Offley was compelled to wait another day for his planned discussion with the governor. Thus at last he had time enough at his disposal for thinking matters through and preparing a formal report for John P. Brown, American chargé d'affaires at Constantinople in the temporary absence of Minister George P. Marsh.

He proceeded to describe the events that had taken place up to the moment of writing.

Winding up his recital with an account of the murder of Baron Hackelberg, he closed the report with a few comments which, simple at first glance, reflected considerable shrewdness and eventually served as the anchor of a line of argument developed by the Department of State. In this first summary report Offley, not a diplomat, or an international lawyer, correctly diagnosed the case and gave firm orientation not only to Chargé Brown but to the entire diplomatic chain of command when he stated: ". . . it is clear that Koszta is not an American citizen, but it is certain he is a refugee living in a foreign land and has renounced all allegiance to the Emperor of Austria, and has declared on oath his intention of becoming a citizen of the United States. It is true that [Hungarian exiles] were not, according to the convention betwixt Turkey and the European powers, to return here; but Koszta's return, contrary to the convention, does not give Austria the right to act as she has done; and all she had the right to do was to demand from the Turkish authority his expulsion from this country, and it was only Turkey who had the right of interfering with him."

As so many times since, a modest agent of the American government in a faraway post of limited importance, a public servant duty-bound to think freely and report honestly, a man personally unknown in policy-making circles and never to receive public plaudits, set down views which percolated upwards until they turned up in state papers of historic significance under the signature of the secretary of state himself. The thoughts and even some of the very words of hard-working Mr. Offley were to be used by Secretary Marcy in one of the most stirring diplomatic notes in the Department's note-studded history.

The consul remarked that "the precarious state of the refugees residing here has been greatly increased by these doings . . . The other consuls have also written to their embassies on the same subject . . . Steps ought to be taken which you consider proper for the release of said Koszta and for the future protection of those unfortunate exiles who are in this land."

Ingraham too was writing a report on that day, although as yet only an unofficial one. In accordance with the promise he had made to Mr. Langdon of the Smyrniote delegation to keep him posted, he wrote the gentleman that "I am as sensible as you are of the gross outrage committed upon the person of Martin Coszta by the Austrian Consul and his hired ruffians; and it is a disgrace to the Turkish Government to suffer it . . . The American Consul . . . informed me that [Koszta]was a Hungarian refugee and had no evidence of his being a citizen of the United States . . . On board [the *Hussar*] I asked why he had left [America] before he had remained the time required by law [for the acquisition of full citizenship]. He told me he came to Smyrna for the purpose of establishing himself in business . . . Anything I can do in behalf of this unfortunate man, I shall be most happy to aid you and the Americans residing in Smyrna."

The commander made no attempt to conceal from Langdon and his associates that he was in somewhat of a quandary, nor did he minimize the obstacles blocking any unorthodox solution at the moment: "Should the claim be made that Coszta is an American by adoption, it will have to be enforced; and how can this be done when by law he has forfeited his claim?" *

In the early evening Mr. Blackler, an American resident at Smyrna and a member of the American-British delegation that had visited Ingraham aboard the *St. Louis,* was returning home from the inner city. Shocked like everyone else by the Hackelberg murder, the tragedy incensed his feelings about Weckbecker, the man responsible for the cause which led to the lynching.

Blackler's house faced the wharf. As he reached the gate, he noted the approach of several Austrian sailors led by two officers, all wearing the insignia of the *Hussar* and all walking somewhat unsteadily. Blackler, entering his front yard, slammed the iron gateway behind him, and unable to resist an urge to give vent to his resentment toward Austrians in general, turned and shouted:

"Down with tyranny! Long live Kossuth!"

His young son's head bobbed up in an open second-floor window. The boy merrily chimed in:

"Down, down! Hurray!"

The naval group, resentful because of the hostile attitude of the population which spoiled their shore leave, and irritable under the effect of liquor consumed as a palliative in quantities larger than the usual, were thrown into a rage by the American's provocative outburst. Rushing to the gateway, they banged away at it first with their fists, then with rifle butts. One of the officers yelled orders for the sailors to line up with rifles ready to shoot, while the other had already fired several shots from his service pistol in the general direction of doors and windows. Fortunately, his aim was much too unsteady, and the bullets hit neither Blackler nor his little boy. But now a volley was in preparation, possibly to be followed by an invasion of the house.

It so happened that the Prussian consul at Smyrna was taking his evening constitutional in the same street, at the same time, and

* The original of this letter is lost, but a transcript was prepared and sent years later by Langdon to a son who eventually released it for publication.[39] The son, William R. Langdon, is a retired consul general, former American political adviser in Korea.

happened to be close by when the pistol shots rang out. He rushed toward Blackler's house and shouted in a baritone stentorian enough to do proud even Frederick the Great on field maneuvers: "Halt! Halt!"

The resounding command in their native tongue affected the Austrians at once, in a manner demonstrative of the correctness of Pavlov's theories about conditioned reflexes. Frozen for a moment, they turned around just as the consul reached them. Shaking his fists, he gave them as thorough a dressing-down as only an ex-major of Grenadiers, which he indeed was, could administer in all its glory. Cowed by his orders to leave immediately, officers and men slowly straggled away while the consul continued to bellow after them a formidable assortment of Prussian profanities.[24]

The effect that could have been created by the injury or death of the American or his child, at a time when an eruption of tempers had already produced one lynching, is both easy and frightening to imagine.

Saturday, June 25, began with a conference in Consul Offley's study, attended by himself, Attaché Griffith and the consuls of Britain, France, Holland, and Piedmont.

British Consul Brant informed his colleagues that he had sent a report to Lord Redcliffe, ambassador at Constantinople, summarizing the events of the past few days and suggesting that "it is now high time that the question of refugees in Turkey be defined by the offices which represent the Courts of Europe. Let us hope that a satisfactory solution will be found for an affair which is an outrage to justice and humanity."

All others present expressed full agreement with these sentiments. Offley said that he had been waiting to hear from the American chargé before taking further action, but added that he planned to visit Ali Pasha that morning in order to obtain his unofficial views. He called attention to the fact that the funeral of the unfortunate Baron Hackelberg was scheduled to be held that afternoon, and suggested that the consuls would do well to warn everyone under their authority to stay away from the ceremony. Things might happen . . .

Recognizing the wisdom of this recommendation, the others agreed to send out appropriate notices. Since only a few hours remained in which to do this, the meeting was adjourned.

Offley went to the *Konak*, hoping to find the pasha in an agreeable mood.

The governor of Smyrna, his nerves having recovered during the holiday from the effect of the tempestuous interview with the Austrian consul general, was his usual friendly self on receiving the American. However, the news which he gave his visitor as soon as they had seated themselves on a divan was quite unpleasant.

As Offley wrote Brown on June 27, "His Highness applied to me . . . requesting that I should arrest Ferdinando Baschish, a Hungarian refugee holding a passport given by our Legation;* and that he and the other refugees under [local] protection should be sent to the local authorities to be examined by them in regard to the murder that had been committed . . . Baschish is the servant of the British chaplain of this place. In compliance to the governor's request I immediately sent Mr. Griffith to effect the arrest as requested."

Something in the governor's account must have convinced Offley of a certain likelihood about the guilt of the man named, else he would hardly have ordered the arrest without any further ado, "immediately." But the records reveal no more about the background of Baschish than the meager information in the consul's report about his identity. The surname is not a Hungarian one. The first name, Ferdinand, was odd for a nineteenth-century Hungarian to have. Whoever he was, his possession of an American passport was disturbing to Offley who certainly had enough on his hands already as far as controversial documents were concerned.

But soon an element of comedy entered the picture:

"On going to the house," reported the consul, Griffith "found

* It was the man's possession of an American passport that had prompted the Turks to make a formal request, in order to avoid any infringement upon extraterritorial privileges regulated by the American-Turkish treaty of 1830.

the man there." Baschish appeared to be either too innocent or too brazen to flee; he "left the room to dress himself in order to go with Mr. Griffith; and, on the latter finding that he delayed to return, he was told that the man had disappeared."

The attaché, greatly embarrassed, rushed out of the house to talk to the policemen whom "he had placed . . . to guard it." The policemen told him that "the man had not left the house." But he was nowhere to be found in or near it. Did he perchance have an accomplice among the police? Or were the police simply careless? It was only a few weeks previously that the newspapers had a field day at the expense of the local law-enforcing authorities when the rifles of a police squad, stacked in neat little pyramids in a park while the men were throwing dice, disappeared in full daylight.[38]

A province-wide alarm was issued for the arrest of the fugitive. American authorization was given the Turks to "seize Baschish wherever he might be found."

Offley's increased concern about certificates of various kinds still in exile hands was reflected in a further message to Chargé Brown about the queer case of the vanishing servant: "I now beg you to inform me if any refugees holding American passports should be seized by the local authorities to be put under trial for the murder of the Austrian officer, what am I to do in the case? Am I to give them up to the Turkish authorities, or am I to protect them?"

Brown had to do considerable soul-searching before giving his answer to the blunt question, since it was none other than he who had given a passport to Baschish. According to his letter to Offley on July 1, "on looking over the list of passports given by the Legation, I find one dated the 24th January, 1851, to 'Baschish' for America, which was vized [officialese for "granted visa"] the 25th of the same month. I presume that this is the person to whom you allude as 'the servant of the British chaplain,' and who has been demanded by the local authority of Smyrna as suspected of having been implicated in the murder of the Austrian officer . . . I apprehend that I could not expect that an official intercession for [Baschish] on my part could be approved by the President, as he is only possessed of a passport given him by this Legation for the purpose of departure to the United States. The protection possessed by Baschish is at most but a nominal and temporary one, and may be disputed, with reason, by the Austrian consul in case he is or has been an Austrian subject."

However, the humane aspect still emerges: "I would not . . . recommend you to cast him off or withdraw entirely your protection or interest in him. Humanity forbids it, especially if you have reason to believe him innocent of the accusation imputed to him. You may, however, allow him to be judged by the local authority, and use the matter of the passport as a reason for being present or represented at court."

But Baschish, rather fortunately for all concerned except possibly the Austrians, never turned up again.

In the early afternoon the consul paid another visit to the governor, this time in the company of Commander Ingraham. It was now the commander's turn to play a passive part similar to that of Offley on the occasion of their joint visit aboard the *Hussar*.

The governor's opinions had not yet crystallized. At any rate, that is what he said. But at the end of an admirable specimen of Near Eastern circumlocution, he ventured the guess that former Austrian subjects now without consular protection would probably have to be given up to the Austrians.

Offley, registering alarm, spoke up in defense of the exiles. Ingraham, perturbed though he must have been, remained silent. The pasha kept reiterating that they and everyone else had his sympathy. The Americans left.

The consul appealed to the chargé to use his influence "in order that this act may be hindered. Amongst the refugees there are many upright and good men who have behaved in the most exemplary manner since their arrival here. There are also many who are not Austrian subjects and who were until lately under the protection of the Sardinian and other Consulates, but who have been abandoned under these circumstances when they are more in need of protection than ever . . . I would take the liberty of suggesting that in case the local authorities should put the refugees to a trial, it would be well to use your influence conjointly with the English and French ambassadors, in order that it may be carried on impartially and in the presence of a *dragoman* [interpreter] of those powers, so that justice may be done them."

For Ingraham, it was enough to see that matters were getting more muddled as time went on. "Words, words, words" were inundating the solid fact that a man, at least possibly an American, and certainly not yet proved guilty of anything, had been forcibly removed from the territory of a neutral power and was being held in chains on a foreign ship within sight of the *Konak* and within the range of fire of the guns on the *St. Louis*.

His mind may have flashed back to the unforgettable orator named Kossuth whom he had seen and heard at Philadelphia while in charge of the Navy Yard there. His ears had rung to the cheers of immense throngs of free Americans as the spellbinder thundered: "Those who strive for freedom are brothers, wherever they be . . . The lesson [Americans] give to humanity will not be lost . . . Will God's merciful arm not raise up a power on earth to protect the law of nations when there are so many to violate it?" [40]

Atop the buildings of the various consulates flags were at half mast on the afternoon of Sunday, June 25.

The funeral of Baron Hackelberg was under way.

At the head of the procession a group of Austrian marine drummers marched slowly, beating their muffled instruments. A heavily armed detachment of sailors followed, carrying muskets topped by fixed bayonets. Contrary to military custom, even the pallbearers, fellow officers of the victim, carried heavy pistols. The coffin rested on a two-wheeled cart draped in black and pulled by two white horses wearing black headgears.

The consul general of Austria and the consul of Prussia walked directly behind the cart. Virtually the entire complement of the *Hussar* followed, led by Captain von Schwarz, chanting psalms of David and traditional songs of mourning as the funeral cortege proceeded through the main streets of the city toward the Church of the Franciscans.

The circularized warning of the consuls about possible disturbances and the desirability for their respective citizens to remain at home proved effective. Not more than a handful of westerners appeared in the crowds lining the streets.

The tragic death of the young man seemed to have had a calming effect on the taut nerves of the populace. Not the slightest disturbance occurred during the funeral. In fact, the Hungarians proved chivalrous enough to purchase a huge wreath of red roses and lay it before the altar of the church. The wide black ribbon on the wreath bore this inscription:

Adjon az Ur örök nyugodalmat! ("May the Lord give you everlasting peace!")

An observer was apt to notice two small initials under the huge, golden block letters of the inscription. If he happened to know that in Hungarian usage the family name always precedes the given name, he did not have to think twice about the initials K. M. to realize in whose name the wreath had been sent.[38]

THE MAILBOAT

June 25-29, 1853

THE principals were now forced to bide their time. Weckbecker was waiting to hear from Baron von Bruck, chief of the Austrian diplomatic mission to Turkey. Offley was expecting instructions from Brown, American chargé at Constantinople. Ingraham was scanning the horizon for signs of a possible Austrian attempt to spirit Koszta away from the port.

And all the while, waiting in mental anguish and amid physical hardships was the American Hungarian aboard the *Hussar*.

The Austrian consul general was much discomfited by the backfiring of several points in his original plan of strategy. He had not foreseen such complications of a legal and diplomatic nature as those which Koszta's "first paper" now appeared to entail; nor could he have anticipated the identification of the kidnapers by eyewitnesses. A special disappointment had been Ali Pasha's unwillingness to propose or approve any action when — subsequent to Koszta's capture, to be sure — Weckbecker reported the "presence" of an alleged Austrian criminal in town. Finally, there was the remarkable coincidence of the arrival of an American warship the morning after the abduction, stimulating anti-Austrian sentiment in town and bringing close collaboration between Offley and Ingraham.

The Play

And yet another development arose in the evening of June 26 to plague the man who had masterminded the capture of the Hungarian.

Jovicich and Luca paid a nocturnal call on their clandestine employer and in place of the originally fixed ten thousand piasters as payment for services rendered, they now insisted on getting exactly twice as much. They threatened to expose the consul general in case he refused to pay it. They claimed that the attitude of the population, so unmistakably shown in the murder of Hackelberg, placed their lives in danger; that they had become outcasts for whom the best thing to do was to leave Smyrna forever.

Weckbecker, faced with the prospect of having to pay the thugs at least partly out of his personal funds, made every effort to put them off. He failed. After long and noisy wrangling, a bitter compromise was made: he handed over fifteen thousand piasters.[24]

Spurred by this new frustration, he started a campaign against all exiles. His influence in Turkish official circles and among local merchants was not inconsiderable, as shown by the fact that, at his behest, the Smyrna Paper Factory discharged fourteen exile workers, the Lloyd Shipping Company dismissed twenty-two, and scores of others were summoned to local police stations, subjected to rough interrogations, sent to jail for alleged vagrancy or other trumped-up charges, or held under so-called protective arrest of indefinite duration.

Among the first ones ordered to appear at precinct stations were leaders of the delegation which had visited Ingraham on June 23: Fumagalli, the language teacher; Storari, the engineer; Antinori, the ornithologist. Summoned were also the Criccal brothers, one of them a teacher of music, the other of "dance and manners"; Genna, violinist in the small but loud Smyrna Philharmonic Orchestra, who later wrote a grandiose, virtually unplayable, and never-performed tone poem dedicated to Ingraham; Konduriotis, a landscape gardener, grand-uncle-to-be of a future president of Greece; Hungarian ex-Captain Virágh; and many others. Ceccherelli, a tailor, father of seven children, was held in a police jail charged with "defiance of official authority by refusing to answer questions"; he knew only a few words of Turkish and in addition was completely deaf.

French Consul Pichon, upon learning of some of these cases, declared that he would request his government to authorize him to place all Italians under his official protection.[24] As dean of the local representatives of the Western governments, he called on the governor of Smyrna and demanded an end to the persecutions.

This intervention proved fruitful because it coincided with the pasha's receipt of advance information about an impending official investigation of the activities of his underlings, to be conducted by a special commissioner. Within a few days, molestations of exiles were stopped, all arrested persons released, and black-listings by Weckbecker ignored.

But the exiles remained restive, fearing that a possible adverse outcome of the Koszta case might again jeopardize their precarious freedom. On June 27 their leaders submitted a new petition to the consuls of the United States, France, and Great Britain, pointing out that some of their associates were endangered by "lack of usual papers because of various irregular ways in which they had been forced to emigrate," while others held "passports which some of the Consulates refused to recognize either because the passports had expired or because new regulations are in effect." They added: "In view of differences in religions, customs, and laws, it is impossible for us to have recourse to the local government. We therefore hereby invoke the good offices of your embassies at Constantinople, begging them to issue us valid documents which will grant us status as Europeans [sic]." [24]

Thus the whole complex problem of the status of exiles, involving conditions of political asylum, validity of letters of protection, and other vexing questions, was once again revived at this late date in the wake of the sudden misfortune of an erstwhile *emigré* who was now perhaps an American — and then again, perhaps he was not.

"It's here!"

Observers posted at the piers by the exiles breathlessly reported the arrival of one of the mail steamers which commuted regularly between Smyrna and Constantinople.

Within minutes of that early morning hour on June 29, a crowd gathered near the point where the sacks of incoming mail were to be put ashore as usual. One of those sacks was likely to contain a certain tensely awaited letter of crucial importance.

A quarter hour later Offley found that letter in the consulate's dispatch pouch. Dated June 27, it read:

"I have received your letter of the 24th instant, respecting the outrageous and inhuman conduct of the Austrian Consul of your city towards the Hungarian refugee Martin Koszta who, though not possessing the full rights of a citizen of the United States, has nevertheless, by the oath of allegiance which he has taken to the Government of the United States, claims upon your friendly aid and intercession. I have addressed a letter to the [Austrian] Internuncio [i.e. minister] in which, after expressing my opinion freely of the barbarous conduct of the Consul, I interceded for Martin Koszta's immediate release from the brig-of-war and return to the United States.

"I have to request that you will continue your officious intercession in behalf of Martin Koszta, both to the Austrian Consul and the Commander of the *Hussar* . . . I should have supposed that the neutral soil of the Sultan would have demanded more respect from the Austrian Consul, and though the victim unfortunately does not possess a passport of the United States, yet his declaration of allegiance . . . merits the regard of the American Consulate and your friendly sympathy.

"The act of the Austrian Consul has, very naturally, excited the indignation of the inhabitants of Smyrna, as it has of everyone here. The effect everywhere which it will make, will be the most unfavorable to the Austrian Government, and nowhere less favorable than in the United States.

"No Convention was made, as you apprehend, apparently, between the Government of the United States and the Porte, that the refugees should not return here; nor do I know of any between them and the Porte."

79

As soon as he finished reading Chargé Brown's letter, Offley grabbed his hat and hurried to the *St. Louis* for another conference with Ingraham. His subsequent report outlined what then took place:

"On receipt of this letter I went aboard the *St. Louis* and communicated its contents to Commander Ingraham. During my interview with him as to the means to be adopted in behalf of Koszta, one of the officers of the corvette entered the cabin and told the Commander that the Austrians were loading their guns.

"Commander Ingraham then gave orders to load the guns of the *St. Louis*. He and I decided that I should go to the Austrian Consul and endeavor to effect the release of Koszta, or that he should at least be kept there until we should hear further from the Legation of the result of its letter to the Austrian Minister.

"I, therefore, called on the Austrian Consul, and my efforts for [Koszta's] release having proved unavailing, I then requested that he should be kept here until further instructions from Constantinople.

"He at first told me that he could not comply to my wishes, having received orders to send Koszta by the steamer that was to leave on that day to Trieste.

"Under these circumstances, I suggested the propriety of his keeping Koszta here at least for 8 days, but he refused to grant my desire, and it was only after much opposition on his part that I was enabled to obtain a promise that he should not be sent away before Saturday the 2nd instant."

That evening a small caïque pulled up to the side of the *St. Louis*. A rope was thrown down, on which a native messenger climbed aboard. He pulled out a letter from somewhere underneath his *burnus*, handed it to the officer of the day, bowed deeply, climbed back into his conveyance, and paddled away.

The letter was unsigned:

"Citizen Captain:

"It is our hope that by this time the Commodore Stringham [commander of the American Mediterranean Fleet] will have received an accurate account of the events of the 22d, set down for him by an eye-witness. Europeans residing here have no recourse other than to rely on you, hoping that you will take some measure to save the victim.

"Tomorrow at dawn he is to be placed on board the Austrian Lloyd steamer and taken to Trieste." [24]

Did Ingraham know who the writer was?

Had he made arrangements beforehand through the grapevine to establish sources through which information about moves planned or made by Captain von Schwarz would reach him?

One might even ask, does the salutation "Citizen Captain" suggest a French writer? Perhaps Madame Vigny?

Within a few minutes a letter from the commander was on its way to the Austrian captain:
"Sir:

"I have at this moment received a letter stating M. Koszta was to be sent on board the steamer tomorrow at daylight, to be sent to Trieste. I have been only waiting to hear from the Minister at Constantinople before I took some action in the case of Koszta, as he has a paper stating his intention of becoming a citizen of the United States. He came here in an American vessel, and has been some time in the United States.

"I earnestly protest against his leaving this port before something has been heard from Constantinople.

"Respectfully,

[signed] INGRAHAM, Commander." [41]

Captain von Schwarz had hardly finished reading this note when sudden movements made by the *St. Louis* were reported to him by his officer of the watch.

Rushing up on deck, he saw that Ingraham was deploying his ship between the *Hussar* and the Austrian Lloyd steamer.

Ships could no longer pass between those two.

And Koszta could no longer be transferred unobserved from the brig to the steamer.

THE ULTIMATUM

June 30-July 2, 1853

EARLY risers in Smyrna on the morning of June 30 were electrified when they noticed that the American corvette had changed its position.

"Great was the excitement in town," reported the newspaper *L'Impartial*, "the shores lined with people anxious to note the results of the *manoeuvre* . . ."

The crowds dispersed toward noon, realizing with disappointment that only an intensification of the previous watchful waiting on the part of the Americans seemed in prospect. But they retained the hope that sensational events could not be far off.

The persecution of the exiles had been stopped by Ali Pasha just in time for the arrival of a high-ranking representative of the Sublime Porte. The emissary came to investigate the situation as a result of a joint request to the Turkish Foreign Office by the Western diplomatic corps at Constantinople. Chargé Brown had reported: "Opinion here is strongly in our favor. The conduct of the Austrian Consul is so despicable that there is a profound sense of indignation here, and everywhere, against him. All the Turks, even the Persian chargé d'affaires, say that the 'Yenghi Duny'd' (New World) is not to be so trifled with . . . I am in hopes that the Internonce will be staggered by the 'declaration' [of intention] and my argument, though the Austrians will with reluctance relinquish their victim . . . Lord Redcliffe and M. de la Cour [British and French ministers, respectively] promised me to act together . . . and to speak with the Internonce on the subject. The Sardinian Minister is also, I believe, warmly interested."

Some of Brown's informants in Turkish cabinet circles told him that Chekhib Effendi, "a person of high rank and experience," one of the Porte's outstanding experts in international law, had been assigned to go to Smyrna "as a Commissioner in this matter."

The American chargé had addressed several communications to the Austrian minister, Baron von Bruck. Enclosed with one of the notes was a blank form of a declaration of intention, with Koszta's name and the date of his original "first paper" filled in by Brown. Having found the form in the legation's collection of sample documents, he inscribed the data in order to combine general illustration with specific information. And to the secretary of state he wrote: "The brutal conduct of the Austrian Consul will, I trust, be disavowed by the [Austrian] Minister at this capital; but I doubt whether the unappeasable thirst for the blood of the unfortunate Hungarian will permit him to do justice to my intercession in favor of the present victim . . . to save the life of one who, though not wholly a citizen of the United States, nevertheless has strong claims upon my official interference in behalf of his existence."

On June 30, a reply came from the baron.

It was unfavorable.

"The explanations you have kindly furnished me on this subject and for which, Sir, I cannot but thank you, can not, however, produce any change in the measures that have been taken in regard to said individual whom it is impossible for me to consider under any circumstances as belonging to a foreign jurisdiction inasmuch as the ties which bind him to Austria have not been legally dissolved. Martin Koszta . . . will be immediately conveyed to Austria . . . I think it my duty to remind you . . . in case you should intend to continue your applications in his behalf, that any overtures to that effect would be entirely useless unless directly addressed to the Imperial Cabinet by the Representative of your Government at Vienna."

The envoy concluded with a statement which sounded almost as if it had been specially designed to incense Brown: "I assure you, Sir, that the individual in question will find his surest guaranty of just and indulgent treatment in the wisdom and foresight of Austrian law and especially in the clemency and magnanimity of my august Sovereign."

Brown had been not only officially but also personally close to matters relating to the late Hungarian revolution. Both he and his chief, Minister Marsh, had established friendship with numerous Hungarian leaders. Both during and after the Hungarian war they had ample opportunity to observe the extent and nature of the Austrian "wisdom" and "magnanimity" glibly cited by the baron. Even at this late date, four years after the end of the revolution, countless people in Hungary were in prison for such "crimes" as undefined "unreliability" reported by informers and punished by the military satraps of the subjugated country. Public executions were still frequent as the results of star chamber procedures. The circumstances of Koszta's abduction alone were sufficient to show the sort of "wisdom, foresight, clemency" to which the internuncio found it proper to refer. And now the Austrian suggested that Koszta throw himself at the mercy of his persecutors.

As at Smyrna, the issues were finally drawn also at Constantinople between Austrians and Americans, embroiling in sharp dispute Bruck, Brown, and Marsh, each a man of forceful personality, unusual talents, and colorful background.

Karl Ludwig Freiherr von Bruck (1798–1860) had attained aristocratic rank through his success as a businessman. Founder of the Austrian Lloyd Company of Trieste and later of several chains of banks and railroads, he was raised to the baronetcy by the court for his achievements as one of the principal organizers of Austrian domestic and foreign commerce. He had been, in turn, a member of Parliament, confidential adviser to successive cabinets, and minister of commerce before the receipt of his appointment as envoy to Turkey in 1853. He was again to become a cabinet member in 1855 as minister of finance. His career was to end tragically in 1860 when, while still in charge of the latter portfolio, political enemies and social rivals accused him of illegal manipulations and he was summarily dismissed. A few hours after his disgrace, he committed suicide. A government commission appointed to investigate the alleged malfeasance of office worked on the case for several months and in its final report established the baron's complete innocence.[42] His widow was given a high decoration — and the affair was closed.

Von Bruck's direct American adversary in the affair of Koszta, John Porter Brown (1814–72), was diplomat, linguist, orientalist, grandson of a noted naval captain of the American Revolutionary War. An uncle, Commodore and later Admiral David Porter, upon receipt of appointment in 1832 as minister resident at Constantinople, took his nephew along to the Turkish capital. Young Brown quickly learned Turkish and Arabic, became dragoman and consul in 1836, consul general in 1857, secretary of the legation in 1858. He acted as chargé d'affaires of the legation on nine occasions, including that of the Koszta case. In 1850 he helped secure the first Turkish diplomatic mission to the United States by convincing Grand Vizier Reshid Pasha of the advisability of sending accredited agents to inspect American naval and military establishments. He gained considerable repute as an orientalist, translator into English of numerous Turkish and Arab works of history and poetry, and wrote several excellent guidebooks. He proved himself an official of ability and audacity in delicate diplomatic affairs. After four decades of service in the Moslem world, he died of heart disease at Constantinople in financial circumstances so strained that his widow, a somewhat eccentric lady who chose to conceal her need from American officials and personal friends, accepted help from the sultan's exchequer to enable herself to pay her late husband's debts as well as her own passage back to America.[43]

George P. Marsh (1801–82), American minister to Turkey — absent from his post on a special tour of duty during the greater part of the events involving Koszta — had been a child prodigy. By the time he was seven, voracious reading had nearly ruined his eyesight. Unable for long periods to use his eyes, he learned by listening to others read. At Dartmouth College, which he entered after only a few months of formal schooling, he was the most brilliant student in his class. In his spare time he learned French, Spanish, Portuguese, Italian, German, and the Scandinavian languages, becoming later one of the two most formidable linguists in the American Foreign Service during the nineteenth century.* After graduation with highest honors in 1820, he entered law school, was admitted to the bar in 1825, soon became highly successful not only in the practice of law but also in business, and still found time to pursue scholarly activities such as the writing of philological studies and dictionaries. In 1834 he was elected to Congress as a Whig; later in the same year he was appointed minister to Turkey, and when Kossuth and his entourage left their Turkish asylum for England and the United States, it was Marsh who made arrangements for their departure and issued them special American passports. After his recall from Turkey in 1854, Marsh lectured at Columbia University on English philology and etymology. In 1860, President Lincoln sent him to Italy as America's first minister to the new kingdom; he held the post during the remaining two decades of his life, died at Florence, and was buried at Rome.[44]

With men such as these in the picture, the diplomatic duels precipitated by the Koszta case promised to be exciting. Intense professional interest was focused on the unfolding figurative game of chess.

* The other was Caleb Cushing (1800–79), the first American minister to China and a behind-the-scenes participant in the final phase of the Koszta case. He had mastered the Manchu language so completely that he was able to negotiate the Treaty of Wang Hsia without the aid of interpreters. He could converse fluently in French, Spanish, Italian, and German, and had a working knowledge of Russian, Swedish, and Dutch. Acting as counsel before the Geneva Arbitration Tribunal in 1871–72, he shifted repeatedly from English to French and Italian for hours without betraying the slightest mental fatigue.

In our own times, top-ranking Foreign Service officers of special linguistic talents include the only American envoy ever to surmount the difficulties of the Hungarian language: Christian M. Ravndal, minister to Hungary from 1951 to 1956, at present Ambassador to Ecuador. He is also proficient in German, French, Spanish, Norwegian, Arabic, Turkish, and Swedish.

86

In the early afternoon of July 1, Offley sent word to Ingraham about the unexpected arrival in town of a recently elected member of Congress. The chance visit offered an opportunity to seek advice from a new quarter of great importance, at a time when not even the Department of State, much less congressional circles, had as yet received reports about the happenings at Smyrna.

Caleb Lyon, "squire of Lyonsdale," elected from New York to the House of Representatives in March 1853, future first governor of the Territory of Idaho (1864–66), was widely known in the Foreign Service as a world traveler and a student of the Middle East. Ingraham might have heard of him as a powerful congressional advocate of naval expansion.

The commander went to the consulate to meet with Offley and the visitor. After a thorough briefing, Congressman Lyon expressed the view that while something certainly had to be done for the American Hungarian, Chargé Brown's opinions should be first awaited. He requested to be kept informed about developments during the next week or so while attending to the business that had brought him to Smyrna: a survey of recent excavations of ancient Roman aqueducts in the outskirts of town.

Around six o'clock the next morning, July 2, exile observers hurried to their leaders to report that the mailboat had again come in. A messenger, sent to Offley to forewarn him, had the consul awakened only a few minutes before the official courier himself reached the consulate with the pouch.

A large envelope from Chargé Brown, marked "Confidential — for eyes only," and embellished with large seals of red wax, yielded one letter addressed to Offley and another to Ingraham, as well as transcripts of several recent notes from Brown to Baron von Bruck.

Within a few minutes the consul appeared aboard the *St. Louis*, hurried to the cabin of the commander, and handed him the letter marked "For Commander Ingraham, personal," dated June 28.

". . . The public here are quite as indignant at the brutal conduct as they were in Smyrna. Mussulman, Christian, and Jew

87

execrate the conduct of the Consul and accuse him as the cause of the bloodshed [i.e. Hackelberg's murder] which resulted from the brutal arrest and treatment of Koszta.

"I believe that under the circumstances you have a right to persist in demanding him from the Austrian Commander. The *Porte* would wish to leave the matter open between us and the Austrians, and if we could see the poor fellow carried off and hung, to let us take the ignominy of the transaction on our own shoulders. If I thought you would be governed by my instructions . . ."

Brown well knew that he could give no outright orders or instructions to the naval officer. But, speaking hypothetically: ". . . my instructions . . . would be to demand him, in the most formal and positive language, of the Austrian Commander . . ." — and he was prepared to associate himself with Ingraham in such action: ". . . in my name as representative of the United States, and after having him in your possession, leave the matter to be adjusted between the two Governments . . ."

Brown's views mirrored those Ingraham had held from the outset: to force a temporary arrangement, pending settlement of the dispute on a cabinet level between the United States and Austria. The term "force" had but one meaning in the commander's dictionary. And what followed in the letter indicated that the able linguist at Constantinople possessed a copy of the same dictionary and was not loath to use it when the occasion demanded: "In case of a refusal to deliver him . . . I would take him out of the vessel . . . Such a course will meet with the most profound applause from this Government, and from every foreign Legation here except that of Austria, and cannot but call for strong gratification on the part of our Government and people at home."

A final word to Ingraham: "All you have already done has elevated the character of our country and our navy."

And another, indirect, to his civilian comrade-in-arms: "I do not doubt that [Offley]will support you in all you do."

The time for action was here at last.

The initiative passed into the hands of the master of the *St. Louis.*

88

Final preliminaries follow.

Offley reports: "We agreed that [Ingraham] should go on board the *Hussar* to have another interview with Koszta."

At 7:30 A.M., the commander arrives aboard the Austrian brig. Von Schwarz greets him stiffly.

Permission is given for the interview with the prisoner, and Koszta is brought up on deck.

In Ingraham's words: "He seemed much better at this interview than at the last. I asked Koszta how long he had been in the United States. He told me one year and eleven months. I then asked him if he had intended to settle in the United States; he answered 'yes.' I then said, 'do you demand the protection of the American flag'; he told me he did."

Ingraham's rejoinder, "Then you shall have it," draws no more than stony silence from the Austrian officers standing by.

The commander turns to the captain and calls upon him to release Koszta within three hours: not later than eleven o'clock.

Von Schwarz's curt, irritated answer is that, as he has already indicated, the matter is entirely up to Consul General Herr von Weckbecker.

The American has nothing more to say; nor does his antagonist.

Salutes are exchanged — and the last discussion between the two officers is over.

Back on his ship, the commander informs the waiting Offley of the verbal demand given by him to the Austrians. The consul, disturbed by the brevity of the time limit set, says that perhaps he could now get somewhere with Weckbecker; perhaps the obvious imminence of American action would now prompt the consul general to make concessions.

Ingraham does not object to a renewed effort at conciliation; he is willing to extend the time limit to four o'clock.

It is now close to 8:30 in the morning. The commander walks to his small desk in the corner of the cabin. A peremptory demand must be phrased in words likely to gain the approbation of thirty million plain-speaking Americans.

As he gazes, pen in hand, alternately at the sheet of white paper before him and through the porthole out to sea, he may recall many things with a certain bearing on the situation.

One of the chief causes of the War of 1812, in which he saw service as a very young cadet, was the British "impressment" of seamen, the forcible removal of naturalized Americans of British birth from American vessels on the high seas.*

And what about that resounding message from Secretary Webster in answer to bellicose Austrian remonstrations against the appointment of a special American emissary to Hungary back in 1849? That emissary, by the way — Mr. Mann of Virginia — is now Secretary of State Marcy's chief deputy back in Washington. Webster stated at the time, in one of the most spectacular examples of stump-speech diplomacy, that had the imperial government subjected Mann to treatment as a spy — which the Austrians in their note had in fact branded him — "the spirit of the people of this country would have demanded immediate hostilities to be waged by the utmost exertion of the power of the Republic, military and naval." [45]

And Ingraham may remember certain views expressed by his boyhood idol John Paul Jones, which so accurately described his own present predicament: "It often happens that sudden emergencies in foreign waters make [the naval officer] the diplomatic as well as the military representative of his country, and in such cases he may have to act without opportunity of consulting civil or ministerial superiors at home, and such action may easily involve the portentious issue of peace or war between great powers . . ." [46] †

* Citing the belligerent's right of search, British boarding parties removed from ships of foreign neutrals all seamen deemed British, considering this action indispensable to the maintenance of their sea power in their war with France. Use of the English language seems to have been the main test applied in the cases of likely-looking seamen, as shown by the fact that out of an estimated ten thousand persons "impressed" from American ships, only about a thousand proved to be British subjects.

† If it had not been for his untimely death, the great naval hero could conceivably have made use of these lessons himself. He was "appointed Consul of the United States at Algiers, June 2, 1792, by the President alone," as an entry in the State Department's appointment index states. Two weeks later, at the age of forty-five, he died.

The ultimatum now to be written seems destined to form a sequel to Webster's declarations about American feelings concerning the cause for which this man Koszta had fought. Will the ultimatum become a curtain raiser for an armed clash between American and Austrian naval forces? Will John Parker's words to the minute men at Lexington — "if they mean to have a war, let it begin here" — assume new meaning at this time, at this place?

The memories and questions are many, the responsibility fearful. But the note must be written.

Perhaps the fact that Ingraham is no diplomatist makes it easier for him to compose it. Of few others could it have been so aptly said that "the traits of character that distinguish the naval officer: simplicity, candor, and directness, affect his negotiations and give them a sort of unity. The sailor-diplomat is pre-eminently a 'shirt-sleeve' diplomatist. He is a stranger to the devious and tortuous methods of procedure which so long disfigured international state-craft. Being a fighter by profession, he does not underestimate the importance of a display of concrete force when temporarily filling the peaceful office of a diplomat." [47]

What, exactly, shall Ingraham cite in the note as the authority upon which his ultimatum rests?

From the Austrian viewpoint, his own authority as commanding officer of the *St. Louis* may not suffice; Schwarz himself constantly refers to consular and diplomatic authority as the fountainhead of his own role in the controversy. Very well; Ingraham will add Brown's authority to his own, on the basis of the chargé's letter. Expediency in the tactical moves allows reference to Brown's emphatic suggestion as a directive — which it would in fact be, were it not for American peculiarities of chains of command which are inexplicable to the Austrians.

But how is he to describe Koszta's citizenship status?

The man is not an Austrian; this is the basic American position. Koszta is a quasi-citizen of the United States, perhaps; a legally accepted candidate for American citizenship; a conditional almost-citizen; a domiciled national; call him what you will, quibble as you please. But the Austrians recognize only two designations:

citizen and alien. Very well, then: citizen it is, American citizen; challenge it if you will. America could not save the Hungarian fighters a few years ago; perhaps America can now save one of them, the particular one named Martin Koszta.

The commander begins to write:

"Sir:

"I have been directed by the American chargé at Constantinople to demand the person of Martin Koszta, a citizen of the United States, taken by force on Turkish soil and now confined on board the brig *Hussar*, and if a refusal is given to take him by force.

"An answer to this demand must be returned by 4 o'clock P.M.

"[signed] INGRAHAM, Commander,

U.S.S. St. Louis." [41]

He thrusts the pen aside and reaches for a small brass bell standing in a corner of the desk, a facsimile of the bell which announced the birth of American freedom some seven decades before at Philadelphia. Grasping the wooden handle, he shakes the little bell.

Brandywine limps into the cabin.

His master's instructions are brief.

A minute later a midshipman is leaving for the *Hussar*, with an envelope containing the note.

An American ultimatum, formal, written, first of its kind, is on its way into history.

THE SHOWDOWN

July 2, 1853

NINE o'clock in the morning. Offley has just left the *St. Louis*, taking with him a copy of Ingraham's ultimatum to show to Weckbecker.

A courier from the *Hussar* arrives aboard the American vessel with a note from Captain von Schwarz to Commander Ingraham. It is an immediate answer to the ultimatum:

". . . I altogether depend upon the Consul General concerning the matter respecting the prisoner Martin Koszta. I shall send to him your letter of this day and I shall state to him to come to an understanding with you himself.

"In case of any violence against His Majesty's brig *Hussar* or schooner *Artemisia*, I must protest, and I should consider it again as a hostile step for which you would be held responsible altogether.

"[signed] SCHWARZ."

Is there anything left to be said?

Situation report from the French newspaper of Smyrna: "The captain of the *Hussar* took such measures as were necessary for defense, and the schooner *Artemisia*, with which he did not cease to exchange signals, unfurled its sails and maneuvered so as to be ready in case of need to come to its consort's assistance . . . It would be impossible to describe the emotion and anxiety of the people lining the shore. So great, however, was the sympathy which the cause of the prisoner excited that no one thought of the danger which threatened the town should the ships have engaged so close to it . . ." [48]

The noon hour is approaching.

Ingraham receives word from Offley that although no headway whatever has yet been made in his discussions with Weckbecker, he will continue to press his appeal to the Austrian's better judgment.

Another messenger arrives on board, with a note from Congressman Lyon written at a small port west of Smyrna. He has been awaiting a boat there to travel to Greece: "I cordially approve of the measures of Mr. Brown in taking the exile Koszta per force, and I do hope you will do so. So far as my humble power goes, I will defend it . . . Do not let this chance slip to acquit yourself nobly and do honor to our country . . . The eyes of nations are upon the little *St. Louis* and her Commander . . ."

He closes with a brief, impassioned plea: "For God's sake, and for the sake of humanity, stand for the right!"

From the diary of Passed Midshipman — eventually Rear Admiral — Ralph Chandler of the *St. Louis*:

"When Captain Ingraham came back and told what he had done [as to the ultimatum], there was no surprise expressed, but we all saw that unless the man was given up there would be bloodshed, and every man on board seemed anxious for a fight. The time was put off until 4:00 P.M. for his delivery into our hands and we had ample opportunity to get ready for action.

"The Austrian force consisted of the brig *Hussar* of sixteen guns, the schooner *Artemisia* of twelve guns, and a steamer of four guns. None of the guns of the Austrian were of as large calibre as ours, but their number exceeded ours by twelve guns. If that excess were all in one battery, for instance, if it were one thirty-two gun ship instead of the three separate ones we were to contend against, our chance would of course be much better for we could always avoid a raking fire and would not be obliged to fight both batteries at one time. In the other case one vessel might be on each side of us and another ahead or astern, and in either position we would be exposed to a raking fire. It was evident that in the case before us our plan of tactics was to get underway and fight at long range until one or more of our opponents were disabled; and that being accomplished, we were certain of victory.

"This was the plan Captain Ingraham adopted and prepared to put into force. Slip ropes were got on the chain ready to cast off at any moment from the anchor, the men were called to quarters, shot and shell passed up to the guns, and everything soon assumed a warlike aspect. Before all this was effected, however, we left our old berth and stood closer in just ahead of the *Hussar* and came to again within less than half a cable's length from that vessel, and only veered to twelve fathoms of chain, so that the fifteen-fathom shackle would be near at hand to slip with.

"The schooner, as soon as she was informed of our Captain's demand, weighed her anchor and stood off and on across our bows for the rest of the day, and the steamer got up steam ready to tow either of the other vessels into position. No one can doubt that these were all hostile maneuvers and tended to show that resistance would be shown to the last.

"Our guns were loaded each with a round shot and a shell, the men armed with cutlasses and pistols, and the ship put in readiness for action. Bulkheads were knocked down, yards slung, and rigging staked down, and the array of amputating instruments that were displayed on the steerage table by the doctors was enough to chill one's blood. We were all in a great state of excitement, but not an expression of fear or regret did I hear . . .

"The people on shore heard of our intention and it produced much consternation among them as they had fears of our firing by chance into the town, and many of those men who were loudest in their advice to capture Koszta now thought better of it and would rather a little diplomacy and forbearance were exercised. But it could not be.

"Either Koszta must be delivered into our hands or we would take him, and so matters stood at half past three . . . We were all certain of victory . . . but many a gallant life would have [had to] be sacrificed and many a family at home plunged into mourning for a beloved son or husband." [35]

Another midshipman of the *St. Louis*, and likewise a future rear admiral, also recorded the ominous preparations. The diary of this young man, Richard Worsam Meade — nephew of General Meade, victor of the Battle of Gettysburg — furnishes details and reflections largely identical with those cited in Chandler's.[49]

Two o'clock in the afternoon.

Offley pays a final, desperate visit to the Austrian consul general.

Much wear and tear of nerves is discernible on both sides. Weckbecker camouflages his growing uncertainty and confusion with an attitude of haughty rigidity. Offley, normally a man of few words, cannot stop talking. Finally, face reddened, temper lost, the American shouts: "All right, listen! Ingraham is determined to go to the finish, and he is a professional fighting man. You and I are civilians. But you refuse to take a single step toward reconciliation. Do you then desire bloodshed?"[24]

Only an hour remains till the expiration of the ultimatum — and the beginning of the shooting.

Ingraham and his aides are on the bridge, watching the *Hussar*.

Activities aboard are more intense with every passing minute and can be clearly seen from the deck of the Austrian brig.

The drummers of the *St. Louis* are beating general quarters.

Shot-boxes are being uncovered.

Now the drummers sound action stations.

Men race to shot-lockers and open them, exposing to view a great number of round-shots, grape-shots, cannister-shots.

Cannon balls are piled into pyramids.

The master-at-arms passes out pistols and a variety of equipment necessary for the crew to repel boarders.

Sharp words of command sound from the bridge:

"Now hear this! Now hear this! Load your guns!"

Only one more command — "Light your matches!" — remains to be issued before a point of no return is reached and a signal to fire envelopes the scene in flames.

"Powder monkeys" run forward with cartridges of powder which the loaders put in the muzzles of guns and follow it with a heavy round-shot, then the spongers-and-rammers push both home, while the quarter-gunners prepare their long matchsticks.

Ingraham takes another glance at the huge pocket watch he is holding in his left hand. It shows ten minutes of four.

An aide exclaims:

"Commander, sir . . . Look!"

He straightens and looks up and ahead.

A small boat is being lowered from the *Hussar*.

A rope ladder is let down.

Several figures climb into the boat, all of them in uniform.

All — except one.

Martin Koszta.

A roar goes up from the crowds on shore.

The entire complement of the *St. Louis* breaks into one long echoing hurrah.

All — except one.

Ingraham, cap removed, raises his eyes to the blue skies over Smyrna harbor.

✈ THE AGREEMENT

July 2-7, 1853

OFFLEY and Weckbecker reached the waterfront just in time to see Koszta taken toward shore and hear the jubilant outcries of the multitude.

Exile accounts depicted the scene as follows: "The crowds which had gathered along the shore, certain that there would be cannonfire during the day, assembled almost as by magic in numbers mounting to ten thousands in the great square of the Bella Vista Café and the adjacent streets: Europeans, Greeks, Turks, Armenians, Hebrews, women, children, persons of all ages and conditions gathered there . . . All eyes were looking sea-ward. A boat was put over the side of the Austrian brig. In the stern of this boat sat the Hungarian, Martin Koszta, in chains, flanked by a naval officer on the left and four infantrymen in the bow. The boat moved toward the Bella Vista wharf and was closely followed by an American boat bearing four officers. Behind this boat were many small craft . . ."

The procession was as colorful as the scene dramatic. When the lifeboat of the *Hussar* reached shore, "one of the interpreters of the French Consul gave his hand to Koszta and helped him alight. The Austrians made an attempt to accompany the prisoner, but their efforts were in vain, for the scornful shouts sent up by the crowd drove them back toward the water. Is there anything in the world more powerful than public opinion?

"The decree was solemnly proclaimed and was greeted with applause and shouts of joy on the one hand, with hisses and curses on the other. Extolled and pitied, Koszta crossed the great square of the Bella Vista, followed by the American officers who, with ineffable affection, waved their kerchiefs to the people."

Koszta still wore his chains on hand and foot when he was put ashore. When the French consul demanded that the chains be removed, it was found that "the keys were not at hand . . . A messenger was despatched to fetch them from the Austrian long-boat, and when the smallboat started moving, it was greeted with further shouts of 'death to tyranny!'"

And finally, "the news of this victory flashed through all parts of the city . . . A powerful universal and resounding cry of public rejoicing went up which rang through the whole city: 'Long live America! Long live the liberators of the people!'"

When the American consul visited him for the second time on that hectic day of July 2, Weckbecker, pressed by the threatening deadline set by Ingraham, seemed to have reluctantly decided at last that there was a limit to the value of Koszta as a prisoner; that the Hungarian was not worth a bloody clash between American and Austrian naval units and the incalculable consequences of such a collision. He had undoubtedly never been authorized to go to endless lengths in the affair. He had already done more than enough to justify before his superiors a withdrawal in the last critical moment, a withdrawal which could yet prove but a tactical one; it was now up to the imperial diplomatic corps to see to it that ultimately the Austrian viewpoint should prevail.

It was almost three o'clock, about an hour before the expiration of the time limit set in the ultimatum, when he scribbled a note and sent it by messenger to Captain von Schwarz. He did not acquaint Offley with its contents, but merely remarked to the American in tones as measured as was possible under the strain of the moment that he was agreeable to a suspension of activities

99

until final disposition could be made by the respective governments. In reply to Offley's query as to whether this meant that Koszta would be released in the meantime, Weckbecker alluded vaguely to neutral hands which might now have to play a role in the affair. He suggested that they write a joint note to the other heads of consulates in town, requesting them to come to the *Hussar* for a conference at which details could be worked out.

A note to that effect was quickly sent to French Consul General Pichon. He, and others notified by him in turn, arrived at the bay a few moments before Koszta reached shore in the armed company of the Austrians. It was not until then that Weckbecker announced to all the officials present that Austria was desirous of leaving Martin Koszta under the personal authority of Monsieur Pichon until the entire matter could be finally settled.

Offley recalled later in his report to Brown dated July 4 that ". . . Captain Ingraham . . . approved of the condition stipulated betwixt the Austrian Consul and myself. I need hardly say that the excitement in town was very great. An immense concourse of people were present on [Koszta's] landing and 'vive l'Amérique' and her gallant officers who saved Koszta from Austrian barbarity, was in the mouths of all present, and the heartfelt thanks of all the European population have been given to our country on this occasion.

"It is fortunate for Koszta that force was not used for his release, as it is very probable that he would have been shot by the Austrians on the first attack that might have been made on the brig . . . I feel certain, now that Koszta is out of the clutches of Austria, that he will not fall again in her hands."

To feel "certain" about anything was hardly justifiable under the circumstances. No one in Washington had as yet any knowledge, after all, that anything out of the ordinary had been taking place in the faraway port of Smyrna. The name of Offley would hardly have elicited even recognition at first hearing from anyone of important station at the State Department. Ingraham, writing the secretary of the navy the day before the consul penned his remarks, was certainly far from "certain" about things to come:

The Play

"I have taken a fearful responsibility upon me by this act; but after Mr. Brown had informed me that Koszta had taken the oath of allegiance to the United States and forsworn all allegiance to Austria, that he was an American and had been under the protection of the Legation at Constantinople, I could not hesitate to believe he was fully entitled to protection. It was a case of life and death, for if Koszta had been taken to Trieste, his fate was sealed; and could I have looked the American people in the face again if I had allowed a citizen [i.e. a possible citizen] to be executed and not use the power in my hands to protect him for fear of doing too much?

"The manner, also, in which he was given up, and the convention that he should be held by a third party until his nationality should be established, is evidence that they [the Austrians] were not sure of their ground.

"Should my conduct be approved, it will be one of the proudest moments of my life that I have saved this gallant man from a cruel and ignominious death; on the other hand, should my course be disapproved, I must bow to the decision; but whatever might be the consequence to me, I shall feel I have done my best to support the honor of the flag, and not allowed a citizen to be oppressed who claimed at my hand the protection of the flag."

Offley to the secretary of state: ". . . The Governor of this place, Ali Pasha, sent his *dragoman* to express the satisfaction he had felt on Koszta's release. No measures of interference were taken by the local authorities in this matter, and the other authorities felt highly pleased at the happy result."

The pasha's satisfaction was short-lived. It lasted only for one day, because on the very next morning he was removed from office. The Porte, acting on the basis of Chekhib Effendi's findings about the recent persecution of exiles at Smyrna, held the governor responsible for the excesses of some of his underlings. An immediate trip by Ali Pasha to Constantinople to sway his cousin the sultan brought no result other than the receipt by "the very illustrious former Governor and perpetual Court Councillor" of a high decoration for "past services of great value rendered to the Sublime Porte."

Ingraham wrote Minister Marsh on July 3:

". . . And now, you gentlemen of the pen must uphold my act . . . I know I have taken a very heavy responsibility; but as [the Austrians] had more guns than I had . . . and three steamers to help them, they will not like to own it was fear that made them deliver up Koszta; so we must suppose it was a sense of returning justice . . . I suppose the [Austrian] Minister will make a terrible complaint against me to our Government; but as they chose to yield, and I did not do what I threatened, I think they had better keep silent.

"The French Consul, I think, approved my course, although he does not say much. Some of the others shake their heads . . . The Austrian Consul, to show his spite to the last, did a thing we never could have supposed possible — landed Koszta in chains. The French Consul, however, had them removed immediately."

The report closed with a surprising postscript added on the Fourth of July: "The Austrian vessels of war have hoisted the American flag in honor of the day."

This gesture of Captain von Schwarz, made almost certainly in the face of a strenuous protest by Weckbecker, was the only act of chivalry displayed by the Austrian during the entire controversy. It was as typical of traditional naval concepts of sportsmanship as Koszta's delivery in chains was of Weckbecker's malice.

Beyond the brief postscript, Ingraham made no comment about his opponent's gentlemanly move. But through the rest of his long life, he never permitted an unkind word to be spoken in his presence about the gruff but *korrekt* Captain August von Schwarz of His Imperial Majesty's Navy.

Also on the Fourth of July, according to Midshipman Chandler's diary, "the American citizens at Smyrna gave a dinner to Captain Ingraham and his officers. There was a general jollification, and there was a popping of bottle corks instead of the big guns. And last night [July 6] we had a ball on board for some of the residents of Smyrna."

L'Impartial reported that "our local Philharmonic Orchestra went on board a launch which was brilliantly illuminated for the purpose, and proceeded to the *St. Louis* to serenade her gallant commander. The emotion caused by the affair has not yet subsided. The incident continues to form the subject of every conversation."

The exiles closed their own chronicle of the adventure with these words: "In this way, thanks to the power of a free government and a liberty-loving people, his chains smitten from him, Martin Koszta, whom the 'most benign emperor' had condemned to the gallows, was snatched from the talons of the Austrian eagle. History will record this day of triumph . . . America, the land of the free, has with this deed added yet another star, symbolic of the resurrection of the people, to her banner of freedom." [24]

Straining ropes and creaking pulleys spread the sails of the *U.S.S. St. Louis* to the breeze as it slowly slid out of the harbor.

Scores of rowboats speckled the bay; hats and kerchiefs were waved by thousands on shore; shouts of farewell fused with shreds of music, as the ship receded from view.

For the people of Smyrna, the show had ended. For the consuls, another act of it was about to begin.

The text of the convention arrived at between Offley and Weckbecker — and sent in its final form to Washington on July 4 — included a stipulation accepted by the Austrians with great chagrin. It was to the effect that Koszta's "board and maintenance" during his retention in neutral hands was to be paid by Austria. This constituted a personal victory for Offley. The complete text, in the official English translation, read as follows:

"The Undersigned, the Consul General of Austria, and the Consul of the United States, beg the Consul General of His Majesty the Emperor of the French to receive in deposit in his prisons * the so-named Martin Koszta (Martin Costa) detained on board the Austrian brig-of-war *Hussar*, whose nationality, and consequently the relations of protection, are being discussed between the respec-

* In the French Hospital, designated as a temporary place of detention and cited in that sense further down in the document.

tive embassies in Constantinople as well as between the Consulates at Smyrna.

"They beg the Consul General to take charge of this deposition with the following conditions:

"The individual aforesaid shall be consigned in the course of this day, and as soon as possible, to a detachment of soldiers belonging to the Austrian brig, who will conduct him to the landing of the French Hospital where he shall be delivered into the hand of the Consul General of France or of the person whom the latter may depute to receive him. The prisoner shall not be at liberty to communicate with anyone outside, with the exception of the undersigned Consuls, and in the Hospital he shall be especially entrusted to one person whom the Consul General of France shall designate. The costs for the board and maintenance of the prisoner, which the Undersigned leave entirely to the discretion of the Consul General of France to determine, shall be discharged by the Undersigned Consul General of Austria.

"It is expressly understood that the Consul General of France is not to deliver up the prisoner Martin Koszta (Martin Costa) except upon the requisition of both the Undersigned.

"[signed] E. S. OFFLEY, Consul of the United States; WECK-BECKER, Consul General of Austria."

"And now," as Ingraham had written to Minister Marsh, "you gentlemen of the pen must uphold my act . . ."

To him, standing on his bridge and peering back into growing distance of space and time, the moral of the trying days and nights at Smyrna might have seemed to be what a contemporary of his was to express in these words:

"The quarrel is done — God avert such another.
The lesson is brought we should evermore heed:
Who loveth the Flag is a man and a brother,
No matter what birth or what race or what creed." *

* From the poem "At Fredericksburg" by John Boyle O'Reilly (1844–90), Irish revolutionary who was sentenced to death by the British, was transported to a western Australian penal colony to serve twenty years there as a result of a commutation of the death sentence, escaped to the United States in 1869, became a prominent editor and poet, and in 1876 organized an expedition which rescued all Irish prisoners from the western Australian convict establishments.

The Reviews

THE REVIEWS I

TEXAS was annexed in 1845, Oregon acquired in the following year, the Mexican War won in 1848 . . . In three hectic years, the area of the United States was increased by more than two thirds,* and in 1850 California was made a member of the robust Union. Young America, happily bounded on north and south by weak neighbors, and on east and west by fish, was "conscious of a glorious destiny both in physical growth and in world power. Spread-eagleism was the order of the day . . . Patriotic emotions . . . aroused together with humanitarian sympathies led to a widespread conviction that the time had come for the United States to lift its voice against the autocracy and privilege of the Old World." [50]

Boundless energy generated incessant movement and mounting ambition. The nation, wrote Senator — and future Secretary of State — William H. Seward to his wife, "seems almost divided into two classes: those who are going to California in search of gold, and those going to Washington in search of office." [51]

Rapid physical expansion and economic development ran parallel with a steady rise in self-confident nationalism and brought

* The acquisition of Texas, the clear title to Oregon below the 49th parallel, and the gaining of the Rio Grande boundry, upper California, and New Mexico increased our territory by over 1,200,000 square miles, more than 66 per cent.

variegated forms of aggressive diplomacy. The popular temper was accurately if grandiloquently characterized by an editorial writer of the *New York Courier and Enquirer* when he wrote: "Republicanism on this continent has reached a point where it neither fears the frown nor will it tolerate the insults of any power or combination of powers on the face of the earth." [52]

The nation flexed its diplomatic muscles in three major clashes with the Habsburg empire within four years after the tragic end of the Hungarian revolutionary war, and each had its cause in that almost universally lamented debacle.

The first occurred in 1850 as an aftermath of the already mentioned appointment of Ambrose Dudley Mann as special American diplomatic agent charged with observing the war and authorized to determine the moment suitable for American recognition of Hungarian independence.*

The American move had been doomed to failure. For one thing, the Austrian intelligence service succeeded in obtaining Mann's secret instructions; for another, the Kossuth regime had fallen by the time Mann arrived at his listening post in Vienna.

Now, more than a century later, it is no longer a secret how Austria's agents were able to deliver their master stroke.

Available is a confidential memorandum from Foreign Minister

---

* At the time of Mann's appointment in 1849, Secretary of State Clayton received a letter from a young officer who had graduated at West Point only three years before, requesting appointment as military observer to join Mann. The officer, George B. McClellan, future commander in chief of the Union Army, wrote his letter at Philadelphia on August 19, six days after the Hungarian collapse which was not yet known in America.

McClellan was to be involved in a curious incident more than a decade later with the only Hungarian general of Kossuth's forces whose invincibility the Austrians had been forced to admit. General György Klapka, only twenty-nine years of age in 1849, had successfully withstood all Austrian attacks as defender of the key fort of Komárom for more than two months after the collapse of the Hungarian armies everywhere else. He was finally offered honorable terms of surrender, and personal freedom to leave the country. He went from Hungary to Switzerland, later became a Prussian major general and still later a Turkish general. Shortly after the outbreak of the American Civil War, when he was still only forty-one, Secretary of State Seward decided to invite "the hero of heroes" to join the general staff of the Union Army. According to a letter from Klapka to McClellan in 1861, a representative of Seward had approached him in the matter. He preferred to deal with McClellan directly and informed him that

Prince Schwarzenberg to the Austrian chargé at Washington, dated November 5, 1849, according to which "the information we possess on the subject [of Mann's mission] reached us from such a reliable source, we cannot indulge any doubt as to a proceeding which at first we found difficult to credit."

It appears that about the time when Mann's secret instructions were issued, the head of the American legation at Vienna, William H. Stiles, left the legation in care of an Austrian subject named Schwarz who had a lengthy record of satisfactory performance as an attaché and had close contacts, regarded by the Americans as advantageous to them, with the Austrian Foreign Ministry. The records show that Mann suggested to the State Department on October 11, 1849, that Schwarz should be removed from the legation, and remarked that the archives of that office should never have been entrusted to an Austrian subject.[53] The results of an investigation left little doubt that Schwarz was responsible for the leakage of Mann's secret orders through one of the most flagrant security breaches in the history of our Foreign Service.

In one of their numerous protests about American activities concerning Hungary, the Austrians openly accused the United States of what was certainly not far from the truth, namely, of "being impatient for the downfall of the Austrian Monarchy," and

---

he was willing to join but — as in the case of the Austrians — "only on certain conditions" which were (1) a bonus of $100,000; (2) an annual salary of $25,000; (3) to serve as chief of staff to McClellan, but only until he, Klapka, learned enough English, at which time he would take over McClellan's position as commander in chief of the Union Army. McClellan wrote in his memoirs: "He failed to state what provision he would make for me, that probably to depend upon the impression I made upon him." McClellan showed Klapka's letter to Lincoln who "became very angry" and the matter was dropped.

"Klapka the Incredible," as McClellan referred to him afterward, returned to Hungary after the country's rehabilitation through the Compromise of 1867. He had left a son in England where he had spent several years. The son attained fame on his own as the editor and playwright known under the name of Jerome K. Jerome, the middle initial standing for Klapka.

Not long after his return to Hungary, the general was elected to the House of Representatives. The last military assignment he undertook was the reorganization of the Turkish army in 1877, for which he was made honorary personal adviser to the sultan. He died at Budapest in 1892, preceding Kossuth by two years.

they went so far as to threaten this government with "retaliations" for "demonstrations hostile to Austria in favor of Kossuth, the rebel chief." [54] In his reply, Secretary of State Webster caustically reminded the imperial government that at the time of the American Revolution "Washington was considered by the English Government as a rebel chief"; observed that the American people could not "suppress either the thoughts or the hopes which arise in men's minds in other countries from contemplating the successful [American] example of free government"; and flatly rejected the threat of retaliations with the blunt retort that our people were "quite willing to take their chances and abide by their destiny." [55]

The second collision between the two governments, in 1851, was caused by an official invitation to Kossuth to visit the United States as the nation's guest. As will be shown, this resulted in a personal break between the Austrian chargé and Secretary Webster. The third, set off by the fracas at Smyrna in 1853, added yet another somber color to Austrian-American relations, and it moved the man on the street even more than its precursors on the turbulent record.

In each of the three controversies it fell to a man of small physical stature, but considerable dignity and long experience, to represent the Austrians before the American Department of State. He was the Chevalier Johann Georg von Hülsemann.

From 1838 till the death in 1841 of Baron Mareschal, Austria's minister to Washington, Hülsemann served as secretary of the legation here, and afterward as chargé. He became minister in 1855 and held that post through the first two years of the Civil War. At the time of his first arrival in America, he was an eager and vigorous young diplomat, personal protégé of the formidable Prince Metternich. When he finally departed from the legation at Washington, he was a nervous wreck.

Hülsemann served his emperor well. He did his utmost against hopeless odds to counteract admiration for Hungarians and antagonism toward Austrians on the part of the great majority of Americans. His incessant efforts to influence a segment of the press in Austria's favor brought some success. A few important publications, such as the *Quarterly Review* of New York, the *North American Review* of Boston, the *Catholic Register*, and the *Cincinnati Gazette*, adopted many an argument persuasively advanced by Hülsemann in circles of the socially prominent, through letters to editors, and to more or less isolationist members of Congress. This accomplishment, however, was insignificant in the face of overwhelming American sentiment favoring the Hungarians, which refused to die down even after the final defeat of Kossuth's forces. Popular hostility toward Austria continued to receive stimulation from a steady flow of press reports about the cruelties of Hungary's oppressors as well as from colorful feature stories depicting the predicament of the Magyar heroes in exile.

The Indiana legislature called upon the federal government to use its influence to secure a general amnesty from Austria for the Hungarian patriots.[56] Ohio petitioned Congress to send an ambassador to the sultan to solicit the liberation of Kossuth and his companions and bring them to America.[57] New York instructed its congressional delegation to support any resolution granting land to Hungarian exiles.[58] Masses of citizens of St. Louis and other large cities signed petitions to Congress demanding that land be given to Hungarian ex-revolutionaries in the United States.[59] Senator Case of Michigan, in a stinging attack on the Austrian government on January 4, 1850, urged that a rupture of diplomatic relations with the empire be taken under advisement; Senator Foote of Mississippi, and others, gave immediate support to the proposal, and even former President Tyler declared himself in favor of a break — as did the former secretary of war William L. Marcy, who became secretary of state a few years later and, as such, had to dispose of the Koszta affair.

Approval by President Fillmore on March 3, 1851, of a joint congressional resolution "for the relief of Louis Kossuth and his associates, exiles from Hungary," authorizing the government to send an American naval vessel for the Hungarian leader to convey him from Turkey to the United States, caused a further deterioration of relations with Austria. When at the end of that year Kos-

DARING DIPLOMACY

suth and his retinue arrived in America, many of the highest public officials and leading social, religious and cultural figures of the country openly contributed to the immense personal success of his nationwide tour. The irritation of the Austrian government grew apace as Kossuth was received at the White House and in Congress, and was tendered a congressional banquet where Daniel Webster, as principal speaker, delivered an impassioned eulogy of the Hungarian leader and his cause.

There seemed no end to the pin-pricks to which the Austrians felt themselves subjected by the Americans who named townships and counties for the Hungarian hero in Illinois, Iowa, Indiana, Missouri, Michigan, Ohio, Pennsylvania, Wisconsin.* Vienna continued to protest, Kossuth continued to orate, and the American people continued to cheer. Speaking "a curiously expressive, stately, powerful, pathetic English which sounded as if it belonged to a higher time and to loftier interests than ours," [60] the Hungarian struck notes violently discordant to Austrian ears: "Either America will regenerate the condition of the Old World, or it will be degenerated by the condition of the Old World . . . How could the fire of despotic oppression, which threatens to consume all Europe's freedom, civilization, and property, fail to affect in its results America? How can it be indifferent to you whether Europe be free or enslaved? Whether there exists a Law of Nations, or no such thing any more exists, being replaced by the caprice of an arrogant mortal who is called Tsar, Emperor? No; either all the instruction of history is vanity, and its warnings but the pastime of a mocking bird, or this indifference is impossible." [40]

Longfellow remarked that Kossuth's spellbinding eloquence made the people of America "go clean daft"; Henry Clay wrote a letter to the Hungarian explaining his earlier refusal to attend a

* To this day, Kossuth, Miss., Kossuth, Pa., Kossuth County in Iowa, and a great many Kossuth streets and avenues mark the memory of the enthusiasm for the Hungarian. American diplomats of today may be interested to know that the father of George Kennan, ambassador to Moscow under President Truman, was named Kossuth Kent Kennan; he was born in 1851. "My grandfather's action in giving him this name," wrote the former ambassador recently to the author, "was the direct result of the widespread interest in Kossuth following the events of 1848."

112

meeting at which the former was to speak, in this manner: "Your wonderful and fascinating eloquence has mesmerized so large a portion of our people wherever you have gone that I feared to come under its influence lest you might shake my faith in some principles in regard to the foreign policy [of formal neutrality] of this government." [61]

Day in, day out, Kossuth thundered his inflammatory precepts. Protests lodged by the Chevalier Hülsemann in person invariably met with indifference or rebuff. One note, especially well sprinkled with Viennese condiments, moved Webster to burst out in his reply: "The power of this Republic at the present moment is spread over a region one of the richest and most fertile of the globe, and of an extent in comparison with which the possessions of the House of Habsburg are but as a patch on the earth's surface . . ."[62]

No one in a responsible position had ever addressed words like these to the Austrian imperial court, and Webster's dander appalled even some of his own confidants, one of whom drew this explanation from the secretary: "If you say that my 'Hülsemann letter' is boastful and rough, I shall own the soft impeachment. My excuse is two-fold: 1. I thought it well enough to speak out and tell the people of Europe who and what we are, and awaken them to a just sense of the unparalleled growth of this country; 2. I wished to write a paper which should touch the national pride and make a man sheepish and look silly who would speak of disunion. . ."[63]

Austrian Foreign Minister Prince Schwarzenberg gave unprecedented authorization to Hülsemann on November 4, 1851, to move from Washington to some other location, should he find the capital's atmosphere insufferable. On his part, the chargé felt convinced that the imperial government had "all possible reason to break with the United States." As a result of the speech Webster had made at the congressional banquet in Kossuth's honor, the Chevalier addressed a private note to President Fillmore himself on January 2, 1852. He called it "a last effort to maintain good relations between the two countries." In it, he proclaimed that if the president's response "be not such as I have hoped, I beg you then to consider my diplomatic functions as suspended."

The chief executive called Hülsemann to the White House in the hope of conciliating him. He stressed that Webster had spoken not in an official but in a strictly personal capacity. But Hülsemann declared point-blank that if Webster continued as secretary of state, he, the chargé, would leave the country. He added that Russian Minister Count Waldemar Bodisco had assured him of his full solidarity by stating that in that event he too would resign. The Chevalier insisted that President Fillmore offer certain reassurances, and that he do this publicly in the form of a statement to his unofficial organ, the *Republic*. The president indignantly reprimanded Hülsemann for his importunities in general and his tone of voice in particular, whereupon the chargé marched out of the presidential study in such a huff that he left his stovepipe hat behind. A special messenger carried the personal property to the Austrian legation a few hours later — without the president's compliments.

Webster, furious over Hülsemann's personal encounter with the chief executive, served notice on the diplomat that he should confine his future contacts with the American government to formal correspondence with the secretary of state.

The vituperative reply which the secretary must have expected to get failed to come, for just previously the chargé had received instructions from the foreign minister to the effect that the dignity of the imperial court required a suspension of relations between him and Webster. Accordingly, from that moment onward the Chevalier refused to have any contact, official or personal, verbal or written, with the secretary of state. Official business between the legation and the State Department had to be handled by officers of lower rank, and the unprecedented impasse lasted until Webster's death in the fall of 1852.*

* Hülsemann was spending an extended vacation near Vienna when news of Webster's death reached him. To reporters asking for his comments, he said tersely: "The Americans have lost a noted — orator . . ." The Chevalier's sarcastic emphasis of the oratorical side of Webster's manifold personality is buttressed by a description of Webster's last hours. According to his friend and

The United States sloop of war St. Louis *in the harbor of Smyrna, July 2, 1853 (lithograph, 1853)*

Right. *Francis Joseph I, emperor of Austria. (From a portrait, 1853).* Below left. *Lajos Kossuth, governor-president of Hungary. (Portrait by Aurel Rasko, New York).* Below right. *The Hungarian Holy Crown.*

American-Austrian altercations caused many frustrating difficulties for American travelers during those years in the far-flung territories of the empire. Hülsemann's suggestion to the Foreign Office on January 18, 1852, that every American be regarded as an agitator against Austria unless proven otherwise had found ready acceptance and duly filtered downward to all echelons of the sprawling bureaucracy. Americans were exposed to endless inconveniences relative to internal travel permits, police registrations, hotel reservations, and even delivery of personal mail. Their most cursory contacts with Austrian official personnel became as unpleasant as the emperor's obedient servants could make them.

When Webster died, the Viennese Foreign Office believed that the disappearance of Austria's most vociferous American antagonist would open the way to an amelioration of relations with the United States. But Hülsemann soon warned his government: "The adventurous spirit of this country [the United States] will lead to trouble . . ."

His forecast proved correct. New trouble between the two nations was ushered in by the new year, 1853. Fresh quarrels developed, first over restrictions imposed upon American travelers in the emperor's Italian provinces, then about the flare-up in Smyrna harbor which involved former Kossuth-officer Martin Koszta.

Called upon to handle the new disputes on the highest diplomatic level were the old pro-Hungarian William L. Marcy, now secretary of state, and the former special emissary to Kossuth's cabinet, Ambrose Dudley Mann, now the secretary's deputy.*

---

biographer Curtis, the dying statesman, surrounded by his family and friends, delivered a lengthy discourse on religious matters; this so exhausted him that he could neither speak nor move for some time afterward. On regaining some strength, his first and nearly last words were "Have I — wife, son, doctor, friends, are you all here? — have I, on this occasion, said anything unworthy of Daniel Webster?" The audience replied in chorus: "No!" The dying giant smiled, and soon expired.

* Appointed to the newly created position of assistant secretary of state in the spring of 1853.

THE REVIEWS II

HAD Koszta's misadventure taken place yesterday, whether at Smyrna, Timbuctoo, Tananarive, or any other however distant and outlandish place on earth, the Department of State would have known about it within the hour. Instructions to its representatives would have been drafted and dispatched before midnight; action at the other end of the line would be under way today, with a steady flow of reports reaching the appropriate desks in Washington by cable, radio, and intercontinental telephone.

In 1853, however, when the use of transatlantic cables was still years in the future, surface mail was the only means of communication between the Department and its agents abroad.*

Thus the American government and public learned only at the end of July about what had taken place at Smyrna a month or so earlier. In a note to Consul Offley dated August 6, Acting Secretary of State Mann — in the temporary absence of Secretary Marcy — remarked that the Department had received its first notice about the Koszta case "about 10 days since," and "through the public prints" at that. Even at the date of writing, no official report on

---

* A cable across the Atlantic, most of it laid at a depth of nearly two statute miles, was completed on August 5, 1858. Through it, messages were exchanged by President Buchanan and Britain's Queen Victoria; but the cable was weak, the current insufficient, and the service had to be suspended. The first permanent cable was laid only in 1866.

the matter was yet on hand, and Mr. Mann sternly warned: "The Department has been waiting with much interest, from day to day, to receive from you the official account . . . but as yet nothing has come to hand, although it is well known that private parties in New York have received letters since the date of these occurrences, both from Smyrna and Constantinople . . . Should it appear . . . that there was any delay on your part in writing to the Department, or in embracing the first opportunity of sending despatches, the fact will be at once reported to the President . . ."

It was, of course, easier for American businessmen at Smyrna and Constantinople to get a few informal notes off to their associates back home than for the consul, an official constantly busy with both the delicate case and routine matters, to compose a comprehensive and carefully thought-out report. Such a report he did send to his highest superiors as soon as was possible under the circumstances. It arrived in time to reassure Mann about the consul's sense of duty.

The fact remained, however, that already in mid-July most of the leading newspapers of Europe had reported the incident and its reverberations. *La Presse* of Paris, in its issue for July 14, was even prepared to pass judgment. Perhaps especially inspired by the festive day, anniversary of the storming of the Bastille, the paper declared that "if in fact the captain of the American sloop-of-war has acted in this firm and praiseworthy manner, every one who has two free hands at the service of a noble heart will applaud with frenzy this grand example given by the new world to the old."

But in Washington, only on July 25 did the reader find an account — brief and inaccurate as it was — of the affair, when the *National Intelligencer* reported: "Advices from Smyrna to the 29th of June mention a disturbance there, resulting from the arrest of M. Costa, an emissary of Kossuth, and in connexion with which the Captain of the U.S. frigate *St. Louis* had behaved very gallantly in demanding that the prisoner should be placed under the protection of this Government. In consequence of the riot

DARING DIPLOMACY

Austria had demanded and received from Turkey satisfaction for the insult, and the Governor of Smyrna had been dismissed."

Not until the end of September was the American press in a position to present to the public a detailed description of the events of June 22–July 2. Some of the reports came from the pen of a writer far better known today than he was then, one by the name of Karl Marx.* But even cursory interim reports seemed sufficient to mold public opinion because of pre-existent psychological conditions. Austria had to be wrong; America had to be right. A resounding rebuff was expected by every "red-blooded American" — no other name was deemed proper — to be administered to the Habsburg tyrant for this latest of many outrages.

It so happened that just then Congress was debating a bill for the reorganization of the Navy. From the viewpoint of advocates of naval expansion, the affair at Smyrna could not have taken place at a more opportune time. Supporters of the bill welcomed the unexpected ammunition it furnished.† The need for an enlargement of America's naval power was dramatized by the bravery of an American naval captain in the face of a numerically superior force. The cry went up, "More power to the Navy!"

* In 1848, at Cologne, Marx made the acquaintance of Charles A. Dana, managing editor of the *New York Tribune* — later assistant secretary of war during the Lincoln administration — who was then visiting in Europe. Three years later, when Dana requested a leading German exile in London, the famous poet Freiligrath, to send him reports on European political developments, the latter turned the offer over to his friend Marx. The future author of *Das Kapital* was living in great poverty with his wife and children and had just been evicted for nonpayment of rent. An agreement was reached whereby Marx was to write two articles each week for a fee of two English pounds per article. But his knowledge of the English language was too limited for the task; he had to ask Engels to help him translate the German drafts. The articles were published mostly without a by-line; some of them appeared as leading editorials with little or no revision.

† Viewed in the light of modern American naval might, the proposed expansion was Lilliputian. The bill urged that "the commissioned officers of the Navy of the United States shall be 20 commodores, 68 captains, 97 commanders, 50 lieutenant commanders, 325 first lieutenants," about 500 others including 24 chaplains "and the 12 professors of mathematics now in service . . . but no professors of mathematics shall hereafter be appointed in the Navy." The professors could not have dreamed of the resplendent rehabilitation accorded them in the atomic age through the meteoric rise of their spiritual descendants in modern defense establishments.

118

"I know of no man of experience and character who is more ignorant than he is of all which relates to our foreign affairs. But he has a cool head and a strong intellect, and I place great reliance on his capacity. He may, and I trust will, succeed." [64]

The man thus characterized happened to be the secretary of state.

The man so characterizing him was a former member of House and Senate, former minister to Russia and to Britain, former secretary of state, future president: James Buchanan. He gauged accurately, if bluntly, some of the principal characteristics of the man called upon to lead the showdown with the Austrians over the Koszta case.

Another experienced observer's opinion of the secretary was similar to that of Buchanan: "Mr. Marcy is a person of wisdom and experience, ignorant of foreign affairs; but he knows his ignorance, and in this self-knowledge is his strength." [65]

This critic too, the prominent Senator Charles Sumner, was a good judge of men; and Marcy himself agreed in effect with both Sumner and Buchanan when he admitted that he "had not until recently given much attention to our foreign relations and really was not qualified for the position assigned me. I have been obliged to make up this deficiency with really no leisure to do it, without much assistance from any quarter . . ." Looking back upon his public life, he said he found that "it has all been spent in learning trades, and I fear I have not acquired a high degree of skill in any of them. Tho' not ambitious, I naturally wish to appear to as good advantage in the last [as secretary of state] — certainly the last — as in any of them . . ." [66]

But the protestation of lack of further ambitions was not sincere. Although Marcy was sixty-six years old when he took over the direction of the Department of State, and thus the oldest man in President Pierce's cabinet, it was well known to his associates that he entertained hopes of attaining the presidency. He expected the eventual fulfilment of the dream frustrated at the last Democratic National Convention by the sudden compromise which had brought the nomination of a very dark horse, General Pierce, instead of Marcy, Cass, Buchanan, or Douglas.* Buchanan, the only member of this quartet to become president later, expressed his conviction shortly before the Koszta incident that Marcy would "probably cherish until the day of his death the anxious desire to become President . . ." [67]

About his lack of experience in foreign affairs, however, Marcy was unduly apologetic. Of our fifty-one secretaries of state to date, only eighteen have had previous direct experience in the field of diplomacy.†

He became a successful secretary, and in some respects an outstanding one. The record of his service is a veritable mountain of significant state papers, hardly lower in the eye of the researcher than the highest summit in the Adirondacks — named in his honor Mount Marcy.

Among his notable accomplishments were the successful settlement of the *Black Warrior* dispute with Spain;‡ the regularization of delicate matters of protocol through the controversial order called "Marcy's Dress Circular";§ the so-called Gadsden Purchase;** the conclusion of twenty-four treaties, the largest number

* On the forty-eighth ballot, Marcy received the highest number of votes. On the forty-ninth, Pierce won out.

† Jefferson, Marshall, Monroe, J. Q. Adams, Clay, McLane, Forsyth, Buchanan, Everett, Cass, Foster, Day, Hay, Kellogg, Stimson, Stettinius, Byrnes, Dulles.

‡ The commercial vessel *Black Warrior*, touching at Havana, Cuba, on February 28, 1854, was seized by the Spaniards because its master refused to submit a cargo manifest. Only after the payment of a $6000 fine was the ship restored to its owners. In the ensuing controversy, the able handling of the case by Marcy was nearly frustrated by Soulé, our minister to Spain, who was bent on acquiring Cuba for southern interests and whose tactics brought matters to the verge of war. After much wrangling, the case ended with a payment by Spain of an indemnity of $53,000.

§ In June 1853, Marcy issued instructions to all American representatives abroad to appear at royal courts and on all important state occasions "in the simple dress of an American citizen." A great deal of controversy, many ludicrous practices, and a near-suspension of diplomatic relations between Britain and the United States resulted from "Marcy's Dress Circular." However, it led ultimately to general acceptance of American diplomatic etiquette, and it remains valid in essence to the present day.

** James Gadsden of South Carolina, named to negotiate with Mexico a settlement of boundary disputes, signed a treaty whereby Mexico ceded for fifteen million dollars an area of some 45,000 square miles. The line established marks the present American-Mexican border. The region included parts of present-day Arizona and New Mexico. The treaty, mainly the result of Marcy's firm leadership, was ratified in 1854.

ratified under any administration up to that time; and his adroit handling of the explosive Koszta case.

Having first gained note as an associate justice of the New York Supreme Court, Marcy became a United States senator in 1831. The most lasting mark he made while in the Senate was his introduction of the term "spoils system" into the dictionary of American politics, when in a speech about political patronage he declared that "to the victor belong the spoils." Marcy has long been forgotten; the phrase survives.

He resigned from the Senate to campaign for the governorship of New York, won the election, and served three terms as a highly efficient executive whose abilities as a powerful arbitrator made possible the settlement of the bitter New York–New Jersey boundary dispute. After he retired from the governorship, his effective service as a member of the Mexican Claims Commission increased his stature, and President Polk appointed him secretary of war in 1845. His performance in that position until 1849, including important participation in the formulation of plans for the Mexican campaign, was largely responsible for his appointment in 1853 as President Pierce's secretary of state. True, the President had first offered the post to two others, and to Marcy only when the first choice, former Senator Dix of New York, had to withdraw because of southern opposition to his nomination, and the second, Senator Hunter of Virginia, decided not to give up his seat in the Senate. But Marcy accepted eagerly; the highest ranking position in the cabinet seemed a potential springboard to the presidential nomination.

He had spent only a few months at the head of the State Department when the Koszta incident thrust him into the most spectacular verbal duel of his eventful forensic career.

In August 1853 Secretary Marcy and his advisers read the first full reports of the alarum at Smyrna. Minister Marsh had written under date July 7 that "as all these events took place without my knowledge and while I was absent under special instructions from the Department, it does not perhaps belong to me to express any opinion in reference to them."

But he had added that "the importance of the principles involved in the case, and the magnitude of the consequences which may flow from it, will, I hope, be thought to justify me . . . in support of the course taken by Mr. Brown and Captain Ingraham . . ."

The Navy Department, addressing itself to Ingraham's actions only and steering clear of matters of international law and diplomatic protocol, was delighted about the exploit of the officers and men of the *St. Louis*. Secretary of the Navy James C. Dobbin wrote the commander on August 19: "This Department does not feel called upon to enlarge on the various questions of international law involved in the proceedings concerned. These questions may hereafter become a subject of discussions between the respective Governments interested. I deem it proper at present to content myself by assuring you that the prudence, promptness and spirit which marked the part you bore in the transaction is approved by this Department. It is a matter of congratulation that the affair terminated without a resort to collision and bloodshed . . ."

A few days later Secretary Dobbin reiterated his approval in a communication to Ingraham's chief, Commodore Stringham, who had on his part already endorsed the commander's actions in a letter to the Navy Department on August 2. Stringham, in charge of the Mediterranean Squadron, had given his "entire approbation to the course pursued by Commander Ingraham . . . The disorganized state of the Turkish empire at this period, more particularly the confusion and lawlessness existing in the province of Smyrna, together with the total imbecility of the authorities of the city in permitting the flagrant and illegal seizure of M. Koszta by a foreign power, and their lamentable supineness subsequent to the arrest, rendered in my opinion the demands of Commander Ingraham . . . perfectly justifiable. My only regret is that Commander Ingraham was not enabled to receive M. Koszta on board his ship and await further action in the premises afterward."

But Minister Marsh felt it necessary to do more than merely review past events. He reminded the secretary of state on August 4 that the Koszta case made it mandatory to reappraise and resolve certain long-pending, uncomfortable issues:

"There are at Smyrna and elsewhere in Turkey several refugees who emigrated to the United States under similar circumstances as Koszta, and who have returned after taking the first step toward naturalization, some without passports, others with passports from American Legations, Consulates, or other authorities, describing them as American affiliated citizens.

"There are others who received from this Legation in 1849 and 1850 passports not noticing their nationality at all but merely describing them as persons 'emigrating to America,' and which were given merely to enable the bearers to proceed to Smyrna or other ports where passage could be taken for the United States.

"There is a third and much more numerous class, amounting probably to several hundreds, who came to Turkey in 1849, and were provided with passports from the American Consulate in Rome, describing the bearers as citizens of the United States. Many of these latter passports have been sold or otherwise transferred from hand to hand, and none of those to whom they were issued have any claim to be regarded as possessing any other rights as American citizens than such as this Consular declaration of nationality confers upon them."

Marsh pointed directly to the heart of the matter when he declared in conclusion: "We are likely to have difficult questions in regard to these persons, and I beg, as I have done before and during the administration of the late President [Fillmore], *general instructions* as to the extent to which they are to be regarded as entitled to the protection of this Legation."

Meanwhile, the accidental cause of the deepening perplexity, Martin Koszta, was still held at the French Hospital at Smyrna.

The only visitors he was allowed to have were Offley and Pichon. Neither Lisa, Madame Vigny, nor exile leaders were permitted to call on him for the time being. The main reason for caution was indicated in a note from Marsh to Offley on August 4: "The notorious [illegible name], an Austrian spy and assassin, is said to have

123

gone to Smyrna. I hope Koszta will be on his guard against false friends as well as open enemies."

The American minister had proposed to his Austrian colleague at Constantinople that Koszta be placed on the first American ship sailing directly for an American port, with the stipulation that "he shall not land at any Turkish or European port" and that "if he voluntarily leaves the ship, our protection shall be withdrawn from him." He was "confident" that this proposal would be accepted. But von Bruck disappointed him, replying that "I can neither accept your proposal nor recognize the soundness on which it is founded," and making no constructive suggestion of his own.

Backstage, Weckbecker still had a few strings left to pull. But Offley was on guard; he reported to the Department on August 5 that "since Koszta's transfer to the hospital, the Austrian authorities have made use of every possible intrigue to induce him to escape from here. This has been several times proposed to him [in letters] by persons who I have every reason to believe are Austrian emissaries, offering to conceal him in their houses, whose object doubtless was to have him arrested on leaving the hospital by the Austrian spies who are constantly hovering about the building, and restore him again to the Austrians; but Koszta was timely put on guard by me against all such intrigues on their part."

All the while, Offley was tensely awaiting word from the Department concerning his past actions in the case, aware that the slightest censure on whatever technical grounds would revive earlier machinations aimed at his removal.

At last, nearly three months after Koszta's abduction, under date of August 31, an official expression of the Department's views reached the consul: "While the President regrets the occurrences . . . he does not find, after the fullest attention given to the subject, any just cause for disapproving of your conduct, or that of Captain Ingraham, the Commander of the United States corvette *St. Louis*, or that of any of our diplomatic agents who took part in the matter . . ."

With this communication the last best hope of the anti-Offleyites

was dispelled. The harassed official could now breathe more freely
— until some next occasion of one sort or another.

Although he still had on hand problems constituting a postlude
to the incident on a local level, he believed that no more than
routine administrative steps remained to be taken, and that the
liquidation of the affair within consular jurisdiction would be a
smooth process.

He was completely wrong.

✗ THE REVIEWS III

BY STANDARDS of the period, it was an imposing edifice that served as headquarters for the Department of State between 1820 and 1866, on the corner of Fifteenth Street and Pennsylvania Avenue.* Pictures of it show a building which even today would be considered good-sized and attractive, somewhat resembling the comfortable but not overly pretentious residence of a provincial patrician.

Within it, however, in the year of the Koszta case, personnel did not number above two score, less than the corps of file clerks alone in the formidable Imperial Ministry of Foreign Affairs in the Austrian capital.

The Department was open for business in those days from ten in the morning till three in the afternoon, a fact apt to arouse justifiable nostalgia in its present-day employees.† There were no Civil Service regulations to define employees' status and working

---

* In 1866, the Department moved into the building of the Washington Orphan Asylum, and in 1875 into the so-called State-War-Navy Building next door to the White House. When General William T. "War-Is-Hell" Sherman was told that the building was fireproof, he is said to have remarked dryly: "A pity." [68] Now called the Executive Office Building, it contains offices of White House aides, the Budget Bureau, and other agencies, and the President's press conference room which used to be called Indian Treaty Room.

† Working hours were extended in 1869 to begin at 9:30 A.M. and end at 4:00 P.M. Further periodic revisions brought it to the current 8:45–5:30.

126

conditions, for no Civil Service existed. Legislation marking the end, or at least the beginning of the end, of the inglorious era of the spoils system was not enacted until 1883.* Supervisors were authorized to require employees to work any day for any length of time without overtime pay or compensatory leave; in turn, in case an employee did not have enough work to do to fill out his working day with useful occupation, he was obliged under a standing directive from the secretary himself to request the chief clerk — a *de facto* under secretary — to find something for him to do. No record is extant to indicate that such a request was ever made.

The secretaries of state themselves were not much less heavily burdened than their successors a century later. On top of their main work load from day to day, they had to carry a variety of extra weights which accrued from almost ludicrous marginal duties. Up to 1850, all petitions for pardon had to be submitted initially to the secretary of state; no one knew exactly why. Even during the following twenty years — until the establishment of the Department of Justice in 1870 — many such cases had to await his personal attention. Until 1861, his Department had the duty to compile the *Biennial Register*, also known as the *Blue Book*, of all military and naval officers and civilian officials of the federal government. Until 1855, lists of passengers of all incoming vessels had to be submitted to him. In fact, William L. Marcy, chief of the Department at the time of the Koszta case, was at least lucky in not yet having to handle in person every single passport application and to sign each passport in his own hand. It was in 1856, at least partly as a result of the incident at Smyrna, that it was made unlawful for anyone but the secretary himself to issue and sign passports.†

When the Department, established without specific provision for it in the Constitution, was first organized in 1789, the statute under which it came into being was the shortest and most general-

---

* The legislation had been sparked by the assassination in 1881 of President Garfield. The murderer was a demented office seeker, Charles J. Guiteau, who demanded public office in return for political services allegedly rendered.

† The number of passports now issued by the Department each year averages about a half million.

ized one among all bills devised for the various departments. One peculiar view that seemed to underlie the attitude of Congress well into the first half of the nineteenth century was that with the passage of time, the Department's duties would steadily decrease rather than increase. Many in and out of Congress felt that the signing of more and more long-term treaties of commerce and friendship with foreign nations would inevitably result in a gradual diminution of the work load. One brief glance at the Department's operations today would stagger the good souls who had so grossly miscalculated.

Under Jefferson, America's first secretary of state, the entire staff at the disposal of the head of the Department consisted of one chief clerk, three ordinary clerks, and one translator. The diplomatic corps totaled three ministers. The consular force numbered sixteen persons who received no salary but were allowed to engage in trade.*

Even four decades later, under the Jackson administration, the Department's staff at home consisted of a mere 22 individuals. In 1870, its members still numbered fewer than 60; in 1909, only a little over 200; and as recently as 1922, when the population of the United States was nearly 110,000,000, the Department had about 600 employees, all told.

The agency charged with handling our foreign affairs has always had to carry on its work with a staff at times the smallest and at other times one of the smallest among the executive departments. Salary inequities gave its employees at home and abroad, from the earliest times, another undesirable distinction; and no palliative in the form of popular respect or applause was vouchsafed them. The Department became a convenient target of free and easy

* The first American consul to be appointed was Colonel William Palfrey, paymaster general of the Continental Armies, selected by Congress in November 1780 to serve in France. A special salary of $1500 a year was voted him. En route to his post, his ship was lost in a storm. Congressional sympathy over Palfrey's demise took a curiously inverted form: the salary — for his successor, Thomas Barclay — was reduced to $1000.

The first consul actually to serve under the Department of State was Major Samuel Shaw of Massachusetts. He was confirmed on February 9, 1790; his post was Canton, China.

The Reviews

criticism because of reasons inherent in American psychology, historical inhibitions, and the nature of the agency's mission. Officials who told unpleasant truths, were constantly involved in controversial situations, had to make and implement risky decisions, and habitually associated with foreign diplomats popularly regarded as tricky if not outright diabolical, were not likely to win popularity contests. An agency whose province is trouble abroad is always prone to get into trouble at home. If things went badly with our foreign interests, "those people in the State Department" surely must have messed things up; if departures from established precedent and comfortable custom became apparent, outcries went up about violations of tradition at best and personal loyalties at worst. Attacks from Congress, from the defense establishments, from the press, from civic organizations and specialized pressure groups, from foreign governments, from sundry quarters expected and unexpected, responsible and irresponsible, made it appear at times as if the country simply wanted no foreign policy at all, and in any case no State Department.

Internal difficulties were also numerous. To mention one, the Department kept urging Congress throughout the first half of the nineteenth century to establish a regular salary for consular officers, and Congress again and again failed to act. The most persuasive arguments on the matter, advanced by Secretary of State Livingston in 1833, were in vain, even though the requested appropriation was only $186,000. The year of 1856 had rolled around by the time the legislative bodies girded their collective loins to the task. A salary system was established and provisions were made for the certification by the secretary and appointment by the president of twenty-five "consular pupils of peculiar fitness and qualifications." But in its very next session, Congress reversed itself. It refused to appropriate the necessary extra $25,000 for the "pupils" and repealed the whole section concerning them. With another change of heart, in 1864, the essence of the measure was restored by the creation of a corps of thirteen consular clerks, and two years later consular examinations were established. But the spoils system was

129

as difficult to kill as the mythological hydra; it prevailed throughout the century.*

Monday, August 29, 1853, marked the high point of a heat wave in Washington. The humidity was already oppressive around ten o'clock in the morning, when a pitch-dark hansom pulled up in front of the building of the Department of State. Out of it stepped a smallish, quick-moving gentleman with a huge stovepipe hat in one hand and a large briefcase in the other.

His Excellency the Chevalier Johann Georg von Hülsemann, chargé d'affaires at Washington of His Imperial Majesty Francis Joseph I, arrived to lodge with the American secretary of state the Austrian government's latest protest.

The text of the lengthy document, temporarily withheld from the public, was taken under immediate study at the Department.

In reply to impatient inquiries made by the gentlemen of the press, the Department's spokesman neither confirmed nor denied that a *démarche* had been received. But he was willing to go so far as to state — albeit not in such currently familiar wording as the following, but no doubt to the same effect — that whatever information on subjects of legitimate public concern became available would be released with all possible speed consistent with the national interest and departmental regulations.

Enterprising newsmen tried but failed to obtain information from the Austrian legation itself about details of the representation made by the chargé.

By the middle of September it was the talk of the nation that a violent Austrian protest in the Koszta case had been received and that the secretary and his aides were hard at work on a reply.

---

* A violent outburst of it took place on the threshold of the twentieth century, under the McKinley administration, when out of 272 consuls in office, 238 were summarily recalled. Untried men of little or no aptitude were put in the vacant positions, and examination standards were drastically lowered so that any party hack was able to qualify. An examination of 112 candidates brought the rejection of only one person, in a notable instance.[69] The hapless individual proved incapable of passing even the "life saver" test that could still have assured him a career in the service: he was unable to memorize a relatively short, stereotype sentence designed to prove that the candidate's mind could, in case of absolute necessity, retain specific information.

"Insiders" predicted that the reply would turn out to be a land-mark in American diplomatic history.

The Washington correspondent of the *New York Weekly Tribune* reported on September 28 that "Secretary Marcy's Mani-festo in the Koszta Case will certainly appear between this and Saturday [October 1]."

His newspaper had taken an enthusiastically affirmative editorial position regarding the incident at Smyrna, and that position was warmly endorsed by the *Examiner* which wrote: "The *Tribune* by no means exaggerates the popular feeling on the subject when it says that although it knows not whether Captain Ingraham is a Whig, a Free Soiler or a Democrat, yet certain it is nevertheless that if he had sunk the Austrian ship of war to the bottom, he would have been the next president of the United States . . ." [70]

According to the *Tribune*'s concept of the case, "the whole question as between this country and Austria turns on this point: Was the act of Captain Ingraham aggressive or defensive? Did he commit an outrage, or only resist one? On this question we invoke the judgment of the civilized world." [71]

Clustered around Secretary Marcy as he at least figuratively rolled up his sleeves to get the job done was a group of able men from the top echelon of the small Department under his command.

It consisted of his deputy, experienced and resourceful Ambrose Dudley Mann; chief clerk William Hunter; Francis Markos, head of the Diplomatic Bureau; Robert Chew, chief of the Consular Bureau, the only German-speaking officer in the Department at the time; and, extracurricularly, Attorney General Caleb Cushing, later the first American minister to China, on whose personal devotion and firm grasp of foreign affairs the secretary relied during his whole tenure.

Night after night, lights were seen burning in the secretary's office long after the witching hour . . .

THE REVIEWS IV

THE long-expected thunderstorm broke loose at the end of September 1853 with the joint publication of Hülsemann's note of protest and Marcy's reply.

The *Tribune* had raised in advance a voice of warning and entreaty: "If our Government is entirely right in the matter of Koszta, as we feel sure it is, let us for once exhibit the spectacle of the American people forgetting all partisan differences, all chronic prejudices, all inborn timidities, and rally as one man around the Government of their choice in the defense of weakness against violence, right against despotism, humanity against oppression." [72]

The Chevalier's exposé, dated August 29, comprised some 3300 words, the secretary's rejoinder of September 26 over 11,000.

Sparks of personal animosity shot up from the subsoil of one passage after another in both notes. On reading them, one seems to hear Hülsemann shout and Marcy roar, and see the former gesticulate and the latter pound his desk, in line with their respective characteristics.

To contemporary readers, not a syllable of the mammoth wordage was without timely interest. Today, selections from it to illuminate salient points are sufficient unto the purpose. Fitted into a sequence to form a dialogue in which arguments face each other for thrust and parry, they follow:

Hülsemann: "Our Consul General has caused to be arrested and conveyed on board the Austrian brig of war *Hussar* the Hungarian refugee Martin Koszta . . . who, after having pledged himself in writing not to set foot again on Ottoman territory, broke that pledge by returning some months since to Smyrna . . ."

Marcy: "The facts should be more fully and clearly stated . . . Koszta, by birth a Hungarian, and of course an Austrian subject at that time, took an open and active part in the political movement of 1848–49, designed to detach Hungary from the domination of the Emperor of Austria. At the close of that disastrous revolutionary movement, Koszta, with many others engaged in the same cause, fled from the Austrian dominions and took refuge in Turkey . . . They were . . . confined at Kutahia, but at length released with the understanding or by express agreement of Austria that they should leave Turkey and go into foreign parts. Most of them, it is believed, before they obtained their release, indicated the United States as the country of their exile. It is alleged that Koszta . . . engaged never to return; this is regarded as doubtful. To this sentence of banishment — for such is the true character of their expulsion from Turkey — Austria gave her consent; in truth, it was the result of her efforts to procure their extradition, and was accepted by her as a substitute for it. She had agents or commissioners at Kutahia to attend to their embarkation . . . Koszta came to the United States and selected this country for his future home.

"It is important to observe, there is no exception taken to his conduct after his return to Turkey, and that Austria has not alleged that he was there for any political object, or for any purpose other than the transaction of private business.

"While waiting . . . for an opportunity to return to the United States, he was seized by a band of lawless men . . . It is now avowed, as it was then suspected, that these desperadoes were instigated to this outrage by the Austrian Consul General at Smyrna; but it is not pretended that he acted under the civil authority of Turkey, but, on the contrary . . . on application to the Turkish Governor of Smyrna, that magistrate refused to grant the Austrian Consul any authority to arrest Koszta."

Hülsemann: "The American Consul and the American Commander . . . had it in their power to convince themselves, from the declarations of the prisoner himself, that the latter had not acquired the quality of citizen of the United States . . . It is difficult to conceive how the representative of the United States could have sought to found a proof of the pretended naturalization of Koszta upon a document destitute of all authentic character, seeing that the form of legalization which is affixed to it, and which alone could have invested it with that character, leaves in blank both the name of the tribunal before which the declaration of Koszta must have been made, and the name of the clerk who is supposed to be the despository of the original document; and that, moreover, this pretended legalization has neither signature nor official seal attached to it."

Marcy: "The genuineness of the certificate which he produced . . . has been questioned in consequence of the imperfect copy given by Mr. Brown to the Austrian Internuncio . . . A correct copy has been sent to this Department, and verified by a comparison with the record of the Court in New York, in which Koszta made his declaration in due form of law . . ."

Hülsemann: "In our opinion, Koszta has never ceased to be an Austrian subject. The laws of his country [Austria] are opposed to Koszta's breaking asunder, of his own accord and without having obtained permission to expatriate himself from the authorities of that country, the ties of nationality which bind him to it."

Marcy: "There is great diversity and much confusion of opinion as to the nature and obligation of allegiance. By some, it is held to be an indestructible political tie, and though resulting from the mere accident of birth, yet forever binding the subject to the Sovereign; by others, it is considered a political connection, in the nature of a civil contract, dissoluble by mutual consent but not so at the option of either party. The sounder and more prevalent doctrine, however, is that the citizen or subject . . . may at any time release himself from the obligation of allegiance, freely quit the land of his birth or adoption, seek through all countries a home, and select anywhere that which offers him the fairest prospect of happiness for himself and his posterity.

"When the Sovereign power, wheresoever it may be placed, does not answer the ends for which it is bestowed, — when it is not exerted for the general welfare of the people, or has become oppressive to individuals, — this right to withdraw rests on as firm a basis, and is similar in principle, to the right which legitimates resistance to tyranny.

"Neither Austrian decrees, nor American laws, can be properly invoked for aid or direction in this case, but international law furnishes the rules for a correct decision . . . The law of nations has rules of its own on the subject of allegiance, and disregards generally all restrictions imposed upon it by municipal codes. No State can demand from any other, as a matter of right, the surrender of a native born or naturalized citizen or subject, an emigrant, or even a fugitive from justice, unless the demand is authorized by express treaty stipulation . . . To surrender political offenders — and in this class Austria places Koszta — is not a duty; but, on the contrary, compliance with such a demand would be considered a dishonorable subserviency to a foreign power, and an act meriting the reprobation of mankind . . . A few years since, the Austrian Government refused to surrender to the Porte Turkish rebels who fled into Austria, on the very ground now taken by the Porte, namely, that the treaties did not provide for the extradition of political offenders.

"By the consent and procurement of the Emperor of Austria, Koszta had been sent into perpetual banishment. The Emperor was a party to the expulsion of the Hungarian refugees from Turkey. The Sovereign by such an act deprives his subject to whom it is applied of all their rights under his Government . . . By such an act he releases the subject thus banished from the bond of allegiance.

"The proposition that Koszta at Smyrna was not an 'Austrian subject' can be sustained on another ground. By a decree of the Emperor of Austria, on the 24th of March, 1832, Austrian subjects leaving the dominions of the Emperor without permission of the magistrate and a release from Austrian citizenship, and with an intention never to return, become 'unlawful emigrants' and lose all their civil and political rights at home . . .

"Koszta came to and resided in this country one year and eleven months. He came here with the intention of making it his future abode. The intention was manifested in several ways, but most significantly by his solemn declaration upon oath . . . It is not contended that this initiatory step in the process of naturalization invested him with all the civil rights of an American citizen, but it is sufficient for all the purposes of this case to show that he was clothed with an American nationality, and in virtue thereof the Government of the United States was authorized to extend to him its protection at home and abroad . . .

"Mr. Hülsemann . . . falls into a grave error — an error fatal to some of his most important conclusions — by assuming that a nation can properly extend its protection only to native-born or naturalized citizens. This is not the doctrine of international law

135

. . . This law . . . gives the national character of the country not only to native-born and naturalized citizens, but to all residents in it who are there with or even without an intention to become a citizen, provided they have a domicile therein . . . It is a maxim of international law that domicile confers a national character . . . Whenever, by the operation of the law of nations, an individual becomes clothed with our national character, be he a native-born or a naturalized citizen, an exile driven from his early home by political oppression, or an emigrant enticed from it by the hopes of a better fortune for himself and his posterity, he can claim the protection of this Government, and [the latter] may respond to that claim without being obliged to explain its conduct to any foreign power, for it is its duty to make its nationality respected by other nations and respectable in every quarter of the globe.

"Koszta was invested with the nationality of the United States, if he had it not before, the moment he was under the protection of the American Consul at Smyrna and the American Legation at Constantinople. That he was so received is established by the *Tezkereh* they gave him, and the efforts they made for his release."

Hülsemann: "The act of violence which the commander of the sloop-of-war *St. Louis* committed against the Austrian brig *Hussar*, that real act of war, committed in full peace in a neutral port . . . constitutes an outrage upon the principles of the laws of nations . . ."

Marcy: "The first aggressive act in this case was the seizure of Koszta at Smyrna, committed by the procurement of the Austrian functionaries; the first improper use of a national ship — the imprisonment of Koszta therein — was made by the commander of the Austrian brig *Hussar*. That ship was converted into a prison for the illegal detention of a person clothed with the nationality of the United States, and consequently entitled to [American] protection. If Austria upholds, as it appears she does, the conduct of the commander of the *Hussar*, she is in fact the first aggressor . . . The Austrian functionaries had obtained the possession of the person of Koszta not in a fair or allowable way, but by violating the civil law of Turkey, and the rights of humanity.

"Under the circumstances, their custody of him was entitled to no respect from the agent of the Government which, by virtue of his nationality, had a right to protect him. The alleged authority of Austria, under treaties, being set aside, no one would have questioned Captain Ingraham's right, had he been present, to arrest the proceedings of the kidnappers in the streets of Smyrna and rescue Koszta from their hands; they were acting without and against the civil authority of the place . . . If he could have properly interfered in the first stage of this lawless transaction, he might do so in the last . . .

"It is not just to Captain Ingraham to look at the affair as it was at the precise point of time when the demand for the release of Koszta was made. The antecedent events qualify and legalize that act."

Hülsemann: "The Commander of the United States sloop-of-war *St. Louis* threatened the brig of His Imperial and Apostolic Majesty, the *Hussar*, with a hostile attack by bringing his guns to bear upon the latter, and by announcing in writing that if a certain individual, detained on board, whose nationality was being discussed between the agents of the two Governments, was not delivered over to him at a stated hour, he would go and take him by main force.

"There can be no doubt but that the threat of attacking by main force a vessel of war belonging to the military machine of a sovereign State whose flag she carries, is nothing else than a threat of an act of war.

"Now, the right of making war is necessarily, and from the very nature of that right, inherent in the sovereign power. A right of so momentous a nature . . . can belong only to the body of the nation, or to the sovereign, her representative . . . The articles of perpetual confederacy and union between the States of New Hampshire, Massachusetts, etc., of 1778 contain already the following stipulation in 9th article, section 1: 'The right of declaring war, and to make peace, shall belong solely and exclusively to the Congress of the United States.' This basis of the public law of the United States was preserved and sanctioned by the Constitution of the United States, of 1787, which reserves the power of declaring war explicitly to Congress . . ."

Marcy: "The undersigned yields a ready assent to that part of M. Hülsemann's note relative to the war-making power. The doctrine contained in it is sound and well sustained . . . but the undersigned has not been able to discover its *applicability* to the case under consideration."

Hülsemann: "This act of hostility has been committed in a neutral port of a power friendly to both nations . . ."

Marcy: "The right of Austria to call the United States to account for the acts of their agents affecting the sovereign territorial rights of Turkey is not perceived; and they do not acknowledge her right to require any explanation.

"If anything was done at Smyrna in derogation of the sovereignty of Turkey, this Government will give satisfactory explanation to the Sultan when he shall demand it; and it has instructed its Minister Resident to make this known to him . . . [The Sultan] has investigated [the case's] merits, pronounced judgment against Austria, and acquitted the United States. Yet, strange as it is, Austria has called the United States to an account for violating the sovereign territorial rights of Turkey.

"The Government of the Porte has pronounced a judgment in relation to the seizure of Koszta, which Austria herself is bound to respect. It has protested against the conduct of the Austrian agents in that affair as unlawful, and a violation of its sovereignty . . . Austria arraigns the United States for violating the rights of Turkey in the Koszta affair. Turkey, the offended party, exonerates the United States and protests against Austria, our accuser, for the very same offense . . .

"There exist no treaties between Austria and Turkey which could justify or in any way countenance the seizure or imprisonment of Koszta by the Austrian functionaries . . ."

Hülsemann: "The Imperial Government trusts that the Government of the United States will hasten to instruct its Consul at Smyrna not to interpose any obstacle to the extradition of the aforesaid Koszta by the Consul General of France to the Consul General of Austria at Smyrna.

"The Imperial Government entertains too high an opinion of the sense of justice and of the integrity of the Government of the United States to doubt for a single instant its anxiety to disavow the conduct of its agents under the circumstances mentioned above, and that it will hasten to call them to a severe account and tender to Austria a satisfaction proportionate to the magnitude of the outrage."

Marcy: "The President does not see sufficient cause for disavowing the acts of the American agents which are complained of by Austria. Her claim for satisfaction on that account has been carefully considered and is respectfully declined.

"In relation to international rights, the United States ask no more than has been conceded to others, and will not be content with less.

"Being convinced that the seizure and imprisonment of Koszta was illegal and unjustifiable, the President also declines to give his consent to his delivery to the Consul General of Austria at Smyrna, but after a full examination of the case as herein presented, he has instructed the undersigned to communicate to M. Hülsemann his confident expectation that the Emperor of Austria will take the proper measures to cause Martin Koszta to be restored to the same condition he was in before he was seized in the streets of Smyrna."

THE REVIEWS V

THE ringing American statement evoked unconcealed satisfaction in Western Europe and bitter indignation in Austria and Russia.

At home, the virtually unanimous approbation it won made a much-needed contribution toward the strengthening of the domestic political position of the administration. The man who had been elected to the presidency by the largest popular majority given any presidential candidate up to that time was generally regarded, by the time of the Koszta imbroglio, as an incompetent chief executive. Anxious to place the controversy on record as one effectively resolved by his cabinet, the president followed Marcy's so-called Manifesto with a declaration of his own. He incorporated it in his First Annual Message to Congress dated December 5, 1853. After a summary of the incident at Smyrna and its diplomatic consequences, he stated that "I came to the conclusion that Koszta was seized without legal authority at Smyrna; that he was wrongfully detained on board of the Austrian brig of war; that at the time of his seizure he was clothed with the nationality of the United States, and that the acts of our officers, under the circumstances of the case, were justifiable, and their conduct has been fully approved by me, and a compliance with the several demands of the Emperor of Austria had been declined . . . The principles and policy . . .

140

maintained on the part of the United States will, whenever a proper occasion occurs, be applied and enforced."

Although the overwhelming majority of the press hailed the stand taken by Secretary Marcy and endorsed by President Pierce, several important newspapers registered reservations with respect to one or another detail.

The *New York Tribune*, for instance, strongly objected to Koszta's continued detention at Smyrna, attacking Marsh and Brown for restrictive stipulations of the agreement. It editorialized on December 17: "The conclusion is . . . irresistible that our Government had no right at all to detain Koszta one hour after his liberation from Austria was secured . . . If Austria had no right to him, we had even less pretext for assuming the degrading function of jailor to the object of Austrian jealousy and malignity. In short, the business has been lamentably botched by Minister Marsh and his co-workers, the lofty crest of this Republic lowered and its honor tarnished. We have lost by ill-advised diplomacy nearly all that we had gained by Captain Ingraham's straightforward and manly action."

The *Tribune* seemed unable or unwilling to understand that diplomacy could not be more than "the art of the possible," unlike politics with its pat promises of the unlikely. Ingraham, in his own words, could not have "looked the American people in the face again," had he not used his power and opportunity "for fear of doing too much." But he could have faced neither the people nor the judgment of history if he had recklessly used them in order to cater to sensationalists. He had superimposed restraint upon boldness; he had demanded surrender, but not an unconditional one. The rest, as again he had put it, was up to "the gentlemen of the pen," but surely not to the gentlemen of the press.

Now that the executive branch of the government had fully spoken, the next move, if any, was up to Congress.

The Department's officers abroad were still far from finished with the case of Koszta.

Marsh and Bruck continued to quarrel about ways and means

of arranging the man's return to America. On September 14, about two weeks before Marcy's note came out, the internuncio wrote the American minister that the imperial government had "just authorized me to come to an understanding with you . . . in regard to the release and transportation of Martin Koszta." Evidently, the Viennese cabinet had decided that no useful purpose could be served by an insistence upon Koszta's further detention, and that whatever advantage could yet be extracted from diplomatic skirmishes could be attained only through exchanges on a cabinet level and an eventual reasonable compromise.

The court's gradual turnabout stemmed from an awareness of the vastly increased international prestige of the American Republic, and from internal difficulties in the empire. Austria, still not fully recovered from the shocks of 1848–49, had to contend with possibilities of renewed popular uprisings especially in Hungary where sulky millions were held down only by a standing army of soldiers, a sitting army of bureaucrats, and a creeping army of spies. Additional incentive for an early settlement of the Koszta affair was the hope, expectation, and in some cases firm conviction of numerous intimate advisers of the emperor that the American politics of "Manifest Destiny" would eventually involve the United States in a collision with England, affording great opportunities for Austrian revenge.

Orders for a tactical retreat with dignity were passed down from Vienna.

Koszta, wrote Bruck, could take passage in an American vessel, but the ship must be "sailing on direct voyage to America" without touching any intermediate ports except in case of emergency. Austria reserved the right "to proceed against that individual, according to [Austrian] rights, the moment he is again surprised on Ottoman territory." This reservation, appended as a face-saving device, was certain to bring renewed American defiance, but Bruck was bent on probing the extent to which the State Department might be willing to let Austria save face.

On receipt of Bruck's communication Marsh reported to the secretary that it looked as though a final understanding had been reached, adding that "I learn there are now in Smyrna several American vessels about to sail for ports in the United States and I trust that in arranging the details with Mr. de Bruck, no difficulty will arise of a nature to prevent the embarkation of Koszta by one of them."

He proceeded to make minute arrangements. Questions of funds arose. According to Marsh's report to the secretary on September 14, "Koszta is believed possessed of some funds, but if he proves to be destitute, I hope the instructions I gave Mr. Offley to pay his passage and draw on me for the amount, on account of the contingent funds of this Legation, will not be disapproved by the Government."

Orders went forth from him to Offley four days later: "You will make the necessary arrangements for Koszta's embarkation and passage . . ." And to his own deputy, Brown, on the same day: "You will proceed to Smyrna and give Mr. Offley such aid and directions as he may need in carrying out the general instructions I have given him . . . I will leave the arrangements . . . entirely to your discretion. Your expenses, of which you will keep an account, will be paid out of the contingent fund of the Legation."

Koszta was given an American passport in which no express mention of his citizenship or nationality was made, and in which he was strictly forbidden to interrupt his passage except by authorization in case of emergency. A copy of the passport was sent to Bruck for his information.

Everything was now in readiness for the departure of the American Hungarian. To all officials at Smyrna, Constantinople, Washington, and Vienna, days of relaxation seemed to beckon at last.

But suddenly Marsh was jolted out of his optimistic expectations.

Two things happened, simultaneously.

One: Offley refused to accept the final Austrian reservations.

Two: Koszta refused to return to America.

✦ THE REVIEWS VI

MINISTER MARSH is highly disturbed as he reads a letter from Consul Offley dated September 23:

"I abstain from giving my assent for Koszta's removal from the French Hospital . . . The reserve made by the Austrian Government to proceed against Mr. Koszta . . . whenever he may again be found on Ottoman territory, confirms the pretensions of Austria so loudly proclaimed by her to all Europe, that our conduct was an arbitrary one, and consequently that our claims on Koszta were ill founded. To accede to this agreement would be, therefore, a disavowal of our conduct, by our own free will, and before our Government has pronounced thereon at least to our knowledge, Mr. Brown having told me that the Legation has not received up to the 17th instant any news from the State Department relative to this question.

". . . If we had the right to act as we did, we ought to uphold the principle on which we acted, unless we should receive contrary orders from the Department of State. As the signer of the Convention, I do not feel authorized to give my consent to the agreement when it is against my own conviction; when I firmly believe that the paragraph in this agreement [prohibiting Koszta's return to Turkey] so closely touches the feelings and character of our country. Under similar circumstances, I would rather prefer being

144

disapproved for an excess of zeal than submit the character of my country to a condition that, in my opinion and conviction, does not reflect to its credit . . ."

Imperial Austria's public servants abroad are well-disciplined bureaucrats who execute orders without question. Democratic America's are not.

Offley is unafraid of "excess of zeal," like Ingraham of "doing too much." "After the despatch I have received from the State Department in answer to my report on the Koszta case, it seems to me requisite to postpone any further action until we hear again from our Government. The despatch is dated the 13th of August, as follows: 'Your interesting despatch under date of July 5 has been received, and the important questions to which it gives rise are now under grave consideration.' Whereby I naturally infer that the Hon. Secretary of State will, most probably on an early opportunity, give his instructions and views on the matter."

Koszta himself has taken a stand in the argument between the consul and the minister. In Offley's words, ". . . having read to Koszta the terms above referred to, he replied that if he were to sign such a writing with the paragraph to which I have already referred, it would not be with his 'full and free agreement'; but if, he added, the agreement is approved by the United States Government, he would then unhesitatingly do so . . . As the agreement has been sent by Mr. de Bruck to his Government for its approval, it seems to be but rational that under the circumstances it should also be submitted to our own for the same purpose."

After this challenge of his chief's authority to make a final disposition within his own jurisdiction, the consul declares that he is about to turn directly to the secretary of state: "I shall send by the first mail to the Hon. Secretary of State copies of our correspondence on the subject, and will await his instructions thereto."

The minister has hardly absorbed the first impact of his subordinate's recalcitrance when a second shock comes in the form of a translation of a letter written in French by Koszta on September 24 to Offley:

"You have had the kindness to inform me of the arrangement

made in my behalf of his Excellency Mr. Marsh with the Austrian Minister at Constantinople, the last clause of which charges you to obtain from me written evidence of my full and entire consent to all the terms of that arrangement . . . I am obliged to pledge myself never to return to Turkey, and the moment I am again found upon Ottoman territory, the Austrian Government reserves itself [the right] to proceed against my person according to its rights. Thus, by this arrangement, his Excellency again gives a right to Austria which she does not possess at present, and guarantees rights which he disputes himself to this day, which will never be recognized by Turkey and which will always be disputed by England and France.

"When I left America, no one forbade me to return to the country whose Government has tendered its hospitality to all those who in 1849, on account of their misfortunes, asked its protection. And shall this now be forbidden me? Shall I be prohibited from returning to Turkey [after becoming] an American citizen? . . . At such a price I can accept neither life nor liberty. Never will I give my consent to an arrangement which strikes a blow at the sovereignty of American citizens . . . I cannot give you today my written consent; and I beg that you have the kindness to send this Convention to America, and if the American Government approves it, I, who am so grateful, so much indebted to the Government and people of America, shall deem it my duty to sign it without any further hesitation."

Marsh is nonplussed by this homily. He has a hard time trying to control his temper as he writes the consul a stern note on September 26 to thwart further resistance on the part of both Offley and Koszta: "It is with extreme regret that I perceive you have allowed unfounded scruples to embarrass a question which is attended with much more difficulty and delicacy than you appear to be aware of . . . [Koszta's] return to Smyrna would give Austria no new rights, nor was this reservation inserted with a view to claim any such [rights] . . . All such are reserved for discussion between the two Governments . . . The reservation merely serves to indicate that by consenting to the release of the person, Austria does

Franklin Pierce, president of the United States, 1853–57
(portrait by George P. A. Healy, 1853)

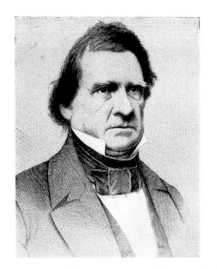

Left. *William Learned Marcy, United States secretary of state from 1853 to 1857 (engraving, 1854)* Right. *The Chevalier Johann Georg von Hülsemann, Austrian chargé d'affaires at Washington (photograph, 1864)*

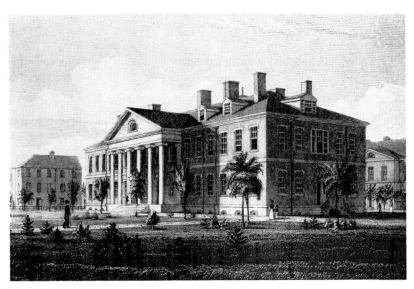

The Department of State building at the time of the Koszta case (engraving at the Library of Congress)

not intend to be considered as waiving the principle for which, though defied by us, she has contended and still contends, namely, the absolute legal jurisdiction over all those whom she claims as her subjects in the Turkish empire. It is not to be expected that in corresponding with the American authorities abroad, the Austrian officials will yield any question of principle . . ."

Offley is neither a lawyer nor a trained diplomat. Marsh, being both, suddenly seems to realize that complicated arguments may boomerang by prompting Offley and Koszta to stick to what appears to them pure and simple. He changes his tune, switching from explanation to command: "You have entirely misconstrued the object and legal meaning of the reservation under discussion . . . Koszta must accept if he expects further aid and countenance from this Legation . . . I now repeat my instructions that in case of further difficulty you are to be guided by the direction of Mr. Brown, if [Brown is] still at Smyrna."

But in conclusion he again permits his tenor to soften; Koszta's written assent, he says, would be "a mere matter between himself and the Legation, and is not intended to be communicated to the Internunciature or Government of Austria."

Yet the consul remains adamant, as Brown, still in town, is pained to find. The latter arranges an interview with Koszta at the hospital on September 30. The substance of their conversation may be found in a note Koszta writes in French and urgently sends to Offley after Brown's visit:

"His Eminence Mr. Brown said these terms were only inserted in the treaty with reference to the American Legation . . . I am not to give any pledge, nothing in writing, but accept my freedom at once — and this very evening start for America. In the event of my refusal, his Excellency [Marsh] will immediately withdraw from me the protection of the American flag and will also tell M. Pichon to refuse me his hospitality and to turn me out of the hospital. As it is impossible for me to depart at once, and as I really want to reflect on this point, I have begged his Eminence to grant me a few days of delay, and also the liberty to consult with you. He has been so kind as to grant me a delay until tomorrow at 12 o'clock . . ."

Apparently, Ingraham's ultimatum has not been the only one to be lodged at Smyrna . . . "This time is indeed very short, and I beg that you pardon me if I entreat that you grant me a few moments and come to me."

Offley hurries to the hospital.

Incidentally, there is a reason why it is "impossiblé" for Koszta "to depart at once" even in case of his compliance with Brown's demand. It is a somewhat peculiar reason, one he did not tell Brown but will explain to his good friend and mentor Offley.

A few days before Madame Vigny persuaded Monsieur Pichon to permit a friend of hers to visit the Hungarian in his hospital room. The friend, a painter of some note from Paris, would paint a portrait of Koszta entirely free of charge. The original would become Madame Vigny's property, but Koszta would be given copies of an engraving to be made of it.

At first, the intended subject shied away from the proposition. But later it occurred to him that acceptance would enable him to give a small but stylish token of his gratitude to some who had been instrumental in his liberation. He could give an inscribed engraving to each of his principal supporters. Inspired by this thought, he agreed to cooperate — and has been sitting for the portrait on and off for several days past. The picture is not yet finished, and the preparation of the required number of copies will take additional time.

Praiseworthy as Koszta's little secret project may be, Offley could hardly countenance it as an obstacle to the far more important matter of getting him back to the United States as soon as possible. But Brown's threat of Koszta's expulsion from the neutral grounds of the hospital, with abrogation of his American protection, arouses the consul's indignation. He protests to Minister Marsh: "The Legation cannot refuse to Koszta its further aid . . . The threats of Mr. Brown that the protection of the United States shall be withdrawn from him and that the French Consul will kick him out of the French Hospital should he continue to refuse to leave for the United States on the terms mentioned . . . could not be put into practice without an infraction on the rights of men. Mr. Koszta begs me to inform you that he continued to keep good his engagement towards you for leaving Smyrna on the terms of your letter of the 4th of August last, which did not contain the proviso of the Austrian Government relative to the reserve it makes of its right to proceed against him whenever he is again found on Ottoman territory . . ."

Marsh, thoroughly provoked, decides that he has had his fill of the importunities of his disobedient subaltern at Smyrna. He reports to the secretary of state on October 3: "I regret to state that the arrangement I had made with the Austrian Internuncio . . . has been defeated by the refusal of Mr. Offley . . . to consent to [Koszta's] release, and of Koszta to accept it . . . Mr. Brown repaired to Smyrna and did his utmost to persuade Mr. Offley as well as Koszta . . . but in vain; upon information of which, I obtained from the French Ambassador an order to the Consul General of France at Smyrna to make all necessary arrangements directly with Mr. Brown. Mr. Brown accordingly commenced a negotiation with the French Consul General for that purpose; but Koszta, acting, as I have reason to believe, solely upon the advice of Mr. Offley, peremptorily refused to embark . . . Mr. Brown, after a stay of nearly two weeks at Smyrna, returned to this city, leaving Koszta in the hands of the French Consul General."

Brown may be even more chagrined at this vexing state of affairs than his chief, in view of his own initial responsibilities in the case during Marsh's absence, which had lasted from Koszta's abduction until well after his release. He explains to Marsh that in his last conversation with the Hungarian, "finding my efforts unavailing, I have given him until noon of the following day for reflection . . . Subsequently [I] sent a friend of Koszta to see and urge him to cease his opposition . . . This person visited him twice on my part . . ."

He discreetly omits to mention that the "friend of Koszta" was Madame Vigny, certainly a shrewd choice on Brown's part, at least at first glance. Whether the lady unselfishly tried to press Koszta to give in for his own good and leave for America as soon as possible, or, on the contrary, urged him to stand firm and remain at Smyrna with her, is a matter of conjecture.

Koszta's obstinacy rests on principles. He knows but one definition of freedom, that which he had learned first as a dream when he was a Habsburg subject in Hungary, then as a bold ambition when he fought for it under Kossuth's banner, and finally as a reality when he partook in it in the United States as a free man. To him, to be free means just that; it means liberty to go where he pleases, when he pleases, provided only that he does not trespass on the rights of others. He is well aware that the importance of his case surpasses that of the individual in its center; he realizes that it may affect countless individuals in the future and many even now. To accept restrictions which, as he sees them, are not only unwarranted and unfair but could later be binding on others, appears to him dishonest. And he is as headstrong a Transylvanian as that peculiar, stiff-necked, colorful branch of the Magyar breed ever produced.

But he does respect authority and knows the measure of his debt of gratitude. Therefore, as he has stated, should the chief of the American State Department approve the position taken by representatives of the Department and instruct Koszta to go, Koszta will go. Otherwise, Koszta will not go.

Offley's support of his protégé remains unswerving. He again risks every consequence of what may come to be judged official insubordination when he writes Marsh on October 5 that "should [Koszta] be driven out of the French Hospital as Mr. Brown intimated, I will give him the efficacious protection of the American flag . . ."

Ingraham has unforgettably shown how to extend that protection boldly . . .

It appears that during the past few days the consul has been doing a bit of tactical scouting. He tells Marsh: "Koszta's expulsion from the hospital . . . is not at all probable. The French Consul read me a despatch from his Government stating that it had approved the charge he had taken of [Koszta's person] and that the only thing that might be regretted would be a disapprobation of the United States Government of the steps taken by its functionaries, in which case —" and now Offley calls Brown's bluff "— in which case the French Government would be under the necessity of giving him its protection."

On October 5, Minister Marsh figuratively rasps his throat and proceeds to read the riot act to the consul: "As the head of the Legation and as a professional lawyer, I cannot consent to be governed by the opinions of Mr. Koszta on questions of the legal effect of written instructions or of municipal or international law, and he must abide by the decision of the Legation or suffer the consequence . . . The Department of State has committed the charge of the matter not to you but to the Legation . . ."

But George Marsh is too good a diplomatist not to sense the moment when a quarrel reaches its danger point. An exit must be found without further delay if departmental interests are not to be very seriously jeopardized. He writes: "I have preferred to ascribe your conduct and that of Koszta in the affair rather to an irritation growing out of your personal relations with Mr. Brown than to a settled purpose of attempting to overrule the decision and the instructions of the only authority responsible in the matter. So far . . . as his written consent is concerned, I have already said to you that it was not intended to be communicated to the Austrian authorities . . . It is proper he should give such assent, but I attach no importance to it, and if [Koszta] supposes there is any danger in giving it, I am willing to waive it."

For the good of the Service as he sees it, the minister defers in effect to the consul who, for the good of the Service as he sees it, has opposed him. "I now expect that [Koszta] will embark by the next American vessel."

Offley receives this on October 7 and promptly writes the secretary of state: "I have thought it my duty to consent to Mr. Koszta's embarkation under the positive assurance of Mr. Marsh that the reserve of Austria is no part of the agreement."

And to Marsh: "I will, without loss of time, attend to the

embarkation according to your previous instructions, under your assurance . . . I have been to see Koszta and he agrees to his departure under the explanation . . . I have likewise seen Mr. Weckbecker, and I do not anticipate any difficulty on his part as to the arrangements for Koszta's embarkation."

But he cannot let the minister's remarks about his relations with Brown pass without a rejoinder that would keep the record straight: "It was painful for me to observe that you seem to consider that my refusal for Koszta's release was caused by 'an irritation growing out of personal relations with Mr. Brown,' and not by the clause aforesaid. The cause . . . can be easily understood on reading my previous letter on this subject."

Now the way is clear to Koszta's departure.

On October 14, a few hours before embarking on the *Sultana*, an American merchant vessel from Boston, the freed man pens a last letter in French to his friend Offley: "In order that it may be well proved that by this [departure] I never intended to acquiesce in a doubt, the effect of which would be to destroy the liberty of the individual, I make my present solemn declaration. Being free like all citizens, I intend to keep and to preserve the right of going and coming wherever my business demands, seeing that *the right of circulation is the first exercise of freedom*, and this without ceasing to enjoy the protection of the noble flag under the aegis of which I have placed myself. I beg, Mr. Consul, that you will bear witness to my declaration in order that no one may attribute any other reason for my departure, and I have the honor to remain, with the liveliest gratitude, Mr. Consul, your humble servant." (Italics supplied.) *

* The words italicized above are virtually the same as those used a half century later by the Supreme Court and then a century later by our second highest federal tribunal in reaffirming the right to travel. In 1900, the Supreme Court declared that "the right of locomotion, the right to remove from one place to another according to inclination, is an attitude of personal liberty . . . Freedom to leave a country or a hemisphere is . . . a part of liberty . . ." [73] And according to a Court of Appeals decision rendered in 1955 in a case involving a refusal by the Department of State to issue a passport, "the right to go from place to place as the means of transportation permit, is a natural right . . ." [74] Fittingly, one of the judges participating in the latter decision was George T. Washington, a collateral descendant of our first president.

In the meantime, the painter had finished the portrait, Martin Koszta's only likeness ever made from life.

The engravings promised were also ready, and Koszta prepared a French inscription to be set over his signature. It may be translated into English as follows:

"Dedicated to Messrs. Captain Ingraham, commander of the American corvette *St. Louis*, Ed. S. Offley, consul of the United States at Smyrna, the Chevalier Pichon, consul general of France at Smyrna, also to Messrs. Blackler, Browning, Burrous, d'Andria, Langdon, McRaith, Mathon, Paterson, Whittall, Wolff, and to all others who contributed their attention and prayers to the cause of my deliverance." [24]

The painting was delivered by the artist to Madame Vigny, while a group of Koszta's exile friends, forming one last committee, volunteered to distribute the inscribed copies among the individual addressees.

Offley's report to Marsh about Koszta's embarkation includes a detail reflecting strangely upon Brown and pointing up once again the consul's dogged determination to keep the American record clean:

"I did all in my power to avoid the arrangements made here between Mr. John P. Brown and the Austrian Consul for Koszta's embarkation, as they would have tended to show that he had been embarked as a prisoner, it having been agreed upon between them that Koszta was to have been conducted aboard by two guards, one of each Consulate. This I positively refused to the Austrian Consul, who then agreed to send his first interpreter, and the embarkation took place in the following manner:

"Captain Watson, the master of the *Sultana*, was on my right, and Koszta on my left; then followed the officers of this Consulate, the French Consul M. Pichon, a number of Koszta's friends, and the Austrian interpreter.

"We were preceded by my *cavass* [Turkish guard] and those of the French Consul. On our arrival at the wharf of the French Hospital, a boat of the barque *Sultana*, with American colors, was in attendance, in which Koszta, Captain Watson, and myself, went on board . . . Early in the morning of the 15th the barque *Sultana* sailed for Boston."

Those to whom Offley referred briefly as "a number of Koszta's friends" included, of course, Madame Vigny, Lisa Cristo, every one of the American businessmen who had been active in his behalf, and Hungarian, Italian, and Greek exile representatives. To avoid popular demonstrations, the local newspapers had not been given notice about the date of the former prisoner's embarkation.

No detailed descriptions of the farewells have come down. Particularly those between the two ladies and their departing friend can be safely left to the imagination of the romantically inclined.

Offley included in his report a brief financial summary, from which later stemmed a blemish to spoil the concluding pages of this section of the record. He wrote Marsh: "I have the honor to enclose a receipt from Captain Watson for one hundred Spanish dollars, the amount of Koszta's passage money, according to your instructions. I have also taken upon myself to pay four Turkish gold pieces of 100 piasters each, which I gave to the *cavasses* who attended on Koszta at the hospital, according to the custom of this place, of which I hope you will approve. I will be obliged to you if you will remit me the above amounts at your early convenience, either in cash per steamer, or in an order from your bankers to their agents here."

Minister Marsh sent an account of Koszta's departure to the secretary on October 20. Unable to forgive or forget Offley's recent self-assertions, Marsh's hurt personal vanity and sense of official dignity prompted him to castigate the consul before the chief of the Department because of "his untimely interference with the arrangement which had been concluded to relieve all parties from the embarrassing position in which they were placed . . . It is impossible for this Legation to maintain a position of respectability or usefulness if ignorant or presumptuous subordinate officials are permitted to overrule its decisions and defy its authority for the sake of giving themselves a factitious importance or of gratifying a private malice against the head or any of the officers of the Legation.

154

"I am aware that the jurisdiction of American Ministers over the Consuls of their nation is, in general, less extensive than that of European Legations over their Consulates; but in the present instance there can be no doubt that the conducting of the whole affair was a matter within the proper competence of the Legation, and I trust that the contumelious treatment of its officers and its authority by Mr. Offley will be visited with such reprehension as it deserves."

Although the basic point could be argued and the anger of the minister at least understood, there was little excuse indeed for the fitful revenge he took on the consul in a manner unworthy of a man of his character and position. While at the outset of this report he claimed that he had "no personal resentments to gratify towards Mr. Offley," he refused to reimburse the consul, whose financial resources he must have known to be slender, for the modest gratuity given to the Turkish guards. As Marsh put it in a letter to Offley, "it was not strictly necessary expenditure and for that reason I cannot allow it as chargeable to the Contingent Fund of this Legation . . . The American Government . . . will, I doubt not, take such notice of your account as it merits."

It was on this discordant note that the American representatives abroad closed their books on the Smyrna incident and assumed the role of observers watching developments at Washington and Vienna.

But Offley received no reprimand of any kind from the Department of State. For one thing, Marsh's heated words became lukewarm by the time of their arrival at headquarters. For another, the consul's arguments and Koszta's self-respecting attitude during the altercation might have met with sympathetic consideration on balance. In any case, silence at Washington was probably tantamount to approval.

By that time, the good ship *St. Louis* was completing another cruise, visiting Egyptian harbors. When it entered the harbor of Alexandria, Ingraham and his men were accorded an uproarious welcome. They were "received amid the joyful ringing of bells and firing of cannon; and when Ingraham entered the theatre [to be officially welcomed] the American flag was flying and he was received with cheers . . ."[75]

He and his crew were serenaded, wined, dined, conducted through the city like visiting potentates, and compelled to accept at least a few of the innumerable and often unidentifiable objects offered them as gifts. They were received in state by one pasha after another, one sheik after another, before resuming their tour of duty which at this time was to end at last on the shores of the long unseen "Home, Sweet Home . . ." *

And Consul Offley?

Very scant is the information that can be discovered about his subsequent service. One item found in obscure records concerns his brief but interesting role in 1855–56 in a transaction so fantastic in retrospect and so little known today as to merit recounting. It involved no less than the importation of camels into the United States for use in a planned United States Army Camel Corps. This is how it came about:

In the fifties, no transcontinental railways or highways existed in this land; hundreds of thousands of square miles in the south-west were totally unknown; the few trails cut across the continent were harassed by Indians. It was commonly supposed that beyond the Mississippi a vast Sahara lay which could not be traversed by mules, horses, or oxen. Some members of Congress recalled in 1852 an idea thought up back in 1848 by Colonel George H. Crossman, deputy quartermaster general of the Army, about the possible importation of camels for public transportation as well as for use in a conceivable Army Camel Corps. At first, bills for appropriations toward the purpose were literally laughed off the floor of the House. But in 1854, after foreign experts assured the Army that the idea was a feasible one, and when Secretary of War Jefferson Davis gave them his support, $30,000 was appropriated "For Importation of Dromedaries to Be Employed for Military Purposes."

Few in Washington, much less elsewhere in the country, had

---

* The nostalgic popular song, it may be noted, was written by one well qualified to sing of homesickness: American Consul John Howard Payne, who served at Tunis from 1843 to 1846 and again from 1851 until his death there in 1852.

even seen a camel. But the French minister here, who had formerly served in Persia, was ready to assist a joint Army–State Department committee in gathering data and drawing up plans. A special commission was sent to the Levant to purchase some of the beasts.

After much inspecting, consulting, and correspondence, one camel was bought in Tunis. But it refused to go aboard ship and had to be hoisted on deck. While the hoisting was in progress, the local authorities intervened, declaring that no camels were to be taken away without the express permission of the Bey of Tunis himself. The American consul general, W. P. Chandler, obtained an audience with the exalted ruler, explained the American plans — and received not only permission but two camels as a gift to the United States.

The ship sailed off, and made a stop at Smyrna. With the help of Consul Offley, and after many difficulties with native traders, thirty camels were purchased. Offley even persuaded several native camel drivers and trainers to join the expedition to America. Major Henry C. Wayne, head of the commission, gave the largest "speed camel" — slated for the cavalry — the name Edward, in Offley's honor.

When the startling cargo arrived at Indianola, Texas, the camels became excited for some reason, soon were uncontrollable, attacked each other as well as the crowds gaping at them, and a few had to be shot on the spot. It took nearly a day to calm the rest of the animals; they were then transported to Camp Verde for training. Although their unsuitability for purposes of military action soon became evident, they surpassed all expectations as carriers.

By 1860, the Army established a caravan system between Texas and California, supplying each military post along the line with camels; twenty-eight camels were taken as far as Drum Barracks, near Los Angeles, for the establishment of the western terminus of the Texas-California Camel Route. Soon a civilian enterprise was founded at San Francisco under the name of Camel Importing Corporation; it began the importation of Bactrian camels, marched them to Nevada, and employed them as carriers in the silver mines.

The Civil War finally dealt a death blow to the enterprise. Confined to farms during the war, the animals gradually decreased to forty-four; these were auctioned off for a final price of $31.00 each, to be exhibited at zoos. The bones of some of them were eventually sent to the National Museum.

Thus it was in connection with the bizarre episode of the still-born Army Camel Corps that Offley's name figured in official records for the last time. About two years before the Civil War, the name vanished from the Department of State Register without indication of retirement or death. Not one picture of him can be found anywhere. He disappeared in the obscurity he had always cherished.

Soon after the incident at Smyrna, public interest through the Middle East and indeed through most of the world was centered upon an international dispute of far greater dimensions, one which in the end did lead to war. Altercations in Palestine between Greek Orthodox and Roman Catholic monks about the custody of Christian shrines served as a convenient excuse for a clash between empires. The tsar's desire to expand southward into the decaying Turkish empire, and British alarm about the territorial and military growth of Russia, had long threatened an explosion. It will be recalled that the cruise of the *St. Louis* on Turkish waters, which turned out to be so eventful at the end of June and the beginning of July 1853, had been directly connected with this situation. In September, the British fleet was ordered to Constantinople; by October, the Russians and Turks were at war, and France and Britain soon joined in. Thus came the Crimean War (1854–56), a source of inspiration for poet laureate Tennyson and for one Miss Florence Nightingale; a bloody demonstration of insane heroics and gallant incompetence by soldiers under stupid leadership; a catastrophe causing the loss of half a million lives and an expenditure equivalent to two billion American dollars.*

As the first shots of that war were being fired, Martin Koszta —

* A popular contemporary caricature depicted British soldiers with heads of lions, their generals with heads of jackasses, and cabinet ministers without any heads.

registered on the *Sultana* as "nationality: American; occupation: gentleman" [76] — was on his way back to the United States where the next reverberations of his adventure were to echo in the halls of Congress.

He had stirred up a nest full of some of the most vicious hornets ever to buzz such provocative words into ears of legislators as expatriation . . . naturalization . . . declaration of intention . . . rights to protection abroad . . . abuse of citizenship privileges . . . control of aliens . . . restriction of passports — words disconcertingly suggestive of past negligence, present complacency, and future troubles.

SINCE all American citizens are expatriated foreigners one or more steps removed, expatriation and naturalization are fountainheads of our national existence.

The implications of expatriation played a direct role in bringing about the American Revolution. Among the many grievances listed in the Declaration of Independence against George III, the Founding Fathers included one concerning the king's order of 1773; they charged that he "has endeavored to prevent the population [i.e. the populating] of these States, for that purpose obstructing the laws for naturalization of foreigners . . ."

The New World view of the freedom of the individual to seek his liberty and his happiness wherever these could be found was diametrically opposed to the English principle of perpetual allegiance to the Crown. The American concept was one of citizenship; the English, of subjectship.

In the words of Mr. Justice Iredell of the Supreme Court of the United States, pronounced in 1796, "a man ought not to be a slave . . . He should not be confined against his will to a particular spot because he happened to draw his first breath upon it . . . He should not be compelled to continue in a society to which he is accidentally attached, when he can better his situation elsewhere, much less when he must starve in one country and may live comfortably in another."

160

In sharp contrast, the British maxim that "no man may abjure his native country, nor the allegiance which he owes to his sovereign," was cited in the sixteenth century by Queen Elizabeth's attorney general as one "long accepted" in common law. It had its origin in the dogma of the "divine" nature of kings, and on the basis of that odd notion the subject was forced into perpetual bondage. The queen's attorney, Sir Edward Coke, declared that "ligeance and obedience of the law to the sovereign is due by the law of nature; *ergo*, it cannot be altered." [77]

In other words: stay, and obey, and give up all hope that you can ever do otherwise. In terms simpler than Coke's but just as inflexible, the great Blackstone stated that "an Englishman who removes to France, or to China, owes the same allegiance to the King of England there as at home, and twenty years hence as now. For it is a principle of universal law that the natural born subject of one prince cannot by an act of his own — no, not by swearing allegiance to another — put off or discharge his natural allegiance to the former." [78]

A slight grace-note in this virtual funeral dirge of individual freedom was Blackstone's assumption that a subject might conceivably be able "through a concurrent act of the prince," in case the ruler was willing, to divest himself of his native allegiance. But the feasibility of this sort of royal cooperation, in the face of "the law of nature," was admittedly so limited as to be practically nil.

On the other hand, the naturalization of foreigners had been an established practice under various conditions both in England and in its colonial empire.

In most of the American colonies of the Crown, each alien naturalized had to be named in a special bill passed by the legislature and approved by the governor.* In 1740, a parliamentary statute introduced a general system of naturalization in all the American colonies, without, however, replacing all the previous naturalization regulations. The naturalization of foreign Protestants and Jews became possible for the first time; no special legisla-

* To cite a few instances, from 1751 to 1774, Rhode Island passed 20 acts for as many aliens; New Jersey, from 1702 to 1772, 37 acts covering 320 persons; Pennsylvania, from 1709 to 1773, 13 acts for nearly 600 individuals.

tive action was required, but seven years' residence had to be proved.

Generally, the effect of naturalization in those times elevated the individual to the level of the native-born citizen, except that he had to accept certain political limitations. For example, in New Jersey, Connecticut, Maryland, South Carolina, and Georgia, such persons were not allowed to hold seats in the legislature. But disabilities of this type were removable, and in any event were never so far-reaching as those in England where the naturalized person was categorically denied all public office, at all times.

When the American colonists declared that they no longer owed allegiance to the British Crown, they stood on English precedent. At the time of the English revolution of 1688, Parliament proclaimed that James II had endeavored "to subvert the Constitution of the Kingdom by breaking the original contract between King and People," and that therefore James was to be considered to have abdicated. It was on similar grounds that the founders of the United States absolved the people of the colonies from all allegiance to George III.

The states, in demanding for themselves the allegiance previously rendered to the king, prescribed oaths of fidelity which were substantially identical with the following formula used in Massachusetts: "I do swear that I will bear true faith and allegiance to the Commonwealth and that I will defend the same against traitorous conspiracies and all hostile attempts whatsoever; and that I do renounce and abjure all allegiance, subjection, and obedience to the king, queen, or government of Great Britain, as the case may be, and every other foreign power whatsoever."

An oath in similar language was approved by Congress in 1776, and the Constitution authorized the establishment of "an uniform Rule of Naturalization." But the first major action of Congress under this grant of power came only fourteen years later, in the act of 1790. The act provided for the naturalization of free, white aliens after two years of residence in the United States.* Applica-

* Extended to Negroes in 1870, to American Indians in 1924, to persons of Chinese descent in 1943, and to Filipinos and Indians in 1946.

tion had to be made to any common-law court in the particular state where the candidate had resided for one year. He was required to satisfy the court as to his good character, and to take an oath to support the Constitution.

During the formative years of our history, the two political parties held opposing views about the desirability of a liberal approach to naturalization. The Anti-Federalists favored the admission of aliens to citizenship through relatively easy processes. The Federalists, however, insisted on difficult conditions and managed to secure the passage of two stringent naturalization laws: one in 1795, another in 1798. In the former, the so-called Declaration of Intention — that key element in the case of Martin Koszta — made its first appearance. In the latter, a system of alien registration was established. And in 1802, it was made a requirement that the alien's declaration that "it is *bona fide*" his "intention to become a citizen of the United States" be made at least two years before his appearance in court to be naturalized.

From the very outset, contradictory practices on the part of federal, state, and municipal authorities created confusion at home and bewilderment abroad. The number of immigrants, and consequently of applicants for naturalization, increased steadily, and especially from the middle of the last century onward rapidly, but legislative attention toward them did not. The whole number of immigrants from 1790 to 1820 was, according to accepted estimates, not above 250,000, and during the 1820s continued to be small. But in the 1830s it began to rise rapidly, in 1842 reached about 100,000 for that year alone, in 1854 attained the relatively enormous maximum of about 430,000, and ten years later, on the threshold of the Civil War, the foreign-born population of the country was about 4,000,000 out of a total population of some 32,000,000.

Wave upon wave of immigrants were "in part forced on us and in part fostered by us. Westward expansion was creating a boom. Manufacturers in the East wanted more and cheaper operatives; railways wanted a reservoir of laborers to build the fast expanding lines; they and the West in general wanted more settlers to develop

the land and to give them business. Not only was literature, much
of it highly deceptive, circulated in the countries which might
possibly supply immigrants, but agents went over to collect them.
Needless to say, the new shipping lines took part in trying to drum
up immigrant traffic." [79]

Free tickets to California — "the true El Dorado! . . . a veritable fairy-land!" — were offered in Paris as lottery prizes, to serve as
incentives for potential immigrants. On one occasion, some five
hundred persons drew such prizes and came to the Pacific coast to
seek the fortunes so colorfully described on handbills.[80] In a later
survey of various practices designed to entice immigrants, the commissioner of immigration himself found that "the peasants of
Southern and Eastern Europe have for a number of years supplied
a rich harvest to the promoter of immigration. The promoter is
usually a steamship agent, employed on a commission basis, or a
professional money lender, or a combination of these two. His only
interest is the wholly selfish one of gaining his commission and
collecting his usury. He is employed by the steamship lines large
and small, without scruple, and to the enormous profit of such
lines. The more aliens they bring over, the more there are to be
carried back if failure meets the tentative immigrant, and the more
likely to follow later if success is his lot. Whatever the outcome, it
is a good proposition for the steamship line." [81]

A balanced picture would, however, include the likewise truth-
ful finding that the immigrants "did find here, for the most part,
conditions so much better than those they had left, that the Land
of Opportunity largely fulfilled their dreams and stimulated their
energies." [79]

Whether through enticement or by independent decision, immigrants kept coming on an ever rising scale, swelling the number
of potential Kosztas and demanding answers to questions affecting
them. And yet, until the reorganization of the entire system of
naturalization in 1906, and sporadically even afterward, the process
of creating new citizens continued to be "carried on in a slipshod
fashion by hundreds of Federal and State courts, municipal and

police courts, without coordination, uniformity, or Federal control." [82]

One particularly troublesome element in the large area of citizenship matters grew out of passport usages. Especially during the first half of the nineteenth century, passports were frequently issued by a wide assortment of authorities and pseudo-authorities to individuals who had merely declared their intention to become American citizens. Exactly when the practice started cannot be clearly established from the files of the Department of State or from records at the National Archives. The Department itself was often guilty of inconsistency, as shown by cases such as that of one Mr. Glazer in 1823. With his application for a passport, this man filed a certified copy of his "first paper." Daniel Brent, chief clerk of the Department — equivalent to an under secretary at the time — sent to Glazer what he called "the passport of this Department." Although he added that "the Secretary regrets that he cannot give a passport" to Mr. Glazer "as an actual citizen," [83] the fact remained that the applicant did get an American passport which, in the eyes of foreign officials, was virtually certain to make him, at worst, a quasi-citizen and, at best, a full-fledged one. Three years later, Secretary of State Clay in a letter to Albert Gallatin, then our minister to England — and himself a naturalized American born in Switzerland — placed strong emphasis on the necessity of completing the process of naturalization before recognition could be granted by this government to individuals as Americans in the full meaning of the word. The secretary wrote: "When the process of naturalization is once performed, the rights of the adopted citizen, so far as foreign nations are concerned, are deemed and held to be everywhere, on the ocean and on the land, the same as those of a native-born citizen." [84]

But the researcher is startled to find that it was this same secretary of state who, just a year or so previously, had issued a curious document to a non-citizen on the basis of a "first paper," in this language:

"UNITED STATES OF AMERICA — To all whom it may concern: Manuel Cartazar, who has resided for several years in the United

States, having declared with all due solemnity his intention to become a citizen of the United States, and to renounce forever all allegiance and fidelity to all other foreign States and Governments, these are therefore to request all whom it may concern to permit the said Manuel Cartazar safely and freely to pass, and in case of need to give him all lawful aid and protection. In faith, etc., 15th March A.D. 1825, etc., H. CLAY, Secretary of State."

The document was never revoked. Foreigners who had occasion to see it could form their own opinion about it; and that opinion undoubtedly was that the bearer had to be, for all practical purposes, an American citizen, but that even if he was not one, the judicious thing to do was to consider him an American. The fact that Clay subsequently issued no other such document was neither relevant nor known to those who, on the basis of this one, had reached certain conclusions of their own. As for our consuls abroad, the secretary kindly allowed them to figure out for themselves just what the "lawful aid and protection" cited in the document was supposed to mean, in what sort of "case of need."

For decades thereafter, impressive-looking certificates of so-called affiliated citizenship were available at the office of the nearest notary public, almost for a song, to be used in foreign countries. A certificate of this type is extant in the form of a notarial appendix to a declaration of intention which bears a date preceding that of Koszta's "first paper" by only three days. Filed in the same New York Court as Koszta's, it is truly something to behold. In it, a notary public named Joseph B. Nones proclaimed that the declaration of intention, onto which he had affixed his formidable seal, "I deem sufficient proof of the affiliated citizenship" of the owner. He compounded his self-aggrandizement by adding in words as pompous as they were misleading that the individual, "having conformed to the requirements of the several Acts of Congress in such cases made and provided, and having received his affiliation certificate [i.e. acknowledgment of his declaration of intent], is entitled to all the benefits and protection of an affiliated citizen of the United States of America."

And then, with a dignity worthy of a foreign minister, he

concluded: "I hereby request all whom it may concern to permit safely and freely to pass the said individual, and in case of need to give him all lawful aid and protection."

Whereupon he affixed what he described as his "National Seal of Office," and presto, the "affiliated citizen" was ready to brandish the document under the nose of any Poo-Bah anywhere on earth, threatening to call out the Marines at the slightest provocation.

Confusion was worse confounded when some states of the Union began to accord important privileges to persons who possessed "first papers."

The homestead laws made it possible for any foreigner who had declared the oft-mentioned intention to secure a deed to a tract of his choice by living on the tract and cultivating it for some specified period of time. In 1850, the state of Michigan gave the right to vote to all who had lived in it for two and a half years or more and had declared their intention to become citizens. Wisconsin did the same for those who had lived there only one year.* Between the middle and the end of the century, persons who possessed "first papers" were permitted to vote in Arkansas, Indiana, Kansas, Missouri, and elsewhere. Under the laws of Delaware, Kentucky, New York, and Washington, such persons enjoyed greater rights in the acquisition of real property than aliens who had no such documents. Particularly interesting is a provision in the federal statute of June 7, 1872, under which an alien seaman who declared his intention to become a citizen and served three years on an American merchant vessel subsequent to the declaration, "*be deemed a citizen of the United States* for the purpose of manning and serving on board any merchant vessel of the United

* Carl Schurz was still an alien when he became a candidate for the office of lieutenant governor of Wisconsin in 1852. Even more unusual was the case of Judah P. Benjamin, presidential elector from Louisiana in 1848, United States senator from 1852 to 1861, Confederate attorney general, secretary of war, and finally secretary of state — all this without ever becoming an American citizen. He returned to his native England after the Civil War, proved his British nationality, and was admitted to the bar to embark on what became a great new career in the law. Oddly enough, he had first won political prominence in Louisiana by fighting for the passage of an amendment to the state constitution requiring that candidates for the governorship be native-born citizens of the United States.

States"; and this law remained in effect until as recently as May 9, 1918 (italics supplied).

Along with the Koszta affair, in the very year of its ocurrence, and bearing a certain resemblance to some of its features, two controversial cases claimed the attention of the Department of State.

A Prussian newspaper editor, Henry D'Oench, erstwhile participant in the German revolutionary movement in 1848, fled to America in the spring of 1850 and filed a declaration of intention two years later. Shortly afterward he sailed for Hamburg on business. The local police arrested him. Extradited to the Prussian authorities to complete a three-year prison sentence imposed on him before he had left for the United States, D'Oench was put in prison and had spent nearly one year there when his brother, a full-fledged American citizen, appealed to the secretary of state.[85] The brother, equipped with arguments based on Secretary Marcy's famous note to Hülsemann, demanded American protection for the imprisoned possessor of a "first paper." In reply, Marcy drew a line between the case of D'Oench and that of Koszta in this manner:

"I have just had a full conversation with Baron Gerolf, the Prussian Minister, in relation to the case of your brother, Henry D'Oench. The position maintained by this Department in the case of Koszta will be acted on in all cases to which they may be applicable; but it is apprehended that there are such circumstances of difference in your brother's case as may embarrass the Government in efforts to procure his discharge . . . The change of national character subsequent to the alleged offense does not release an offender from penalties previously incurred when legally brought within the jurisdiction of the country whose laws have been violated. It may be found that in this respect there is a difference between the case of your brother and that of Koszta. You may, however, be assured that this Government will use all proper means to effect his release." [86]

American consular dispatches on file throw no further light on the case of D'Oench. It is quite likely that the unlucky man had to complete his prison term; the Prussian position, as the secretary intimated, was basically sound from the legal — if uncharitable from the humane — point of view.

By and large the public, apt to lose sight of substance because of outward similarities, was getting a liberal education in the international legal facts of life.

At about the time of the return of the liberated Koszta to the United States, in the fall of 1853, one Simon Tousig, a native of Austria who went back there for a brief sojourn, became the cause of a departmental predicament. His letter of November 23, 1853, to the American chargé at Vienna, imploring that official to rescue him, is among the choice "human interest" documents in the Department's files. With a simplicity as appealing as his orthography was erratic, he wrote:

"Your Honour, You please excuse me when I take the liberty to introduce myself to Your Honour in this present letter. I am compelled to do it, to crave for Your Honour's aid. First I have to tell the whole tale, I am born in Prague and have been a subject to his Majestic of Austria, in the year 1849 I went with a passport (directed to Germania, France, and England) to these Un St of Am, settled myself there (at Metuchen, Middlesex Cou, St of N J) to become citizen of said Un St of America. There was a family in my neighborhood which lost their head, their Father, they are natives of Prague, they want to go back to Prague to their relatives, they had none in Am. A mother and five children, the oldest of them 11 years of age, they want me to accompany them which I did, for which purpose I got a passport from Washington City 1/10–1853. Now comes the point. The police here won't give me my passport to go back to my new home, they say You are a unlawful emigrant and ought to be punished for that, or must be, and secondly You cannot become a citizen of any country before you get leave of your soveregn. And Your Honour: they are going to put the law into me, I think most to plague me, as they do to other American citizens natives or not, they don't like America much. The matters of my process are going likely throuh a dozen of offices or more back and foreward. I have been running since today a week ago, every day from one office to the other, all the answer I got is I can't help you, your matter has to go the legal way. When I told them I am poor, have nothing to live on, then if I ain't in Bremen on the board of the vessel on the 1st of December, so I have to loose that money which I paid to secure my passage, and I have a family in Am, which is waiting for and depending on me entirely.

"Today I went to the police to get my passport directed to Vienna for to beseech Your Honor verbal, but I could not get it. I dare not leave the city till the matter is settled never mind if I or my family which I left in America starve, who does care for them nobody.

"What Your Honour in your kindness and humanity is going to do for me, what I beg and implore Your Honour to do right away for I ought to be off some time this week. Finally I beg very humble Your Honour to make me aquainted with the proceedings when necessary, that I might know what course to take here."

The American chargé, Mr. Jackson, promptly replied after conversations with the Austrian authorities. It appeared that Tousig had first arrived in New York in June 1849, filed a "first paper" there on January 18, 1851, and upon sending the declaration of intention to Washington, a passport was issued him over the signature of Secretary Marcy. As the poor devil wrote Jackson, "that is a true statement as true as the Bible . . . I have no business here, I beg you again help me away from here, the Lord knows I must become sick, I miss the free air of my dear new home, I wish to be there, God bless Your Honour . . ."[87]

Jackson addressed an appeal to the Austrian foreign minister and held several personal conferences with him and his deputies. The tension then existing between the governments because of the affair at Smyrna prompted the chargé to exercise special caution. He courteously and eloquently asked for consideration without brandishing arguments or raising demands. "Respectfully intimating the hope" that he would "receive the benefit of universal principles of enlightened jurisprudence," he observed that Tousig "is an ignorant, uneducated, simple-minded, and unoffending person," and that on this account "I have become the more interested in his fate." He stressed the hope that "charitable consideration may be given to the circumstances of the man" so that Tousig would be permitted to return to America.[88]

In his report to Secretary Marcy, the chargé pointed out that "the Austrian Government may have an especial object in view in holding on to the person of Tousig, and in magnifying the case into an important matter of diplomatic negotiation, to redeem, if possible, the diplomatic honor lost in the Koszta correspondence."

He speculated that since in the Koszta case the Austrians "were convicted of wrong, the destined victim had been rescued from their grasp, they were altogether weak," therefore in the Tousig case "they will stand confidently upon their law . . . The person of Tousig is theirs, they will feel altogether strong; yet both cases, to a superficial glance here in Europe, would be assimilated in a common position to our system of Naturalization . . ."[89]

The secretary's reply held out little hope: "Assuming all that could possibly belong to Tousig's case — that he had a domicile here and was actually clothed with the nationality of the United States, — there is a feature in it which distinguishes it from that of Koszta. Tousig voluntarily returned to Austria and placed himself within the reach of her municipal laws . . . Having been once subject to the municipal laws of Austria and while under her jurisdiction violated those laws, his withdrawal from that jurisdiction and acquiring a different national character would not exempt him from their operation whenever he again chose to place himself under them."[90]

But Austria decided not to impose additional strain on the relations of the two countries. The moderates in the cabinet prevailed over those who advocated the preparation of a vengeful Marcy-Manifesto-in-reverse. Simon Tousig was quietly released, and his passport was handed back to him.

On February 16, 1854, Chargé Jackson gave Tousig a letter of recommendation which enabled him to work his passage back to

America aboard a merchant vessel. As soon as he stepped on American soil once again, in New York, he rushed to the nearest printing shop, had a batch of cards printed, and distributed them to all takers on the streets near the pier.

The text on the cards read: "America saved Tousig — God save America — Thank you, Government!" *

* He had the cards reprinted from time to time and passed them out among acquaintances and strangers alike. I saw one of the cards framed next to the cash register in the grocery store of the late J. O. Tousig, a grandson of Simon Tousig, on Superior Avenue in Cleveland, Ohio, around 1936.

✓ THE REVIEWS VIII

ALONG with the president's message of December 5, 1853, the documentation of the Koszta case was submitted to the Thirty-Third Congress. Since traditionally the more intimate representation of the people was considered embodied in the House, rather than in the Senate, it was in that chamber that the affair, so closely allied to popular attitudes, was expected to be fully debated.

As an opening move, a resolution inspired by the message was offered in the House by Gilbert Dean of New York; it called for an expression of the nation's gratitude to Commander Ingraham for his gallant deportment at Smyrna.

Leafing through the pages of the *Congressional Globe*, predecessor of today's *Congressional Record*, one is alternately or simultaneously amused, irritated, and charmed.

In the exhibition that unfolds between the tattered covers of the tomes, veritable geysers of nineteenth-century Americanese are featured, gushing forth to the accompaniment of almost visible gesticulations rivaling in breadth those of the formidable Shakespearean actors of the period.

Time seemed to lose all meaning as the legislators wrangled over issues often not more relevant to the national interest than the medieval bone of theological contention about the exact number of angels that could stand on the point of a pin.

On the crest of the waves of oratory, up and down bobbed the proposal to award Commander Ingraham an ornamental sword. As the resolution on the subject passed from hand to hand in committee and in the aisles, it came to be rearranged and reworded, watered down and dehydrated, until it metamorphosed into a proposal to give the officer a medal instead of a sword — and doubts soon arose about the propriety of either.

It appeared that Congress was little disposed to delve into the merits and demerits of the Koszta case in general or Ingraham's exploit within it in particular. To let bygones be bygones seemed a wiser strategy to the administration's supporters and opponents alike. The extremely favorable popular reaction toward the affair, which had so fully crystallized by the time the first session of the Thirty-Third Congress got under way, was considered by most as sufficient reward in itself for Ingraham as well as for the Foreign Service officers involved.

In weighing the choice between a sword and a medal, the historical fact was ignored that the former token of approbation was by no means the higher type of the two. Medals rather than swords had been given to those whom Congress had graced with what it considered the most impressive sign of appreciation within its gift. Commodore Truxtun in 1800, Captains Hull, Decatur and Jones in 1813, and Captain Stewart in 1816, each had received medals from Congress; again medals, with a vote of thanks in addition, had been given Captain Preble in 1804, Captains Perry and Elliott in 1813, and Captain MacDonough in 1814. All these heroes were squadron commanders outranking Ingraham, with a record of victories in important naval engagements — whereas no actual engagement was fought by Ingraham at Smyrna.

In any event, as Representative Dean's resolution reached the floor, most members failed to rise to the occasion in any sense other than the physical. Some of them soon resembled all too painfully their most stinging caricatures in the press. Prompted on the one hand to satisfy their constituents' demands that a suitable decoration be given to Ingraham, they were, on the other, careful to avoid whatever political pitfalls could have been concealed beneath Dean's resolution. But, then as now, men of idealism, courage, and forceful convictions were not scarce on the Hill. These men were determined to see that Koszta stayed free, Ingraham received praise, the actions of our Foreign Service officers were approved, the autocrats were taught a lesson, and American history was enriched with a proud little page as a result of the incident at Smyrna.

Habitual visitors to the House galleries during the debates on the resolution witnessed exchanges such as these:

Mr. Bayly: "If the House will look at the resolution, they will find that we thank Captain Ingraham for nothing but judicious conduct in extending protection to a man illegally imprisoned. The ground for the extension of that protection is not settled at all. It was by design, and properly too, that we did not go into that question. We merely thank him for his prompt and judicious conduct in extending the protection of our nationality over Koszta, to which he was undoubtedly entitled. All controverted questions that had been brought up had been carefully left out; and in this case, I do not hesitate to say, properly and judiciously left out."

Mr. Millson: "I have no hesitation in saying that I have never entertained a doubt that the justification of the conduct of Captain Ingraham was complete, but not for many of the reasons which have been assigned. I concur in much of the reasoning contained in the letter of the Secretary of State upon this subject; but I am anxious to see that no resolution passed by the House shall commit Congress to any questionable principle; and for this reason I greatly desire that this matter should be referred to the Committee of the Whole on the State of the Union, and that it shall be taken up some convenient day — at some early day — and disposed of as may seem proper. I make these remarks not with a view of interposing any obstacle to the passage of the resolution, but for the purpose of giving an opportunity of becoming assured for myself that it is in such terms, and contains such sentiments, as I shall be willing to subscribe to. I can see no necessity for any immediate action . . ."

Mr. Bayly: "I thought if we could get [the proposed text] into the Committee on Foreign Affairs, composed of such gentlemen as the gentleman from Pennsylvania [Mr. Chandler] and others who are known to this House — I mention the gentleman in particular because he is known to be what he prides himself upon being, not only a Whig but a Federalist (laughter) — he has been an editor and is an able critic, he understands the use of the English language — I say, I thought that a committee of that sort, if they met together to talk over their phraseology, could, after a while, get [the text] nearly right. Well, we did meet and talk them over. We made suggestions, and we made amendments, and at last we got the resolution in such a shape that the committee agreed to it unanimously; and it has been reported back to the House by the gentleman from New York [Mr. Dean]. [Mr. Millson] wants to send it now to the Committee of the Whole on the State of the Union . . . To talk over the language of it again? To get it right again? Why, sir, this matter of paying a compliment amounts to nothing if it is grudgingly and tardily done. My colleague asks what is the occasion for immediate action? . . . I undertake to say here, we have taken in this matter a new deportment in respect to our foreign affairs. If I may be excused for using technical expressions, this nation has been constantly the plaintiff. We have always been after other nations for what they have done to us. Now, I am tired of seeing this nation eternally the plaintiff. I want a new era. I want to see this nation sometimes the defendant. I say it emphatically, and I wish it to go out to the country. Not only is that my opinion, but I believe it is the opinion of the Committee on Foreign Affairs . . . I approve of Captain Ingraham's conduct thoroughly and entirely. The resolution avoids assigning the reason for that approval, and in my opinion properly so. There is the judgment; every member of this court may assign his own reason for it, and I do not care one cent whether the reason is a good one or not if the judgment is right. It does not matter a particle whether Koszta was an American citizen or not. I presume no one claims that he was a citizen, but he was entitled to American protection; he was illegally seized in violation of the laws of nations; he was imprisoned in violation of law; and I do not care whether he was an American citizen or not. Further than that, I do not care whether he was entitled to American protection or not. I shall not go on with that idea. But I do maintain that there are cases in which we may interfere in defense of humanity, and for the prevention of wrongful injuries, even when we are not bound to interfere. I draw the distinction between where you are bound to do and where you may do it. But, sir, it seems to me that this debate has sprung up too suddenly. This is a matter too important for any man to undertake to speak upon without that decision which preparation alone can afford."

Mr. Orr: "I think that the House is prepared at the present time to vote on the resolution. The resolution does nothing more than simply return the thanks of Congress to Captain Ingraham for a gallant act. It was, sir, an act of gallantry, and it is not necessary that it should be vindicated on this floor upon any other principle — according to the resolution — than upon the great principle of humanity. And what has Captain Ingraham done? He has infused new life and spirit into your Navy; he has caused your flag to be respected on every sea and in every land of the habitable globe. He has done more than your armies perhaps accomplished during the Mexican war — to have this country respected in every land and nation on the face of the earth. In the adoption of this resolution the House does not commit itself, and the country does not commit itself, to any of the debatable propositions which may be contained in the able letter of the Secretary of State [to Hülsemann], in some of which I fully concur. This resolution, sir, does not commit the Government or the country, if it should be passed. Captain Ingraham did not deliberate as long as we have been deliberating here before he determined that Martin Koszta should not be seized by Austrian authority and incarcerated in Austrian dungeons. I trust, sir, that the example set us by Captain Ingraham in doing his duty promptly, will be followed by this House."

Mr. Richardson: "I presume, Mr. Speaker, that there is not in this House or in the country one single man, having an American heart, who does not admire the manner in which Captain Ingraham conducted that matter in a foreign country, with a single vessel, in the face of a foe twice as great as the force he commanded himself. There is about this whole matter something which has made me, for one, rejoice that the whole affair has taken place. Sir, there is more than the conduct of Captain Ingraham. I am glad to see that an American Secretary, in the discussion of this question, and with American authority, came forward to support the acts of our officers. If we are that great and proud nation which we claim to be, it is time that we should have something to say in the law of nations. The American Secretary of State has, for the first time, justified the conduct of an American officer by American law and American precedent. I think that heretofore, in the discussion of these questions, our own country has been at fault if she has not attained the position which she is entitled to among the nations of the earth. I am rejoiced, not only that Captain Ingraham displayed in the face of European authority a gallantry and courage unmatched, in my opinion, in the annals of history, but I am also rejoiced that an American Secretary has placed his justification for the act upon American authority. Now, I wish to inquire of my friend from Virginia [Mr. Millson], who has interposed not an objection to the resolution but an intimation of his desire that it should go to a committee, if there is in the history of legislation a single instance where resolutions of this description have been sent to the Committee of the Whole? The thanks are worth nothing if doled out and forced reluctantly through the American Congress . . ."

Mr. Millson: "I do not wish to be placed in a false position upon this subject . . . No man has defended the course and conduct of Captain Ingraham more warmly and more earnestly than I have done in repeated conversations. But I suggest here whether this tribute will not be more acceptable to Captain Ingraham himself, as the result of the mature deliberation of this House, than as only a spontaneous outpouring of inconsideration . . ."

Mr. Bayly: "If my colleague will allow me, I desire to ask a single question: Does he consider a resolution introduced into this House, and referred to a committee to which it appropriately belongs, and which has undergone its anxious scrutiny, as one that has been precipitately and incautiously brought before this House?"

Mr. Millson: "I reply that while I have all proper confidence in the Committee of Foreign Affairs, and while I consider that my confidence is justified by my knowledge of the materials of which that Committee is composed, yet I regard the Committees of this House as but aids to the House and not substitutes for it; and that this House ought not, in any case, to commit themselves with blind adherence to conclusions to which their Committees may have arrived. It is for these reasons that I desire, as well on Captain Ingraham's as on other accounts, that the question should be referred, rather for the purpose of having the resolution printed than for the purpose of giving rise to any protracted discussion hereafter . . ."

The floor show goes on. Attack follows rebuttal, proposal precedes attack, topic gives birth to new little topics, day in, day out. . .

Mr. Chandler: "While we are deliberating, while we are discussing, the spirit of our good action is evaporating and the whole thing is becoming a mere piece of formal legislation . . ."

Mr. Phillips: "Mere acts of humanity or personal gallantry are

178

not so rare in our Navy as to excite our special wonder or call for this extraordinary testimonial of the Government . . ."

Mr. Smith: "I hope that this or any other resolution of a similar character . . . may not pass this House now or on any other occasion . . . I remember, sir, that on a former occasion in this House I was a minority of one upon a question [to extend a welcome to Kossuth in the Capitol] wilder, more frantic, and more enthusiastic than this, therefore I do not dread minorities, as you may know. It seems that the friends of this resolution cannot be satisfied with any form of resolution . . . Sir, what do you propose to do? You propose to thank a man in this extraordinary manner for doing simply his duty. It is not at all surprising that we should manifest some consternation and surprise when we see any man doing his duty. Any set of two hundred and thirty-seven men who would deliberately waste fifteen days of the public time, in the first month of their session, ought to be surprised that any man should do his duty under any circumstances. (Laughter.) . . . I remember, sir, that two years ago this whole country was wild with enthusiasm about Kossuth; and now it seems to be going wild about Koszta; parallel cases . . ."

Mr. Churchwell: "Remarkable debate! the enlightened world will be astonished when it shall have read the debates of the popular branch of the American Congress of today . . . We find American history crowded with those great events which justly make us proud of our country. In that record there is no incident perhaps more brilliant than the act of the gallant Ingraham in the port of Smyrna . . ."

In column after column, on page after page, allusions and reminders, analogies and admonitions splash right and left like drops of an endless rainfall.

Lengthily discussed or briefly cited are, among countless other things, Lieutenant Hunter's capture of Alvarado . . . tokens of regard given by Queen Victoria to selected worthies . . . Pericles at the feet of Aspasia . . . General Wool and the battle of Buena Vista . . . the promotion of Scott to lieutenant general . . . Samson in the lap of Delilah . . . opinions of international legal luminaries like Pufendorff, Vattel, and Grotius . . . proverbs and maxims culled from Greek and Latin classics . . . Cuba and its "Africanization" . . . the retirement of Lord Palmerston . . .

And the end is not yet.

Mr. Dean, sponsor of the original resolution which is now hardly recognizable, untiringly rises time and time again to the defense of the battered remnants. One morning he shouts on the floor: "If we pass this resolution, as I trust we shall, while we thank this gallant Captain, we declare, as the representatives of the American people, that we approve the act in the light of all its surrounding circumstances, and affirm those great principles of natural and international law on which it is to be justified . . . I believe the time has come when we should, and when we must, concur in these principles. The executive branch of the Government has already done so in the letter of Secretary Marcy which has so often been referred to, a letter which, let me say, is destined to an immortality almost equal to the Magna Charta or the Declaration of Independence, if it is not sacrilege to compare anything to the Declaration of Independence. This letter, sir, is another Magna Charta, one that has been long needed, an American Magna Charta for adopted citizens!"

The congressman from New York exudes genuine pathos as he characterizes Ingraham's action, in a supreme effort to secure the passage of the resolution: "No single battle has ever added such luster to the American name. It has given us a respect abroad which could not be secured by the most successful naval engagement . . . The spot on which a person entitled to the protection of our Government stands, whether at home or abroad, is as inviolable as the sanctuary of the gods!"

The applause and cheers in the galleries are so prolonged that the speaker has difficulty in restoring order and must warn the public that a recurrence will not be tolerated. But it is noticeable that a considerably larger number of members on the floor have applauded Dean now than before. It seems that his passionate outburst has at last broken the ground for an early approval of the resolution. Indeed, after his speech a final vote is taken.

The resolution is passed with an overwhelming 173 against 9. The text now reads as follows:

The Reviews

"BE IT RESOLVED by the Senate and the House of Representatives of the United States in Congress assembled,

"That the thanks of Congress be, and they are hereby, presented to Duncan N. Ingraham, commanding the United States sloop-of-war *St. Louis*, for his judicious and gallant conduct on the second day of July last, in extending the protection of the American Government to Martin Koszta by rescuing him from forcible and illegal seizure and imprisonment on board the Austrian brig *Hussar*.

"RESOLVED, That the President of the United States be, and is hereby, requested to cause to be made a medal, with suitable devices, and presented to Captain Duncan N. Ingraham, as a testimonial of the high sense entertained by Congress of his valor, promptness, and judicious conduct on the above mentioned occasion.

"RESOLVED, That the President of the United States cause the foregoing resolutions to be communicated to Captain Duncan N. Ingraham in such terms as he may deem best calculated to give the effect to the objects thereof."

On March 2, 1854, the Senate received a special message from the White House, enclosed with which was — in compliance with

COURTESY MARINERS' MUSEUM, NEWPORT NEWS, VA.

The two sides of the gold medal awarded by Congress to Commander Ingraham in 1854

181

a Senate resolution passed on February 2 — a report from the secretary of state on the Koszta case. It was referred to the Committee
on Foreign Relations.

About five months later, on July 15, 1854, the House received
formal notification from the Senate that the latter had passed the
House's version of the resolution "with an amendment [requiring]
the concurrence of the House."

On August 3, the clerk of the House reported the disillusioning
results of the final revision: "First amendment: strike out the first
section. Second amendment: strike out the third section. Third
amendment: Amend the section by striking out . . ." — and so
forth. What then took shape was this:

"BE IT RESOLVED by the Senate and the House of Representatives
of the United States in Congress assembled,

"That the thanks of Congress be, and they are hereby, presented
to Commander Duncan N. Ingraham of the Navy of the United
States, as a testimonial of the high sense entertained by Congress
of his gallant and judicious conduct on the 2d July, 1853, in
extending protection to Martin Koszta by rescuing him from illegal
seizure and imprisonment on board the Austrian brig *Hussar*."

The two words, among others, which most accurately depicted
in the earlier version Ingraham's behavior at Smyrna were now
omitted. Missing from this final text were "valor" and "promptness."

One year, one month, and one day after Koszta's liberation, on
August 3, 1854, President Franklin Pierce "approved and signed
House Resolution No. 7, directing the presentation of a medal to
Commander Duncan N. Ingraham." *

The officer named briefly noted for his private files:

"I am in receipt of the medal the Congress saw fit to give me. It is
a handsome one." [91]

---

* The first — and only other — recipient from South Carolina of a congressional gold medal was Colonel William Washington, a cousin of the first president, who had distinguished himself in the Revolutionary War and later settled
at Charleston where some of his descendants intermarried with some of
Ingraham's forebears.

THE REVIEWS IX

T H E effect of what happened at Smyrna in the summer of 1853 made itself felt again and again long after the active participants of the case passed away. Even today, when the adventure of a century ago is no longer known, shadows of Marcy and Hülsemann, of Koszta and Ingraham, lurk behind many a measure affecting the lives of present and future generations of Americans.

After the Marcy-Hülsemann exchange, the State Department's officers both at home and abroad were subjected to an apparently endless series of fusillades by individuals convinced that new privileges were due them as a result of the controversy. Secretary Marcy, with the feather of victory safely in his cap, began to make sporadic withdrawals to positions of caution.

As early as September 1854, in the face of a torrent of demands for American passports by owners of "first papers," he felt compelled to declare what should have been both declared and rigorously enforced long before, namely, that a declarant of an intention to become a citizen was not entitled to a passport calling him an American citizen.[92] Through the remainder of his tenure of office he had to make one effort after another to draw and re-draw lines of demarcation within which to confine the "first paper," and to educate applicants in regard to those elements of the Koszta case which were peculiar unto themselves. Widespread attribution of

Koszta's liberation exclusively to his "first paper" — which in fact had served as proof of domicile only — was sired by ignorance and nursed by wishful thinking. Few understood, or cared to consider, the decisive factor: that Koszta had never returned to the land of his original allegiance but was captured in a third country where unilateral Austrian exercise of police authority was completely illegal. The secretary had to preach far and wide even in 1855 that "had Koszta been within the jurisdiction of Austria when he was seized, the whole character of the case would have been changed, and the forcible taking of him from the legal custody of Austrian officers could not have been defended on any principle of municipal or international law." [93]

But he remained less than lucid whenever it came to defining just how far our representatives abroad were to be allowed or expected to proceed in extending protection to apparently rightful claimants. To our minister to Prussia, for instance, he wrote that the Department did not intend to deny these officers "the right of extending a certain degree of protection to those possessing only the inchoate rights of citizenship. The nature and extent of this protection, however, must depend in a great degree upon circumstances, and these will vary in almost every case." [94]

This meant that in the event of a sudden new flare-up similar to that at Smyrna, our officials in the area could not have directly within sight a guiding light any brighter than that which had so faintly flickered in the previous instance. It was, if anything, only confusing that Secretary of State Cass, who succeeded Marcy in 1857, declared with unmistakable reference to Ingraham's action that "our naval officers have the right — it is their duty indeed — to employ the forces under their command not only in self-defense, but for the protection of the persons and property of our citizens when exposed to acts of lawless outrage, and this they have done . . . and will do . . . again when necessary." [95]

But Cass himself had to stress three years later in a communication to our minister to Switzerland that the impression of the American consul at Zurich about Marcy's position in the Koszta affair was quite erroneous. It was a mistake to think, wrote the secretary, that Marcy had "entertained the opinion that a declaration on the part of an alien of his intention to become a citizen of the United States 'entitles the declarant, while abroad with the intention to return, to the same rights and privileges as a citizen of the United States.' [This view] is the result of some misapprehension originating I know not how. I have never expressed and am very far from holding any such opinion . . ." [96]

As the years passed, the Department had to continue to wrestle with the ghosts of 1853. In 1869, Assistant Secretary Davis felt it necessary to prepare a lengthy paper on the then sixteen-year-old Koszta case, arguing that "it is true that in the concluding part of [Marcy's] masterly despatch he did say that a nation might at its pleasure clothe with the rights of its nationality persons not citizens, who were permanently domiciled in its borders. But it will be observed by the careful reader of that letter that this position is supplemental merely to the main line of the great argument, and that the Secretary rests the right of the Government to clothe the individual with the attributes of nationality, not upon the declaration of intention to become a citizen, but upon the permanent domicile of the foreigner within the country."

An emphatic admonition followed: "To extend this principle beyond the careful limitation put upon it by Secretary Marcy would be dangerous to the peace of the country. It has been repeatedly decided by this Department that the declaration of intention to become a citizen does not, in the absence of treaty stipulations, so clothe the individual with the nationality of this country as to enable him to return to his native land without being necessarily subject to all the laws thereof." [97]

Another sixteen years later the Department was still troubled by the thought that some overenthusiastic naval man might apply the kind of threat of force Ingraham had used at Smyrna. Writing to the American consul general at Guayaquil, Ecuador, on May 1, 1885, concerning one Julio R. Santos who was — be it noted — not a mere "first paper" holder but a fully naturalized American imprisoned in Ecuador for alleged revolutionary activities, Secretary of State Bayard explained: "This instruction will be handed to you by Commander Mahan of the *U.S.S. Wachusett*, who revisits the waters of Ecuador by direction of the Secretary of the Navy for that purpose. Commander Mahan will be instructed to remain within reach pending the prompt disposal of Mr. Santos's case, and in the probable event of his release, he will be afforded an opportunity to return to the United States on the *Wachusett*, by way of Panama, should he so desire."

But on June 17 he belatedly hastened to add: "You will understand that the mission of the *Wachusett* is one of peace and good will, to the end of exerting the moral influence of our flag toward a discreet and mutually honorable solution, and in the event of Mr. Santos being released, to afford him the means of returning to the country of his allegiance and domicile. The purpose of her presence is not to be deemed minatory; and resort to force is not competently within the scope of her commander's agency. If all form of redress, thus temperately but earnestly solicited, be unhappily denied, it is the constitutional prerogative of Congress to decide and declare what further action shall be taken."

If one had eyes sharp enough to discern two shadows behind Secretary Bayard's back as that gentleman penned these lines, and recognize them as the shadows of Ingraham and Offley, he could also detect a smile on those ghostly faces . . .

Year in, year out, an almost unbroken line of applicants confronted American legations and consulates with claims of privileges on the basis of Koszta's case. A wealth of interesting records in this connection are to be found in the journals of Benjamin Moran, secretary of our then most important legation: the one in London. Appointed to that post only four years after the incident at Smyrna, Moran soon found that misconceptions based on it contributed greatly to the various reasons which made his lot, like that of the policeman immortalized by Gilbert and Sullivan, "not a happy one." Here are a few typical items from his diaries, each chosen to exemplify an entire series of cases: *

* Reprinted from *The Journal of Benjamin Moran, 1857–1865*, ed. by Sarah Agnes Wallace and Frances Elma Gillespie, by permission of the University of Chicago Press. Copyright by the University of Chicago.

"Feb. 9, 1857. — A Prussian who had been years in the U.S. came with a passport from the Mayor of N.Y. which I refused to visé as it simply said he had declared his intention to become a citizen." *

"Oct. 14, 1857. — A General Haug, an Austrian, was here this morning with a passport from the [American] Consulate at Rome as a citizen of the U.S., but as it was irregular, having been issued in 1849 to go to the U.S. only, I refused to visé it . . .

"March 9, 1858. — We have had several Germans lately for passports who have only declared their intention, but could not give them passports . . .

"July 23, 1858. — A Greek came to have a blank passport filled up which he got from [American Consul] Croskey 4 years ago, but as he had never been in the U.S., I took it from him and sent him away protectionless. He was very obstinate."

"June 27, 1859. — A fellow by the name of Canzi, an Italian who had declared his intention to become a citizen but never completed it, comes here every once in a while for a visé, thinking no one knows him and he will get it that way. He has not been in the U.S. since 1853, is doing business in England, and is a bad fellow."

"Feb. 29, 1860. — A Mr. Luciani, an Italian, was here today with a passport from our Paris Legation, although he was never naturalized. This . . . shows how careless [certain officials] are."

Aug. 9, 1860. — A very gentlemanly person by the name of George Felletti, a Venetian who had declared his intention . . . at New York in 1851, and obtained a passport as an American citizen from Fernando Wood, Mayor of New York, 15 Sept. 1855, was here for a visé this morning, but I could not give it to him. He has been absent from the U.S. ever since, has been traveling as an American citizen, and seemed to think it hard that I did not acknowledge him. The case is of common occurrence, and the mayors who give such passports ought to be deprived of office."

"March 4, 1861. — There is a lot of swindling Notaries Public in N.Y. who extort large sums of money from foreigners for a species of false passport. A young German by the name of Fred'k Ruprecht was here this morning with one of these doc[umen]ts, No. 17, 521, issued by a man named Michael Louis Hiller, at New

---

* Mayors were often guilty of anomalies of this type; see also the entry for August 9, 1860, quoted later above. Even some forty years later, certificates of "identification" based on declarations of intention were issued by the mayor of New Orleans to persons who subsequently used them abroad as passports. Acting Secretary of State Hill severely reprimanded the mayor on December 5, 1899, declaring that he was infringing on the law. Thereupon the practice, apparently the last of its type, ceased.

York, for which he paid $2. Ruprecht had only declared his intention on the 14th Feby., and Hiller gave him this passport on the next day. It is a specious thing with a big eagle at the top, and headed 'United States of America: To all to whom these presents shall come, Greeting,' and goes on in the name of the said Hiller to certify that the said Ruprecht 'has declared his intention to become a citizen of the United States,' the [word] citizen, etc., being in a prominent line. At the bottom is a seal, and the signature of Mr. Hiller. The whole affair is a manifest swindle and should be put an end to. If Hiller gets $2 apiece for these things and has faithfully numbered this, the scamp has pocketed $35,042 for these false papers. Some time since, I got another of a similar type from a German by the name of Christian Schleyel who got it in N.Y. of a scamp by the name of Leopold Lorenz and paid $3 for it. Schleyel was naturalized and this doc[umen]t certified that he is the holder of a 'Certificate of Legitimation.' It is disgraceful to any country that such men are in office and permitted to swindle."

"Feb. 10, 1864. — Dr. Thomas Airey, a short thickset Englishman heavy with vulgar jewelry, who has two or more diplomas from American Herbalist Medical Colleges and has declared his intention to become a citizen, has been here this morning to obtain . . . assistance in compelling the Medical Registrars of England to register him as a practitioner . . . I explained that we could not interfere to prevent the operation of English law . . . He then told me that the Judge who 'naturalized' him said he was a citizen . . . This is another of the impositions constantly practiced at home by those who administer our naturalization laws. Dr. Airey believes he took an oath of citizenship, and had never before had it explained to him that the proceeding was only preliminary and not final."

Sometimes the claims were so cryptic as to defy at least the first attempts to understand them, as shown by a brief but eloquent example from the year 1864. Here is a letter from the files of our consulate at Marseille: "Mr. Consul: I am notified the Government had registered. And they register me. I told them I am American Sub Jack. They said nevir mind. Yours truly [illegible signature, no address]."

There the consul sits; there the claim is; any minute the claimant may arrive to explain in person what he wants and to teach the consul how to respect his rights as an American "Sub Jack."

Along with conflicts and irregularities in the areas of immigration and naturalization, both the federal government and a number of states were much concerned about discrimination against naturalized citizens. Successive administrations kept urging Congress to pass legislation not only in this direction but generally toward regulating the entire complexus of citizenship. Some states made efforts of their own to prevent the use of two different scales in the weighing of the citizens of America. Maine, for example, resolved shortly after the Civil War that "wherever the American doctrine is denied and the rights of naturalized citizens are violated thereby, it should be regarded as an offense against the United States . . . Justice and honor alike demand that the Executive of the Government should take immediate and efficient measures to restore such naturalized citizens to all the rights and privileges belonging to native-born citizens."

Wisconsin demanded that "no distinction be tolerated between native-born and duly naturalized citizens of the United States," and Maryland urged that Congress "pass such laws as honor, justice and the true policy of the country demand in fully securing to all naturalized citizens the same rights of person and property both at home and abroad which are now possessed by the native-born."

On January 27, 1868, the House Committee on Foreign Affairs sharply rebuked other governments that insisted on maintaining the principle of perpetual allegiance with regard to naturalized Americans. It claimed that since foreign countries permitted emigration, they also must have recognized expatriation as a logical consequence.

On the day of the report's appearance General Banks, chairman of the committee, submitted a bill "concerning the right of American citizens in foreign States." It contained not only a resounding declaration of the principle of the equality of native and naturalized Americans, but also a startling retaliation clause.

Under the clause, if an adopted American should be denied recognition of his exclusive American citizenship and taken under arrest by his native country, or if his release should be unreasonably delayed or altogether refused, the president could order the retaliatory arrest of any subject of that country who happened to be within the jurisdiction of the United States at the time.[98]

The bill, with its explosive tit-for-tat clause, was adopted in the House by an overwhelming vote of 104 to 4. But when the matter came before the Senate, long and violent debate ensued over the retaliation clause. Many feared that it might easily result in giving the president the power to declare war, a paramount prerogative of Congress. Because of such fears, the proviso was rewritten to the effect that in interposing on behalf of Americans, the president might use only "means not amounting to acts of war." In this sense, the bill was passed in the Senate by a vote of 39 to 7, the House concurred, and the measure became effective on July 28, 1868.

The definition of the American position concerning expatriation, formulated and put into effect in 1868, was dignified and unequivocal. It has been called an Emancipation Proclamation for Adopted Americans:

"Whereas the right of expatriation is a natural and inherent right of all people, indispensable to the enjoyment of the rights of life, liberty, and the pursuit of happiness; and

"Whereas, in recognition of this principle, this Government has freely received emigrants from all natives and invested them with the rights of citizenship; and

"Whereas it is claimed that such American citizens, with their descendants, are subjects of foreign states, owing allegiance to the Governments thereof; and

"Whereas it is necessary to the maintenance of public peace that this claim of foreign allegiance should be promptly and finally disavowed,

"Therefore, any declaration, instruction, opinion, order, or decision of any officer of the United States which denies, restricts, impairs or questions the right of expatriation, is declared inconsistent with the fundamental principles of the Republic." *

* Although the United States became the foremost champion of the doctrine of expatriation as a natural right, Congress did not provide either in the legislation of 1868 or in any other law until as late as 1907 for the conditions under which an American citizen might be deemed to have expatriated himself.

If bolder or nobler sentiments have ever been proclaimed in fewer words from a platform of decorous whereases, chroniclers have overlooked them.

In that same year of 1868, something of a miracle took shape in England: a turnabout as radical as any the British had ever decided to make in the face of their ancient traditions and conservative temperament. It was ushered in by the appointment of a Royal Commission to inquire into and report on problems of naturalization and allegiance. As a result, a statute of epochal significance was passed in which Parliament recognized the right of expatriation.[99]

Britons and Americans reached across the ocean to shake hands in perpetual agreement over the right of every human being to seek his fortune wherever his heart and mind would lead him.

This development was part of a chain reaction. Treaties affecting naturalization were concluded in 1868 between the United States on the one hand and, on the other, the North German Union, Bavaria, Baden, Hesse, Belgium; in the following year, Sweden and Norway joined the signatories; and on May 13, 1870, Great Britain followed suit.

Thereupon, at long last, the Austrian court also decided to abandon an increasingly untenable position, entered into a treaty with the United States, and ended a lengthy era of much bitterness and strife.

When American and Austrian representatives affixed their signatures to the protocol, perhaps they gave a mental salute to two irascible gentlemen named Marcy and Hülsemann who had not lived to see the day.

The last traceable occasion for a nationwide resuscitation of memories of the Koszta incident was provided by the arrest of an American national in 1879. The case had but one thing in common with Koszta's: possession of a "first paper," and generally turned out to be rather ludicrous. But it raised much clamor from press and public, and found its way into historical and legal textbooks.

In November 1879 at Piedras Negras, Mexico, a Mexican native named Felipe Burnato, permanent resident of the United States for fourteen years and proud owner of a "first paper," was arrested together with four companions. The group was charged with the smuggling into Mexico of not more and not less than eighteen bottles of beer.

The Mexican collector of customs, exercising his law-enforcing prerogatives, meted out to the hapless devotees of the brew a penalty of five years of forced military service, and caused them to be transported to the nearest battalion. The true reason for this severity appeared to lie less in the illicit import of a quantity of beer hardly large enough to quench the thirst of a few border guards on one day's tour of duty, than in the five men's nativity. The Mexicans regarded them as renegades who had disgraced their motherland by their adoption of the nationality of the enemy of 1846–48.

The American minister at Mexico City received information through his own contacts about the arrest of the group; no official information was sent to him by the Mexicans. After initial denials, the Mexican authorities finally confirmed that the arrests had taken place. Lengthy correspondence ensued between the minister and the Mexican Foreign Office and hard-to-reach provincial officials. When a formal American demand for the release of Burnato in particular — whose nationality status seemed clearest of the group of five — could be lodged with the Mexican government, almost a year had passed since the original arrests. Like Koszta in Ingraham's ultimatum to the Austrians, Burnato was described in the note with somewhat of a tactical point-stretching as "a citizen of the United States."

The Mexicans replied that an application for release should be addressed, of all places, to the Mexican judicial tribunals. The Department of State declined to accept this extraordinary suggestion. It continued to press its demand through our minister until an unexpected turn came to the relief of both sides, with some embarrassment for the Mexicans. It was found that Burnato, and all but one of his associates, had been discharged from the Army some three months before the formal American note was received by the Mexican Foreign Office. Burnato had been "begged out by his wife," he in turn had "begged out" three of his companions, and the fifth beer addict managed to desert the battalion and disappeared without a trace.[100]

Thus ended this odd Pan-American beer-barrel polka, but not before the American press had filled many a column of Sunday issues with colorful particulars of the affair at Smyrna a quarter of a century before.

In the State Department, occasional voices of high authority were raised even on the threshold of the twentieth century in endeavors to confine the ghosts of the Koszta case to what was regarded as their proper place. The tenor of relevant statements reflected the changes that time had wrought in both foreign and domestic attitudes.

In 1897, for example, Marcy's manifesto was described as illustrative of a "somewhat extreme position taken by Mr. Marcy" which "has since been necessarily regarded as applying in particular to the peculiar circumstances in which it originated." [101] So said Secretary of State Olney. Gradually, the case of Koszta came to be telescoped into what might be expressed thus: "There had been but one Koszta incident," to which probably many would then have added that it was one too many, anyhow. After all, in retrospect, with glory shed and color faded, it was only an unpleasantness; it was a messy business reeking with recklessness, lacking a realistic approach on the part of functionaries; and so forth.

True, the case was fit to be filed with accounts of the kind of unpardonable recklessness and unrealistic attitude that sometimes prompt such outbursts as "Damn the torpedoes, full speed ahead"; "I regret that I have but one life to give for my country"; or "You may fire when ready, Gridley"; and even such utterly undignified eruptions as that of the World War II commander of outnumbered and surrounded American troops when he replied to a formal call for surrender with no more than "Nuts!"

And yet, however unfortunate the incident itself was regarded by those eager to bury it in official archives, the act of 1907 reaffirmed the basic position taken by Secretary Marcy. It acknowledged that the acquisition of domicile in the United States, when coupled with the declaration of intention as its proof, may entitle an individual to American protection even though the process of naturalization had not been completed. This law declared that "when any person has made a declaration of intention . . . as provided by law and has resided in the United States for three years, a passport may be issued to him entitling him to the protection of the government in any foreign country." The passport, valid for six months, could not be renewed, and the protection could not be extended within the country of the person's earlier allegiance. The same law included a ban long overdue, prohibiting the filing of a declaration of intention anywhere except in the office of a clerk of court, and required that lawful entry into the United States be proved before making such a declaration.

By the time the law was enacted, a vital element in Marcy's stand had long been sustained by the Supreme Court of the United States.

The case that drew coincidental interpretive comment on the Koszta case from the highest tribunal in the land was decided during the October 1889 term of the Court when Mr. Justice Miller, delivering the opinion of the Court *In Re Neagle*,[102] called the Koszta affair "one of the most remarkable episodes in the history of our foreign relations" and raised the question: "Upon what Act of Congress then existing can anyone lay his finger in support of the action of our Government in this matter?"

It will be recalled that during the debate in Congress over the medal proposed to be awarded to Ingraham, Representative Bayly frankly stated: "The ground for the extension of that protection is not settled at all. It was by design, and properly so, that we did not go into that question."

But now, thirty-five years later, the Supreme Court did not turn its collective face away from that question. Mr. Justice Lamar pronounced approval of the position taken by the executive branch of the government back in 1853, replying to the question in these words: "We answer that such action [in Koszta's case] was justified because it pertained to the foreign relations of the United States, in respect to which the exclusive representative and embodiment of the entire sovereignty of the nation in its united character is the Federal Government . . . In reply, therefore, to the question, what law expressly justified such action, we answer, the organic law, the Constitution, which expressly commits all matters pertaining to our diplomatic negotiations to the treaty-making power."

The time which had elapsed since the occurrence of the incident at Smyrna placed its basic issues in clear perspective, supplying final answers to its dominant questions in this way:

Was Martin Koszta an Austrian subject when he was seized by the Austrians?

With respect to this crucial question, Marcy felt that his answer, firmly in the negative, was well grounded. Not only had Koszta emigrated with the consent of the Austrian government; he had been forced into exile, disowned and banished by that government. He had acquired domicile in the United States through compliance with the conditions prescribed by law, namely, acquisition of residence and establishment of proof of intention to remain permanently or indefinitely.[103] And where a domicile is established, it continues until a new one is acquired.[104] Moreover, according to the presumption of the law, the domicile is retained until its change is proved, and the burden of proof is on him who alleges the change.[105]

Could Koszta be legally seized in Turkey, in any event?

He could not. Not even if he had been an Austrian or a fugitive prisoner of war. Not unless a treaty covering such cases had existed between Turkey and Austria. And no such treaty was in existence at the time. The Austrians, in seizing him, committed an offense both against Turkish sovereignty and against the law of nations.

What were Koszta's relations with the United States?

Admittedly not those of a citizen. But he was entitled to Turkish protection, and he had papers certifying to what seemed tantamount to American nationality. The papers gave him the character of an American, as far as the Turkish authorities were concerned. If he was not entitled to those papers, the matter was subject to a decision between Turkey and the United States without Austrian participation. The American government maintained that Koszta's domicile, conjointly with certain elements in his particular case, conferred on him a type and degree of American national character even though he was not an American citizen. It based its views on a combination of grounds; it did not assert that domicile alone afforded either a sound or a complete criterion of national character. Important to note in this connection is the fact that the rules of domicile determine the status of a person from the international legal viewpoint without any necessary connection with citizenship. Domicile is simply a fact determined by residence and intention, while citizenship results from birth or from law. A person may be a citizen of the Kingdom of Ruritania, have his domicile in the Planetarian Republic, and reside in Outer Baldonia.

Would it have been rightful for Ingraham to use force?

It would not have been rightful for him to use "active and aggressive force." But had he used retaliatory force, it would have been primarily for Turkey and not for Austria to complain, as long as the use of force occurred in Turkish territorial waters. One might even argue that on the high seas Ingraham would have been entitled to use preventive force to avert what the law calls sudden wrongdoing. But the fact remains that he used no more than a threat of force, that the threat of force proved successful, and that, as Marcy pointed out, "if Turkey was satisfied, others had no right to complain."

But still another question remains, one that may have, and indeed should have, occurred to the reader long before this.

Why was Martin Koszta abducted?

Why he? Why there? Why then?

An attempt must be made to find an answer.

THE REVIEWS X

THE records of mid-nineteenth-century Hungarian emigration show only two cases in which Austrians abducted Hungarian exiles from Turkish asylum.

The first such case was that of an unidentified person at Smyrna, in the spring of 1851; as mentioned in an early chapter of this book, his bullet-ridden body was eventually found on the Trieste waterfront.

The second one was that of Koszta, nearly two years later.

Why were these two obscure exiles singled out for physical assault with the intention of forcibly returning them to Austrian territory?

The conjecture is inescapable that some specific motive must have impelled the Austrians to kidnap these particular individuals. Something must have set these two apart, in Austrian eyes, from the thousands of others who had likewise been subjects of the emperor, had participated in the same armed insurrection against the Vienna government, had uniformly violated Austrian laws prohibiting self-expatriation, and were, one and all, anti-Habsburgists whose very existence abroad was symbolic of defiance to Austrian authority and likely to stimulate resistance to absolutism at home.

To the person of Koszta in particular, very special importance

must have been attached, an importance great enough to have
caused the Austrian consul general at Smyrna to involve himself
in the most dangerous of his plots, and to have prompted the
imperial government to exert a maximum effort to sustain its
representative's illegal action. Yet, as Secretary Marcy did not
fail to observe in his manifesto, in none of their dealings concerning the affair had the Austrians intimated, much less claimed,
that at the time of his sojourn in Turkey Koszta was engaged in
any activity objectionable by any valid standard.

Meager is the surviving evidence against which the credibility
of theories about the motive can be tested. The disappearance of
some vital primary sources during World War II in Hungary,
and the inaccessibility of others under that country's present
Communist regime, combine to prevent the filling of gaps between the proof and the must-have-been, between the confirm-
able testimony and the reasonable suspicion. Such reliable if
fragmentary data as do exist tend to confirm the hypothesis that
the Austrians suspected Koszta of possessing secret information
of momentous importance; that he was kidnaped in order to be
cajoled or forced into divulging that information. As a plausible
alternative, mistaken identity may be considered.

The hypothesis about secret information involves elements
which were beyond the ken of the State Department a century ago.
To understand them, the reader must have a nodding acquaintance with a unique object of almost Graustarkian background.
Called the Hungarian Holy Crown, or the Crown of Saint Stephen,
it is a relic of extraordinary historical, legal, religious, and psychological significance.

Even in its physical appearance, the ancient crown of Hungarian
kings is unlike any other described in recorded history. A com-
posite of two originally separate parts of different age, style, and
national origin, its components remain distinguishable as an upper
and a lower part welded together. The upper part, called *Corona
Latina* (Latin Crown), of South Italian workmanship, resembling
a golden skullcap, was sent by Pope Sylvester II to Hungary's first
Christian ruler, István (Stephen) I, in 1000 A.D., as a token of

appreciation of his abandonment of the paganism brought by the Magyars from their erstwhile abode in Asia. It was to serve as a symbol of the identification of the monarch's person and realm with the Vatican. The lower part, a radiate-type crown of Byzantine workmanship called *Corona Graeca* (Greek Crown), was a gift from Michael Dukas VII, emperor of Byzantium, to Géza I, a Hungarian king in the eleventh century.

Although the religious connotations attendant on the double crown made it a Roman Catholic relic, it was held in profound reverence by all religious denominations in the country as the supreme symbol of the nation as a whole. But far more than a mere symbol, it was the legal seat of Hungarian sovereignty, the literal possessor of the Hungarian state, from which the country took its official designation as "the Lands of the Hungarian Holy Crown." *

According to Hungary's ancient laws, the sovereign derived his authority principally not by virtue of succession or election, or as a divine right, but as a result of being touched upon the forehead by the Holy Crown. In principle, the Crown was the national ruler; it was a living force, a moral personality, which retained an unbreakable hold on the people through the centuries and continued to stand high above the nation's leaders and its people, embracing and uniting both under the so-called Doctrine of the Holy Crown.

That the Crown's importance transcended considerations of religious affiliation, and even of monarchical or republican political convictions, may be illustrated by the fact that at the time of the 1848–49 revolution, Kossuth, the devout Protestant, the anti-royalist whose regime proclaimed the dethronement of the Habsburgs as Hungary's kings, himself reverenced the Crown no less than if it had been a living person of awe-inspiring secular authority as well of a supra-denominational holiness. Under his order,

* Although the last crowned ruler of Hungary, Károly IV (Karl I in his simultaneous capacity as emperor of Austria), ceased to exercise his royal functions in 1918, and a regent governed until the autumn of 1944, Hungarian courts of justice continued to hand down verdicts "in the name of the Hungarian Holy Crown" till the disappearance of the country's constitutional identity under a Nazi dictatorship.

the National Defense Council transferred the relic from the capital first to one and then to another large provincial town in order to ensure its safety from enemy troops. When continued resistance to Austrian and Russian onslaughts became hopeless, Governor-President Kossuth authorized his minister of war, Bertalan Szemere, to carry the Crown personally to still other localities as the situation required.

When he was forced to flee abroad, Kossuth faced a dramatic dilemma. On the one hand, he felt it incumbent on him to leave the Crown among the people of the nation which it personified, within the land which belonged to it. On the other hand, he was determined to prevent Francis Joseph I from gaining possession of it and having himself crowned with it. Unless invested with the Crown, the Austrian emperor could not exercise Hungarian royal prerogatives with any semblance of legal authority in the subjugated country. He could not sanction laws or confer privileges. He could only rule by force as a usurper, and not even his person was safe because it was without that absolute untouchability of the sacrosanct which only the Crown's magic touch on the brow could bestow.

After much soul-searching, Kossuth found a temporary solution.

On instructions from him, Minister Szemere and three of his confidants buried the Crown deep in the ground at a selected spot near the point where the Danube breaks through the Carpathian barrier.

Hardly had the war ended in 1849 when the court of Vienna organized a gigantic hunt for the vanished Crown. It mobilized every available secret agent, recruited hosts of informers, tracked down the slightest possible clue, and continued the search for four years with unceasing intensity. On September 8, 1853, the Holy Crown was found by an Austrian search party.

Fourteen years later a general reconciliation came about between Hungary and Austria through the instrumentality of the so-called *Ausgleich* (Settlement) usually referred to as the Compromise of 1867. It made Hungary at once separate from and united with Austria in the form of a dual monarchy — the Austro-Hungarian monarchy — which existed until the end of World War I. As the climactic event of the reconciliation, the Crown was solemnly placed on the head of Francis Joseph I by the Cardinal Prince Primate of Hungary, in conformity with traditional Hungarian ceremonial rules and amid the medieval pomp attendant on this most festive of all occasions in the life of the nation.

With the Holy Crown on his head, the emperor of Austria became constitutional monarch of the people whose greatest national effort at self-liberation he had frustrated with the help of the tsar of Russia.

Early in 1853, rumors were widespread in Europe about an alleged appointment by Kossuth of one or more secret emissaries to dig up the Crown and smuggle it into a foreign country, reportedly the United States.

These rumors were particularly lively during the weeks which preceded Martin Koszta's capture. After that event, speculation cropped up among exile groups at Smyrna about possible connections between Koszta's abduction and the secret of the Crown's whereabouts. References to this can be found in Italian and Greek pamphlets written and disseminated in the town during the fall of 1853.

In the United States, rumors on the subject were first reflected in the *National Intelligencer* which, in its issue for August 1, 1853 wrote that "a letter from Vienna states that Costa is charged by the Austrian Government with having assisted to hide the regalia [the Crown and its appurtenances] of Hungary."

Congress was still debating the merits of Ingraham's rescue action when *Brownson's Quarterly Review* opined in its issue for January 1854 that "the special charge against Koszta, we believe, was complicity in a stupendous robbery, or the purloining and concealing of the Hungarian regalia, and the main motive of getting possession of him was not to bring him to punishment for his political offences, but to obtain from him some clew to the place where the sacred treasures were concealed. Perhaps, after his arrest, he gave the clew, and perhaps his having enabled the

Court to recover them is the reason why Austria has consented to his returning to this country."

This allegation by a prominent publication — even though one which had more than once betrayed a strong tendency to deny or minimize credit due on any account to Secretary Marcy — must have disturbed the government considerably. The implication was as clear as it was damaging that the Americans, who had sallied forth in defense of high principles of justice and freedom, might have been duped by their adversaries. While America reaped applause, did the real victory go to Austria? Was the man whom American courage rescued from Austrian captivity an empty shell thrown away after its invaluable contents had been pilfered? Was Marcy's manifesto no more than a fine exercise of legal acumen and forensic skill displayed after the successful getaway of high-waymen?

A great deal of circumstantial evidence can be garnered from records of the post-1849 emigration to make it highly improbable that Koszta ever knew the secret. He was personally not one whit more important to the Kossuth movement in his exile than, brave soldier that he had been, to Hungarian military or diplomatic strategists as a captain during the war itself. He received no mention anywhere in the voluminous writings of the leaders which came to light to this date. He was never an intimate of any of the principals, and was but slightly acquainted with one or two of the lesser figures among them.

But circumstantial evidence became altogether unnecessary some six decades after the incident at Smyrna, with the emergence of proof which showed that it was definitely not from Koszta that the Austrians had learned the location of the hidden Holy Crown.

The three men who by moonlight, near the whispering river Cserna and the rustling trees along its banks, under the eyes of Minister Szemere, wielded the spades in burying the greatest treasure of the Magyars were Ede Lórody, former mayor of the large town of Székesfehérvár; Ferenc Házmán, deputy secretary of interior; and Rudolf Grimm, son of a confidant of Szemere, who later became a noted painter — and whose sketching talent played an important role in the secret operation.

Házmán and Lórody eventually traveled to the United States. Each made the journey separately, arriving at New York some time after Koszta's original landing there. Házmán arrived on November 10, 1851, and Lórody, together with Kossuth and his entourage, on December 4, 1851.[106]

Lórody returned to Turkey not long before Koszta made his fateful trip to that country. He remained in complete obscurity until 1855 when he turned up as a Moslem convert and a major in the Turkish border guards. Three years later he was killed during a frontier skirmish.

Házmán returned to Hungary after the Compromise of 1867 and remained there until his death in 1894. According to his son, in an interview given by the latter to a leading Budapest daily in 1920, Házmán had repeatedly told members of his family that Lórody had been responsible for the Crown's discovery by the Austrians.[107]

Grimm remained in Turkey until 1867 when he too returned to Hungary; he died in 1885. In 1862, Bishop Arnold Ipolyi, a member of the board of the Hungarian Academy of Science, met him at Constantinople and discussed with him the peregrinations of the Crown.[108] Grimm told the bishop that he had made a careful sketch of the area where the Crown lay hidden, drawn to exact scale and highlighting points of orientation as to the precise spot. He said he gave the sketch to former Minister Szemere on the spot; Szemere showed it to Kossuth when they met in the emigration. Házmán, said Grimm, had arrived earlier at the Turkish asylum, made an immediate verbal report to Kossuth about the burial of the Crown, but when the former supreme leader asked him to describe the exact spot, Házmán, with abject apologies, declined. He said to Kossuth that he had taken a vow not to reveal the secret to anyone at all, which to him meant that not even the former governor could be excepted. He received high praise instead of reprimand. Somewhat later Lórody arrived, preceding Szemere. According to Grimm, he revealed part of the secret to Kossuth without even being asked, informing him of the location of the general area. Months later Grimm heard from Házmán that Lóro- dy had told the latter of his temptation to tell all even to Austrian agents because of his gnawing fear that the sacred relic would be damaged underground by moisture, rust, and mildew. As a matter of fact, this fear later proved well founded because when the Crown was finally brought to the surface, it was in such damaged condi- tion for the exact reasons anticipated by Lórody that its restoration took many months.

As mentioned, it was Szemere who fully revealed the secret information to Kossuth, complete with sketch. But he also told it to others. He shared it with an intimate named Fülepp as well as with Count Kázmér Batthyány and Count László Teleki. In September 1853, when news of the discovery of the Crown reached him, he accused each of these men as well as the wife and certain relatives of Count Batthyány of high treason. Among the causes which finally drove him to insanity in 1865 was his mortification over Austrian possession of the Holy Crown; in the very hour of his death in 1869 he still talked hysterically about "the greatest calamity in the history of mankind."

Not even remotely does Koszta figure in all this. But the decisive testimony which effectively dispels any complicity on his part in the breach of security comes from no less authoritative a personage than General Kempen himself, military commandant and chief of intelligence at the Hungarian capital under Austrian martial-law rule. This testimony came to light only in 1919, after the dissolu- tion of the Austro-Hungarian Empire, when Austria's new repub- lican government opened the state archives to several scholars of high repute. One of the researchers who thus gained access to material previously under guard found and subsequently pub- lished an extensive secret memorandum submitted by General Kempen to the emperor's chief of cabinet on April 24, 1854.[109]

This memorandum describes both the preliminaries and the actual occurrence of the discovery of the Crown. In short:

Spies and *agents provocateurs* of General Kempen and of Police Commissioner Josef Prottman succeeded in penetrating the circles of important exiles in Turkey, England, and France. Some of the operatives had been given the general assignment of reporting on the activities of Kossuth and his intimates, while others had the specific task of collecting clues to the Crown's hiding place. In 1852, certain agents bribed a former liaison officer between Kossuth and his cabinet. This man, half-Hungarian and half-Austrian István Wargha, agreed to send periodic reports to Kempen himself about Kossuth and his close collaborators. He had numerous channels of his own, and his headquarters were in London. He soon reported that he had befriended a former Hungarian officer named Szücs who had "ways and means of his own" to obtain secret information from important exiles and was receptive to bribes. Kempen acted at once — and exact information about the Crown's location reached him in May 1853.

The memorandum suggests that the vital information must have been delivered sometime between May 1 and 19, since Kempen states that on the latter date he issued orders for Wargha's arrest. This move, he explains, was a ruse. He wanted to mislead exile circles in which Wargha's reputation had lately begun to tarnish. The general felt that the arrest, well publicized, would tend to rehabilitate the man in the eyes of exiles and thus enhance his future usefulness to Austria. Kempen desired to use Wargha's services indefinitely if the information about the Crown proved correct. The informer enthusiastically consented to his tactical arrest, aware that a well-guarded prison of the emperor would be as safe a place for him to be in as any in case of a leak in one of his conduits. To Kempen, Wargha's consent to the plan was a sign of the authenticity of the information about the Crown. Also, he figured that to take Wargha's person into custody, ruse or no ruse, was a shrewd precautionary step toward protecting the considerable financial investment that had gone into bribes the man claimed to have paid to unnamed others.

But the accuracy of the precious information, Kempen reports, could not have been checked until the early days of September because of flood conditions in the area involved. Not until that time did the waters recede — and in the morning of September 8 a special committee of investigation, headed by the general's personal representative, Army Judge Advocate Dr. Titus Karger, and accompanied by Wargha as well as a detachment of selected military policemen, appeared on the marked spot.

It should be recalled that by that time Koszta had been out of Austrian hands for more than two months.

On September 8, 1853, the Holy Crown of Hungary was lifted from underground. About a month later it was given a tremendous reception by government and church authorities in Budapest, and was returned to its regular repository in the Royal Castle where highly skilled technicians began lengthy restorative operations on it. And a few months later, the emperor rewarded Kempen by raising him to the baronetcy.

Thus General Kempen's secret memorandum, made available to the public more than a half century after the incident at Smyrna when no one anywhere remembered the name of anyone involved in the affair, exonerated Koszta of the charges circulated on two continents in 1853 and 1854.

It is, therefore, somewhere else that a possible reason for his abduction must be sought.

Ever since the end of the Hungarian revolution, the emperor's myriad agents had suspected secret Kossuth emissaries on every street corner and under every bed throughout the far-flung empire. Every move Kossuth or his close associates made abroad generated new hopes in his people and new fears in the Austrian government. His peripatetic activities during and after his trip to the United States were widely publicized in the West, and news of them trickled into Hungary. His efforts to make alliances with Western powers, obtain funds from them, and organize a huge free corps, tended to rekindle the fire of revolt from embers still not dead under the ashes of national catastrophe. The Austrians were in a constant state of nervousness, from cabinet officers down to mayors, from generals to the lowliest provincial gendarme. Countless spies and informers not only throughout Europe but even in America carried a bewildering number and variety of reports to the mills servicing the emperor's bureau of intelligence.

In the stacks of secret documents in the Austrian court's archives to which access has been gained, two in particular shed revealing light on the scene. Both were prepared in 1850, and scores of other documents show that the measures outlined in them were implemented between the time of their preparation and the date of Koszta's arrival in Turkey three years later.

The first document is a secret dispatch from Marshall Haynau to Prince Schwarzenberg, according to which "one of the most important tasks of the Government should be to track down all secret contacts [among Hungarian exiles]. The Hungarians are scattered abroad: in Turkey, Switzerland, France, Belgium, England, North Germany . . . and in the United States; they maintain their old connections with people in Hungary or are establishing new ones. I consider it urgently necessary to take under broad and well planned surveillance everything originating in those [places] abroad . . ."

The second document is a report from the Austrian minister of interior to the emperor, in which "the Minister of Interior makes a recommendation to the Sovereign to the effect that experienced agents be sent to Turkey to keep after Kossuth's men and to do what the Austrian Consuls cannot, even with the greatest efforts, accomplish. Given enough money, the services of clever people, and the timely application of force, the rebels can be captured. Captives should be shipped to Austria in the fastest and safest manner. Transportation by sea would be best, but all places where Britain has representatives must be avoided en route." [110]

In this light, it would have been both unnatural and a dereliction of duty for Austrian agents not to suspect some sinister motive behind a trip from America to Turkey by a man of Koszta's description. And Consul General von Weckbecker's possession of broad authorization to act could hardly have been questioned.

True, Koszta's person was not significant; but he had happened to move in circles whose members were constantly watched as actual or potential planners or executors of conspiracies.

There were, for example, Házmán and Lórody, reported by Austrian agents ever since the latter part of 1849 as participants in the hiding of the Crown. Both of them had a slight acquaintance with Koszta; both had gone to America not long after Koszta's settlement there; both had traveled to Turkey about the time Koszta went to that country on his business trip.

There was Colonel Ihász, Koszta's former commanding officer and companion in Turkish exile. He had organized a small but successful courier service between Turkey and Hungary in 1850. In the summer of 1851, he became involved in a tragically amateurish project organized by one Colonel Makk and — at the recommendation of Ihász and others — approved by Kossuth, designed to create a secret free corps in Transylvania. Certain letters of accreditation made out for provincial organizers, signed by Kossuth, and countersigned by Ihász — a Translyvanian like Koszta — fell into Austrian hands. With these as clues, investigation led to the discovery of the plot in 1852. Many persons connected with it in Transylvania as well as in Hungary proper were executed, many more imprisoned, and some executions in this connection took place even as late as 1855. Makk himself succeeded in eluding the Austrians and was reportedly hiding in Turkey through 1853, the year of the Koszta incident.

There was ex-Captain Pataki, also a former companion of Koszta in exile, who was captured by the Austrians while attempting to cross the Hungarian border. He insisted during his interrogation that he had come to see his elderly mother who, according to messages received by him, was dying. A check revealed that he told the truth; the mother had died the day before Pataki's capture. But the Austrians wanted to find out who had delivered the messages. Pataki refused to tell. He underwent cruel treatment, including daily beatings, for more than a month, but could not be made to disclose anything about the courier service. On February 2, 1852, he was hanged.

On January 9, 1852, the minister of war at Vienna transferred to the minister of the interior a report signed by an agent named Peter Stojadinovich. This man informed the authorities that five emissaries of Kossuth were preparing to cross the border and organize cells of saboteurs.

In the summer of the same year, former Captain János May, a courier in the "Ihász Chain," was captured at the border. After his first interrogation in prison, he put his straw mattress on fire and burned himself to death rather than face the possibility of breaking down under torture and giving away the names of other couriers.[110]

Koszta, it will be recalled, arrived at Smyrna aboard the *Mimosa* in September 1852. Shortly thereafter, he went to Constantinople and did not return to the Aegean seaport until February 1853 — the month in which something happened in Vienna that rocked the Austrian empire.

On February 13, 1853 the emperor, accompanied by an aide and a group of detectives, was taking a walk on one of the avenues of Vienna when a young Hungarian tailor's apprentice named János Libényi suddenly flung himself upon him with a knife. The stiff, gilded collar of the monarch's uniform averted a mortal wound, but the injury suffered was severe enough to threaten him for several days with loss of his eyesight. On his recovery, the emperor, disliked even in his own capital up to that time, was accorded spontaneous demonstrations of good will; the would-be assassin thus became instrumental in the popularization of the object of his hate. A steady increase in the ruler's personal popularity dated from the incident, even though he refused to pardon Libényi: the youth — twenty-two years of age, like his intended victim — was executed.

It took months for the excitement to abate. The directorate of the intelligence service was reshuffled; the police chief of Vienna was removed. Within five days after the attempt, four executions were held in Budapest alone; mass arrests continued for months. In Vienna, every house where Hungarians lived was put under armed guard. Everyone crossing the Hungarian frontier into Austria, for no matter what legitimate reason and with whatever authorization, was taken into a three-day custody and interrogated with the greatest care before he was allowed to proceed.[110]

Kossuth had personally denounced the attempt at once upon receipt of the news, as did every one of his lieutenants. They likewise denounced the Austrian authorities later when young Libényi was hanged. Several years afterward, Austrian officials admitted that all signs had pointed to a complete absence of any connection between Libényi and the exiles, and that they had felt that whatever Kossuth might have been supposed to do against Austria, he would never have sanctioned any plan of assassination of the emperor or of anyone else. Even his enemies respected his personal character and deep religious feelings. But, in the days of hysteria that followed the attempt, Austrian authorities felt convinced that "the Kossuth dogs" were behind the deed. And it was just then that a former and possibly still active "Kossuth dog" named Koszta made a trip from America all the way to Turkey.

The conjecture that general suspicion led to a specific one on the basis of some of the many wild reports and denunciations then current, and thence to abduction, appears to have psychological validity.

One possibility still remains, namely, that Koszta was the victim of a case of mistaken identity within the setting outlined above. It is interesting to note that Minister Marsh wrote Secretary Marcy on July 7, 1853 that while "it is not pretended [by the Austrians] that Koszta had been guilty of any other offence than participation in the Hungarian revolutionary movements of 1848–49," speculation was rife that "his arrest originated in a mistake of the person."

The speculation, correct or not, was rather realistic as at least one known incident indicates. In that same year, former Colonel Figyelmessy,* a personal friend of Kossuth then temporarily residing in England, one day read with understandable amazement in the London press that he had been recently captured in Hungary while on a secret assignment, and was hanged at the Hungarian town of Hatvan. It was subsequently established that one Thury, a former captain, who bore a physical resemblance to Figyelmessy, was the man executed.[111] Indignation in the House of Commons reached a point where a member demanded that the government formally express "its utter contempt of Austrian methods," and

---

* American consul after the Civil War, first at British Guiana and later at Mainz, Germany.

closed his remarks with the exclamation: "Is there anything more bitter than to die by mistake?"

Was Koszta, too, confused with someone else in that year of at least one such confusion?

Possibly so.

Here the matter rests, covered by the thick dust of a century which saw some of the greatest upheavals in the history of mankind and left hardly a line of the world's physiognomy unchanged. The past hundred years have swept away not only the footprints of the dim figures sought by the latter-day investigator, but also the empires of Austrians, Russians, Turks. The greater part of Smyrna itself, including the buildings and many of the records of the Western consulates, was destroyed by fire in 1922 during Turkish-Greek clashes. And more recently even the "first paper," the freedom-seeker's personal Declaration of Independence, has in effect ceased to exist as part of the American naturalization process.*

---

* The McCarran-Walter Act (Public Law 414, enacted in 1952) abolished in effect the "first paper," doing so in a puzzling manner. According to it, "any lawfully admitted alien resident over eighteen years of age may [but no longer "shall" as in earlier legislation] make . . . a signed declaration of intention to become a citizen," but nothing in the law "shall be construed as requiring any such alien to make and file a declaration of intention." (Sec. 334, Sub-Sec. "f.") Thus the first part of the statement vaguely implies some use which the declaration might still serve, while the second part negates the declaration's historic role and eliminates its practical purpose.

Recently, the "first paper" once again attracted nationwide attention, this time in a novel sense. In the summer of 1955, Dr. Fritz Zwicky, a Swiss expert in rocket and jet propulsion, professor at the California Institute of Technology, was deprived of his Defense Department security clearance because he failed to declare his intention to become an American citizen. A technicality, and not a question of loyalty, was involved. The Armed Forces Industrial Security Regulations require that any immigrant alien, to be eligible for security clearance, "shall have formally declared his intent to become a United States citizen" (Par. 2–203). Dr. Zwicky, the man who pioneered the first attempt to shoot earth satellites into space and received the American Medal of Freedom, announced that he desired to remain a Swiss citizen. His stated reason was that he wished to be able to stay abroad indefinitely at any time of his own choosing, whereas he could not do so as a naturalized American.

Epilogue

EPILOGUE I

COMMANDER INGRAHAM found himself to be a national celebrity when he returned on home leave at the end of September 1853. He was looked upon as the hero of the boldest act to assert the inviolability of American rights since the firing of the first gun in the War of 1812.

In New York, in front of the Naval Club where he spent a few days before traveling to his home at Charleston, South Carolina, group after group of Manhattanites gathered several times each day to give lusty cheers to "the eagle of Smyrna," "Ingraham the Lionheart," or, as he was dubbed by some fellow officer with reference to the time limit of the famous ultimatum, "Old Four-O'Clock."

His known personal reticence, combined with his lifelong lack of interest in politics, allows the presumption that occasional shouts of "Ingraham for President" — mentioned again and again in newspaper reports of his visit at the metropolis — made him indignant if not outraged. But he did permit himself to be persuaded to attend a testimonial dinner tendered in his honor at Metropolitan Hall on September 29, 1853, on condition that he would not be expected to make a speech.

The committee responsible for the arrangements included several former Kossuth officers, among them General Mészáros, former minister of war, and Colonel Asbóth, Kossuth's former aide.

215

It was, according to the *New York Weekly Tribune* of October 1, "a great gathering . . . one which may be of future importance abroad and of political significance at home."

The editors just could not be disabused of the idea that Ingraham would run or be drafted for political office on the waves of popular acclaim . . . "At 7 o'clock the hall commenced filling up, and at 7:30 o'clock its space was densely packed, and those who came afterward stood in the aisles or occupied the space about the doors. The galleries presented a gay appearance, being chiefly occupied by Hungarians, Italians, Frenchmen, and Creoles, with their ladies . . . At the extreme right of the stage the American flag was suspended. Next to it was the national flag of the Italian Republicans. By its side hung the Cuban Lone Star flag. Suspended on the wall, in the rear of the speaker's stand, were two banners as follows: 'Civil Liberty and Religious Independence Throughout the World,' and 'Do you claim the protection of the United States? Then you shall have it! Ingraham — Smyrna — July 2, 1853.'"

Each of a seemingly endless series of speeches brought down the house — except the address of General Mészáros which he later described in a letter to a friend in this manner of candor and humor: "I had to act in the demonstration as one of the speakers. I laid an egg because they could not understand me. Thus my career as a political star seems at an end. Already back in England they failed to understand [my English] and it is natural that my *bon-mots* are even less understandable here. But it is just as well because this means that I will not have to make any more public speeches." [107]

When the commander rose to accept a special medal presented to him in the name of "all exiles in America," the cheers were truly deafening.

Ingraham saluted the crowd, accepted the medal, looked at it, saluted again — and made no speech.

The same night he left for Charleston.

Thousands awaited him in his home town. Many had come from all parts of the Palmetto State on the previous day and slept in borrowed or improvised tents in the city's parks and in open fields nearby, just to be sure not to miss seeing the hero on his arrival.

He probably did not sleep much on that first night at home; serenades were sung till morning under the windows of the old family house.

During his vacation, and for a long time thereafter, countless tokens of respect reached him not only from his own countrymen but also from abroad. As late as the summer of 1854, an item in the *New York Weekly Tribune* (July 8, 1854) told about the arrival of "Richard Winslow, Esq., bearer of despatches from our legations at Paris and London . . . and of a most appropriate and well-deserved present from a very large number of the working classes of Great Britain to Captain Ingraham, U.S.N., as a testimonial of their esteem for his gallant conduct at Smyrna in protecting Koszta from the Austrian authorities. We learn that the fund with which was procured this valuable and interesting token, was raised by a penny subscription among the workmen of the kingdom; it consists of a double-cased, large-sized pocket chronometer in a mahogany case. On the back of the gold case is the following inscription: 'Presented to Captain Ingraham of the United States Navy by some thousands of the British working classes, for his noble conduct in rescuing Koszta, the Hungarian Refugee, from the Austrian authorities. April 1854.' The chronometer is accompanied with an Address, beautifully engrossed and framed."

The state of New York awarded Ingraham a gold medal; the North German government sent him a silver service set; his own home town's gift was a set of six silver goblets; Italy sent a brace of pistols, the British government a silver sword. Few Americans had even been so showered with official and unofficial presents from so many parts of the world.

The commander was appointed chief of the Bureau of Ordnance and Hydrography in 1856, with the rank of full captain. Not until 1860 did he again see service aboard a ship; in that year he was given command of the *Richmond*, a flagship of the Mediterranean

Squadron. But his undoubtedly eager return to his perennial paramour, the sea, lasted less than a year. It was terminated by the War between the States.

His own South Carolina was the first to secede from the Union. In February 1861, Ingraham resigned from the United States Navy to follow his duty once again as he saw it. He accepted the rank of captain — highest under the two admirals of the Confederate Navy — in the small naval forces of the Confederate States of America.

The future offered little for a naval officer of the South. The Confederate naval forces had not a single man-of-war and only a few merchant vessels; its only shipyards were at Norfolk and Pensacola. Even after a greater force had been built, it was not a sea-going one and could be operated only in smooth waters. But Ingraham felt that his place was in it.

At first, he was a member of the board charged with planning the water defenses of the Confederacy. Later he was given charge of the Pensacola Navy Yard, and held the post until the Yard's evacuation. Subsequently he became commander of the naval forces on the coast of South Carolina, with headquarters at Charleston. The courtesy titles of commodore and flag officer were accorded him.

An interesting document in the naval archives recalls one of his energetic actions toward breaking the blockade of the southern coast which was slowly strangling the Confederacy to death. At the time, he was associated with the famous General Beauregard who had ordered the first shot fired against Fort Sumter.

"Headquarters Naval and Land Forces, Charleston, January 31, 1863. — At about the hour of 5 o'clock this morning, Confederate States naval forces on this station attacked the United States blockading fleet off the city of Charleston and sunk, dispersed, or drove off and out of sight for the time the entire hostile fleet. Therefore, we, the undersigned, commanding the Confederate States naval and land forces, do hereby formally declare the blockade . . . to be raised . . . P. G. T. Beauregard, General, commanding; D. N. Ingraham, commanding Naval Forces, South Carolina."

The proclamation of Beauregard and Ingraham was intended

218

to facilitate official recognition of the Confederacy by England and France, one of the conditions for which was understood to have been the breaking of the blockade. However, the blockading fleet soon closed in again.

In this action, Ingraham was outmanned and outgunned, as at Smyrna in 1853. He had only two ironclads, while the Union fleet consisted of ten ships including three regular men-of-war. In the engagement, one Union ship, the *Mercedita*, surrendered to Ingraham under the barrage of fire directed personally by him. He took the word of honor of Commander Stellwagen, the ship's captain, and all of his surviving officers and men, that they would not serve further against the Confederacy, and then released them.

When the war ended, the commodore retired to Charleston. He had served continuously for more than fifty years and was the only survivor among all who entered the Navy in 1812.

Countless friends and acquaintances urged him time and time again to accept public office, but he always refused. After his retirement he never again left the old city in which he was born and which he had defended so bravely.

Day after day he sat in a wooden rocking chair on the veranda of his house on Bull Street, reading history books, talking with visiting kinfolk and neighbors, and gazing out toward the bay. It was there that on the afternoon of October 16, 1891, at the age of eighty-nine, he died in his sleep.

Two days later he was laid to rest at Magnolia Cemetery, next to his wife. Clustered around the grave, in the center of a vast ring of mourners, stood old friends, bearers of historic names: Rutledge, Smythe, Bryan, Marshall, Pinckney, Hasell, Laurens. After the funeral, one of his seven children, Eleanor, wrote in her diary: "I know of no one of whom it can be more truly said that during a long and stainless life he bore without reproach the grand old name of gentleman . . ."

She added two lines of an old sailor ballade the commodore had liked more than any other:

"Though the worms gnaw his timbers and his vessel's a wreck,
When he hears the Last Whistle, he'll spring up on deck . . ."

DARING DIPLOMACY

The *U.S.S. St. Louis* survived her master by fifteen years.

From 1856, when Ingraham left it, till 1858, the sloop was attached to the African Squadron, and from 1859 till 1861 to the Home Squadron. During the Civil War it was a member of the Union fleet and cruised off the coasts of Spain and Portugal. Its mission was to be on the lookout for Confederate ships. Truth in this instance failed to be stranger than fiction: Ingraham, the Confederate naval leader, never found himself facing his former vessel and having the duty to open fire on his old companion of Smyrna days.

In 1865, the *St. Louis* was a member of the South Atlantic Squadron. Later it was laid up at League Island as a receiving ship. In 1895, it was loaned to the naval militia of Pennsylvania and was used until 1906 under the name *Keystone State*.

On August 9, 1906, the old ship, which had seen service on the waters of all continents except Australia, was sold to be broken up. Its name was stricken from the Navy list — and another one of the principal props of the drama at Smyrna made a final exit.*

However, reincarnation after a fashion came to the *St. Louis* — not once, but three times.

An American destroyer by the name of *U.S.S. Ingraham* was commissioned in 1919. It was stricken from the list in 1936 and, in accordance with the London naval treaty, sunk in 1937.

A second *U.S.S. Ingraham*, a modern 1600-ton destroyer designed for a crew of 175, was launched at Charleston, South Carolina, on February 15, 1941. The sponsor was the late Mrs. George Hutchinson (née Harriott Ingraham), a granddaughter of the commodore. The principal speaker at the launching ceremony was a prominent

---

* The leading opponent of the *St. Louis* in the waters of Smyrna Bay, the *Artemisia*, was still in service at the close of the nineteenth century. Admiral Miklós Horthy, regent of Hungary until the last phase of World War II, mentions in his memoirs published in 1953 that in 1895, as a captain in the Austro-Hungarian Navy, he was put in command of the *Artemisia*. Although the memoirs are rich in anecdotes, especially about Horthy's early naval career, no mention of the Koszta case is made in them. Perhaps the admiral never heard of it; or perhaps he chose to forget it because of his devotion — emphasized in the memoirs — to the memory of Francis Joseph I, whose aide he once was and to whom the case of Koszta brought a humiliating diplomatic defeat at the hands of the Americans.

Charleston attorney and member of the state legislature, Lionel K. Legge, now a justice of the Supreme Court of South Carolina, a great-grand-nephew of Ingraham. In the vessel, a bronze memorial tablet was placed by permission of Secretary of the Navy Frank Knox to commemorate Koszta's liberation by Ingraham.* On August 22, 1942, while on wartime convoy duty, the ship perished in the Atlantic; its commanding officer and many of the officers and men were lost.

A special war bond campaign was begun at Charleston to replace the destroyer. On January 16, 1944, a third *U.S.S. Ingraham*, a 2200-ton destroyer for a complement of 350, was launched, carrying a replica of the original memorial tablet. Again the sponsor was the commodore's granddaughter. This ship, still in service, has had a distinguished career, seeing action in the classics of modern American naval annals: Leyte, Luzon, Iwo Jima, Okinawa.

Ingraham, a hundred years after the time when his name was on every American's lips, still sails the seas. It seems that if "old soldiers never die," old sailors will not be satisfied with less.

* This action resulted from a campaign initiated by me and conducted by organizations of American citizens of Hungarian birth or descent.

EPILOGUE II

WHEN the *Sultana* docked at Boston on November 30, 1853,[77] and Koszta once again stepped on American soil to start life anew, no one awaited him at the pier. In this respect, the occasion was a replica of his first arrival; by contrast, however, this time he had some funds in his pocket. The exiles at Smyrna had given him a modest sum as a parting gift; fraternal tradition made it mandatory for him to accept it.

During the long journey back to America, Koszta prepared a statement for the press. The text, evidently corrected by someone before its release to the papers, read:

"Wrested a second time from the tiger grasp of the Austrian tyrant, I owe my liberation mostly to the generous will of the people of this Union who, awakening to the consciousness of their providential mission and destiny, seem determined to protect those bound to their fate by the voluntary oath of allegiance; to this generous will, which has inspired the acts of those entrusted with the executive power, and which found its real manly expression in the heroic soul of Captain Ingraham.

"On touching again the shores of America, I feel it my first duty to give a feeble expression of that gratitude which I cherish in the innermost of my heart, toward all those who have taken active or even sympathizing part in that extraordinary case, in which the

222

American eagle for the first time loosed its thunderbolts for the protection of the weak, for human and international right. Being only an accidental cause of this international event, which has saved me, my gratitude even the most ardent can be of little value to the American people; but the hope, admiration and sympathy of nations longing for liberty, and on the other hand, the confusion and fear of presumptuous and wanton despots, is a reward noble in its sources, lasting in its efficacy, and worthy of a 'people of sovereigns.' "

The *New York Express* printed the statement on December 13, and the *New York Weekly Tribune* on December 14, 1853.

Having thus hailed Columbia, Koszta probably went to see the good Herr Ritter in New York, technically still his employer. If he did, their meeting failed for some reason or other to result in a resumption of the earlier relationship. A few days later Koszta was in Washington, and never thereafter returned to New York.

On December 6, Martin Koszta called at the Department of State.

He was received by Secretary of State Marcy, who must have found the conversation interesting because three days later he introduced the visitor to President Franklin Pierce.

The interviews were not recorded; not even their dates were put on record at the Department. Registers of courtesy calls paid to the secretary or to the president began to be maintained only after the Civil War. But American Hungarians did not fail to record the dates of the calls, noting in their diaries that the former Transylvanian town crier was one of the first of their race to be offered a seat in the office of the highest ranking American cabinet officer and in the study of the chief executive of the mightiest Republic on earth.

A few days later the *Tribune* printed an extensive statement over Koszta's signature. It appeared in the December 14 issue in a dense column-and-a-half of the front page, under the title "The Narrative of Martin Koszta." In an introductory remark, the editor mentioned that the statement "has been addressed to Mr. Pierce by Martin Koszta who lately arrived in Washington."

The text, which took the form of a letter directly addressing the president, opened with thanks "not only for the support of myself but also for the principle which you have established and which will, in the future, enforce respect to all those who have had the good fortune to be placed under the protection of the American flag."

It went on to relate the happenings at Smyrna from the day of Koszta's seizure to that of his embarkation.

A puzzling development followed.

Although nothing in the long statement could have cast doubt either on its authenticity or on its propriety, yet on December 24 the *Tribune* printed the following statement under the heading "A Card from Martin Koszta":

"To the Editor of the N.Y. Tribune:

"Sir: I just now see in the *Express* of Dec. 13 and in your valuable paper of Dec. 14, 1853, a communication under the head, 'Narrative of Martin Koszta.' As I never presented this or any other memorandum to the President, and never did authorize anybody to make such a communication or publication, I feel it my duty to protest against this and similar endeavors to hold out my name, my misfortune, or the circumstances which brought me back to America, in behalf of individual purposes and personal interests. — MARTIN KOSZTA."

Whose benefit could have been served by the forging of a statement which was in no perceptible respect incorrect or improper?

As the editorial columns of the *Tribune* had so often emphasized, the incident at Smyrna involved delicate political questions along with legal and diplomatic ones. Surely, the paper's editor must have convinced himself of the genuineness of the lengthy account before ordering it to be printed.

Assuming that the statement was genuine, only one explanation for its retraction comes to mind. If Koszta had released the statement without first obtaining State Department approval, his disavowal of it could have been the result of an official request. More than the narrative itself, the *Tribune*'s prefatory remark about Koszta's reception by the president could have been the cause of such a request. As Koszta said in his baffling retraction, he "never presented this or any other memorandum to the President." Was this calculated to serve as at least a halfhearted denial that he saw the president, a satisfactory compromise in the matter of a damaging step and a resultant official disapproval?

Noteworthy is the fact that the memorandum stated at its very outset: "I have now the honor to appear before you," and added: "I have proceeded to this city to express in person to his Excellency the President and to his Cabinet . . . deep gratitude . . ." The Department could well have felt concerned about possible Austrian remonstrations in case of an apparently provocative public emphasis of Koszta's reception by the president. And Koszta himself, stubborn but not unreasonable, might have agreed to take a step backward in order to avoid the reopening of diplomatic wounds at an overly late date.

In any event, no sign of further controversy in this matter can be found in the press.

The Hungarian next turned up in Chicago, where he found an old acquaintance, Gyula Kuné, born — like Koszta — in the Transylvanian village of Belényes in 1819.

This man too was a colorful individual with an unusual record. He had served in 1849 as a sergeant in the Fifty-Fifth Battalion under Colonel Ihász and Captain Koszta. In the Turkish emigration he embraced the Moslem faith, later went to England and finally, in 1852, to the United States. Settling down in Chicago, he first worked at the Marine Bank whose president, Jonathan Young Scammon, became a Kossuth enthusiast after hearing the Hungarian leader speak at Chicago and helped many Hungarian exiles to find jobs. In 1860, Kuné became a clerk of the Illinois State Senate and was sent as an alternate delegate to the Republican National Convention of that year where Lincoln received the presidential nomination. He campaigned for the candidate in Illinois and Indiana, making speeches in German. When the Civil War broke out, he requested and received Lincoln's permission to organize the Twenty-Fourth Illinois Volunteer Infantry Regiment. As the regiment's major, he fought through the war; afterward, he wrote for the *Chicago Tribune,* became a member of the Chicago Board of Trade, undertook a lengthy European assignment as press correspondent covering the Franco-Prussian war, wrote a volume of memoirs, and died shortly before the outbreak of World War I.

Kuné mentions in his memoirs [111] that "I was surprised to find here Captain Martin Koszta who during the Hungarian war of liberation commanded a company in the battalion in which I served. This Martin Koszta came near becoming the *Casus Belli* between the United States and the Austrian Emperor . . ."

In December 1854 Martin Koszta got his name into print once again. The Chicago press reported his marriage.

He chose a young widow for a wife. Did she perhaps resemble that other young widow back in Smyrna who had disappeared from his life forever when the *Sultana* drew away from the port on October 15 of the previous year?

The *New York Weekly Tribune* did not fail to spot the news in the Chicago papers and commented in its issue for December 30 as follows:

"KOSZTA AGAIN IN BONDS. From the *Chicago Journal* of the 13th inst., we learn that Martin Koszta recently met with a fall [pun on the lady's name, McFall] and through that means has been again captured. No Marcy-ful interference, however, will be expected since the captive not only submits to his bonds but actually boasts of them. The following is the account of the affair: 'In this city on the 12th inst., by Judge H. L. Rucker, Capt. Martin Koszta was married to Mrs. Lucinda McFall of Chicago.' "

The Chicago City Directory for 1853 lists one John McFall as deceased in that year, the only person by that name in the category of the departed between 1849 and 1853. It appears that Koszta proved irresistible enough for the widow to marry at once on the expiration of the customary period of mourning.

At the time of his marriage and for some months thereafter, the passive hero of the adventure at Smyrna was employed at the small bank of Richard K. Swift, later a general in the Civil War. Founded in 1843, the bank advertised in the City Directory that it "will loan money on bonds and mortgages and other undoubted securities," and that it was located "in the Tremont Building, 2d story, over Clarke's drug store, 102 Lake Street." It probably also made it widely known by word of mouth that visiting clients could behold free of charge a certain famous Hungarian in the flesh.

An odd little coincidence may be mentioned here. Until the day of his marriage, Koszta's address as recorded by the officiating magistrate was 556 West DeKoven Street. A cottage next door, at Number 558, was eventually purchased by a widow named Mrs. O'Leary. This good lady, as perhaps the reader will suspect at once, is said to have had a cow: the very cow which, kept in a small stable adjunct to the cottage, entered history in 1871 as the bovine criminal that caused the great Chicago fire by kicking over a lantern.

Koszta's vagabond spirit was apparently quickly communicated to his wife. Their first wedding anniversary found them no longer in Chicago. The *Daily Democratic Press* of the city reported in its issue for December 5, 1855: "Martin Koszta, the Hungarian refugee, who passed a year or more in this city, and who was married here, is announced through the papers as having arrived at Galveston, Texas, where he intends to make his future home."

In January 1856, the couple bought a farm near San Antonio — and another year later disappeared without a trace. The property was foreclosed. According to the deed records of Bexar County, Texas, Martin and Lucinda Koszta purchased from one Christopher C. Gove on January 5, 1856, a tract of land comprising about 1350 acres, some thirteen miles southwest of San Antonio, together with a farm house, two slaves, horses, cattle, wagons, household goods. The price paid was $9000. The record of foreclosure, dated February 4, 1858, shows that the Kosztas left unpaid a sum of $1800 which they owed to one George B. Browrigg, and that "these people were not living in Bexar County at the time of the issuance of the Sheriff's notice." The property was sold at auction on July 2, 1861.

The next — and last — news about Koszta was printed in 1858, not in the United States but across the seas in his native Transylvania, reporting without details that "Martin Koszta, the Hungarian emigré saved from death in 1853 at Smyrna by American naval captain Ingraham, has recently died amid dire circumstances in Guatemala." [112]

Why in Guatemala? What were the "dire circumstances" of his death there at the age of thirty-nine?

Searching for answers that might furnish at least a reasonably clear terminal point for the bare outline of a life, the investigator finds his way blocked at every turn. The man or his shadow often seems within reach, only to vanish in the last moment and leave no more to rely upon than incomplete reports, rumors, speculations, psychological probabilities.

During the decade preceding the Civil War, buccaneers of diverse origins and ambitions organized a series of expeditions in the United States to take part in Central American revolutions. They were given the name of filibuster, an English corruption of the old Dutch word *vrijbuiter* (freebooter), which originally denoted persons engaged in private warfare against a state and came to be applied in modern American usage to legislators who practice obstruction through dilatory tactics in parliamentary procedures.

The boldest, most talented and colorful of the filibuster leaders was William Walker (1824–60), American physician, lawyer, and editor turned political adventurer, self-styled general and head of state, who first sailed from San Francisco with an armed force for the conquest of Mexican territory. In 1854 he proclaimed Lower California and the neighboring state of Sonora an independent republic, made the Mexican governor his prisoner, and designated himself president. Mexican attacks coupled with American prevention of access to food and other supplies forced the abandonment of the enterprise, and Walker returned to the United States. Tried for violations of the neutrality laws, he was acquitted, and in 1855 organized another force sailing for Nicaragua at the invitation of a revolutionary faction there. Certain officials of the Accessory Transit Company, a Nicaraguan shipping corporation of American businessmen, decided to use him as a tool to get the firm's

Epilogue

control out of the hands of its dominant figure, famed tycoon Cornelius Vanderbilt. They provided Walker with ample funds and transported recruits for him from the United States. In return, Walker seized the properties of the corporation and turned them over to his mentors. Using the ships of the firm, he surprised and captured Granada. His confederate, Patricio Rivas, was made figurehead president of Nicaragua, with Walker as the real possessor of supreme power in the capacity of commander in chief of the armed forces. Walker soon replaced Rivas as president, and successfully withstood the attacks of a coalition of Central American forces led by Costa Rican generals, and aided by Vanderbilt, until the middle of 1857. Meanwhile, however, President Buchanan had placed American naval vessels in the leading Central American ports to prevent the landing of filibuster reinforcements; Walker was forced to surrender to American naval authorities who returned him to the United States. By that time, his exploits had captured popular imagination and there were many noisy demonstrations in his favor especially in the South.

In the fall of 1857, Walker resumed his campaign, landing with an armed force near Greytown (San Juan del Norte, Nicaragua), but was arrested by the commander of an American warship and brought back to the United States once again.

In the summer of 1860, he led a small force to Honduras, was arrested by the British, and, after a trial, was executed by shooting.

Sketchy evidence tends to indicate that Martin Koszta, a resident of Texas in 1857 when lively recruiting for Walker was in progress in that state, might have decided to seek new adventure by joining filibuster groups. Walker's war of "liberation" might have appeared to him in colors not unlike those of the Hungarian revolution in 1848–49. At pro-Walker demonstrations in Texas, the enterprise was probably described in slogans difficult for a temperamental Hungarian ex-fighter for liberty to resist. An unsuccessful marriage, if such was his to the former Chicago widow, could have served as additional incentive for him to seek yet another "new life."

According to a participant and eventual chronicler of Walker's

229

DARING DIPLOMACY

undertakings, C. W. Doubleday, a certain Colonel Lockridge of
Texas was "master of transportation for recruits in Walker's army
and commanding officer of the company of men whom he was
conducting to Nicaragua for Walker's service" [113] in 1857. He adds
that the transport for that particular project was comprised of an
all-Texan group, and that many members of the group were exiles
then living in Texas. He mentions in passing that a friend of his,
"Colonel Anderson, and I, embarked on board the schooner *Susan*
which had already received about a hundred and fifty emigrants."

European exiles in America constituted a large reservoir of
highly valuable fighting men, endowed as they were with rich
military experience acquired in the mid-century revolutions in
Europe. Many of them were still unsettled in the New World
during the late 1850s, roaming especially around southern ports
in search of opportunities to go to seething Central America where
they could work at the one trade which they still knew well and
which required no knowledge of languages, namely, soldiering.
Doubleday says about the exile volunteers that they were "mostly
of the class found about the wharves of Southern cities, with here
and there a Northern bank cashier who had suddenly changed his
vocation. These men were a study, and presented indefinite phases
of character and diversities of education and profession."

The reference to a "Northern bank cashier" accelerates the
investigator's pulse beat. Was it a random reference to describe
one of many types? Or did it stem consciously or otherwise from
Doubleday's acquaintance with a former employee of Swift's Bank
at Chicago, one named Martin Koszta?

A Major W. C. Capers, who acted at the time as "official commissioner of the republic of Nicaragua for the state of Texas,
authorized to solicit funds and raise volunteers for the army of
General Walker," raised in the San Antonio area alone, where
the Koszta farm was located, a unit of more than one hundred
men.[114]

Source material recently located in private American-Hungarian
collections shows that numerous Hungarian exiles joined or at
least planned to join one or another filibuster enterprise, Walker's

230

in particular, in 1854–57. The most prominent among them was General Asbóth, eventual American minister to Argentina, an old acquaintance of Martin Koszta as mentioned earlier. He wrote several of his friends in 1857 that he was planning "to join an expedition about to leave for Nicaragua"[107] — at a time when Walker's last transports to that country were being organized, and when the Koszta farm in Texas suddenly was abandoned.

Walker's last forcible return to the United States took place, as mentioned, in the fall of 1857. It is known that many of his men remained behind, and that some of them decided to participate, as long as they were already in the Central American revolution belt, in some of the uprisings then either in preparation or in progress in Guatemala, Honduras, and Costa Rica. Koszta, if among them, could have gone from Nicaragua to Guatemala and somehow died there amid the "dire circumstances" cited in the Transylvanian newspaper report. With weapon in hand, he might have given his life for a cause possibly as inspiring in his eyes as Kossuth's, and preserved today by no more than a footnote or two in some books on antiquarian bookshelves.

But another noteworthy fragment also beckons.

During the same period, a Hungarian named János Horváth who had served as a corporal under Captain Koszta in 1849 was rising to considerable prominence in Guatemala.

This man could not go into Turkish exile, as Koszta and so many others did, after the collapse of the Kossuth revolution. He was among those who, taken prisoner by the Austrians, were sentenced to forced service of three to ten years in one of the specially supervised regiments of the emperor. He escaped after two years of service, reached France, came to the United States working on a ship as a hand in the engine room, settled down in New York, learned English quickly, and became a member of a Hungarian group there which established the first American newspaper in the Hungarian language. In 1855, Central American revolutionaries in New York, followers of Justo Rufino Barros, eventual president of Guatemala, persuaded him to go to Guatemala with them. He soon turned up as one of the leaders of

Guatemalan volunteers fighting against William Walker's filibuster battalions in Nicaragua. After Walker's surrender to American naval authorities in the summer of 1857, Horváth returned to Guatemala and became a newspaper editor in Guatemala City. Not long thereafter, Koszta disappeared from Texas, and, as reported, he died in Guatemala in the following year — when Horváth and his associates precipitated the first of a series of revolts against that country's regime.*

Were the two men in contact? Did former Captain Koszta go to Guatemala at the invitation of his one-time corporal?

Civil records in Guatemala were not kept until 1877; no grave marked with Koszta's name has been located in the cemeteries of the country's largest cities; no trace of his activities has been found in civil or military records of any of the Central American countries where he might have been active until his death in Guatemala.

An apt motto for this last passage of Koszta's life story could well be the poetic Italian proverb *Se non è vero, è ben trovato* ("It may not be true, but it makes a good story"). Mystery surrounds the end of his life; but his memory is preserved to this day in unique fashion within the country of his adoption whose flag had saved his life at Smyrna.

There is, in the state of Iowa, a township named Koszta. Before the incident at Smyrna, it was called Hoosier Grove, serving as an overnight stop on a stagecoach line between Iowa City and Marshalltown. It was renamed to honor the rescued Hungarian; it had its own post office as Koszta, Iowa, until the early years of the present century, and at one time boasted of five hostels, one of which is still standing as a farmhouse. Its decline began when both the Chicago Northwestern and the Rock Island railroads passed it by — and at present its population numbers a mere three score.

No one among the good people of Koszta, Iowa, knows anything about the man who, in the words of old Kuné, "came near being

* Horváth became special Guatemalan envoy to Washington in 1865 and spent most of his time during the next seven years in the American capital. Emerson and Mark Twain knew him well and repeatedly invited him to their homes. On one of his periodic returns to Guatemala City for consultation with the cabinet, he was assassinated by an old personal enemy.[115]

the *Casus Belli* between the United States and the Austrian Emperor . . ."

Before long, the township, like the forgotten man whose name it bears, will no doubt pass from original obscurity into final oblivion.

Sources and References

↲ SOURCES AND REFERENCES

THE official correspondence relating to the Koszta case is in the following State Department collections: (1) *Manuscript Instructions*; (2) *Manuscript Despatches to Consuls*, under the names of individual countries; and (3) *Manuscript Domestic Letters*, under the names of individual senders and recipients. Records of relevant congressional debates are in *House Executive Documents* and *Senate Executive Documents*, Thirty-Third Congress, First Session. Austrian diplomatic correspondence and formerly secret reports cited are in the *Haus-, Hof- und Staatsarchiv* at Vienna under *Vereinigten Staaten*.

The following sources will be found useful by those interested in details of international legal ramifications of the case, miscellaneous arguments against Secretary Marcy's position on grounds of his confusion about some of the implications, various misconceptions which arose from the executive action because of statements taken out of context, and, generally, theories and practices concerning expatriation and domicile: W. E. Hall, *International Law* (1909), pp. 238–41; J. B. Moore, *The Principles of American Diplomacy* (1918), pp. 300–1, and by the same author, *A Digest of International Law* (1906), III, 835–45; C. H. Hyde, *International Law* (1945), II, 1064–1184; S. F. Bemis (ed.), *The American Secretaries of State and their Diplomacy* (1928), VI, 268–73; E. M. Borchard, *The Diplomatic Protection of Citizens Abroad* (1915), secs. 250–51.

Individual documents and miscellaneous published or unpublished sources used are identified below.

[1] Speech by Victor Hugo at a mass meeting in Paris; *Examiner*, London, August 25, 1849.

[2] William Morris, *A Dream of John Ball* (N.Y., 1899), p. 122.

[3] Giuseppe Mazzini, *Scritti* (Writings) (1864), IV, 351.

[4] Matthew Arnold, *Sonnet to the Hungarian Nation* (1849).

[5] Sándor Petőfi, *Nemzeti Dal* (National Song) (1848).

[6] James Truslow Adams, *The Epic of America* (Boston, 1931), p. 243.

[7] Manifesto of Nicholas I of Russia, April 27, 1849; *The Annual Register* (London, 1850), pp. 333–34.

[8] Abraham Lincoln, *Complete Works* (Gettysburg ed.), II, 127–28.

[9] *Congressional Globe*, January 8, 1849.

237

DARING DIPLOMACY

[10] President Zachary Taylor, *First Annual Message to Congress* (December 4, 1849).

[11] *Kossuth in New England* (Boston, 1852), p. 144.

[12] *Nuova Antologia (New Anthology)* (Rome, December 1923).

[13] G. T. Curtis, *Life of Daniel Webster* (N.Y., 1870), II, 558.

[14] J. B. Siebmacher, *Wappenbuch des Adels von Ungarn* (Book of Heraldry of Hungarian Nobles) (Nürnberg, 1887), IV, 15.

[15] John Bassett Moore, *A Digest of International Law* (Washington, D.C., 1906), II, 560–61.

[16] Imre Áldor, *Vázlatok a magyar emigratio életéből* (Sketches from the Life of the Hungarian Emigration) (Budapest, 1870).

[17] Ferenc Szőllősy, *Kossuth és a magyar emigráció török földön* (Kossuth and the Hungarian Emigration on Turkish Soil) (Leipzig, 1870), p. 78.

[18] *American Historical Review*, XVI, 787.

[19] B. A. Gould, *Investigations in the Military and Anthropological Statistics of American Soldiers* (N.Y., 1869), p. 27.

[20] *Számüzöttek Lapja* (Exile Journal) (New York, October 15, 1853).

[21] Secretary of State Buchanan to Mr. Campbell, July 26, 1848.

[22] Secretary of State Buchanan to Mr. Huren, August 20, 1846.

[23] Secretary of State Everett to Mr. Ingersoll, December 21, 1852.

[24] *Fatti e Documenti* (Facts and Documents), pamphlet issued by Italian exiles at Smyrna in 1853 (copy in my collection).

[25] *Giornale di Smirne* (Smyrna Journal), June 24, 1853.

[26] Mr. Stiles to Secretary of State Buchanan, October 14, 1847.

[27] *American Journal of International Law*, October 1907, p. 897.

[28] Atkinson & Company, Boston, to the Department of State, September 6, 1850; State Department Personnel Files, "Offley, 1850," National Archives.

[29] G. W. Wood to Rev. Anderson, Smyrna, December 26, 1850; State Department Personnel Files, "Offley, 1850," National Archives.

[30] Mr. Offley to Secretary of State Webster, February 14, 1852.

[31] F. C. Bradlee, *A Forgotten Chapter in Our Naval History* (Salem, Mass., 1923), pamphlet (transcript in my collection).

[32] Letter (undated) by Commander Ingraham to his family, in the collection of the late Mrs. George Ingraham Hutchinson, Charleston, S.C.

[33] W. H. Parker, *Recollections of a Naval Officer* (N.Y., 1883), p. 293.

[34] *Giornale di Smirne* (Smyrna Journal), June 23, 1853.

[35] Diary of Passed Midshipman Ralph Chandler; *U.S. Naval Institute Proceedings*, Vol. 53, No. 289.

[36] Mr. Virágh to Mr. Griffith, Smyrna, June 23, 1853, quoted in *I Peripétia Tou Kosta* (The Adventure of Kosta), pamphlet issued by Greek exiles at Smyrna in 1853 (copy in my collection).

[37] *New York Weekly Tribune*, December 17, 1853, p. 1, cols. 5–6.

[38] *I peripétia Tou Kosta.*

[39] *Magazine of History* (New York, December 1941).

[40] F. W. Newman, *Select Speeches of Kossuth* (N.Y., 1854).

[41] House Ex. Doc. 1, 33rd Cong., 1st Sess.

[42] *Der Grosse Brockhaus* encyclopedia (Leipzig, 1929), III, 393.

[43] *Dictionary of American Biography* (N.Y., 1929), III, 139.

[44] *Dictionary of American Biography* (N.Y., 1933), XII, 297–98.

[45] Secretary of State Webster to Mr. Hülsemann, December 21, 1850.

[46] L. P. Lovett, *Naval Customs, Traditions and Usage* (Washington, D.C., 1943), pp. 347–49.

238

Sources and References

[47] C. O. Paullin, *Diplomatic Negotiations of American Naval Officers, 1778–1883* (Baltimore, Md., 1912), pp. 7–8.

[48] *L'Impartial*, Smyrna, July 8, 1853.

[49] Diary of Passed Midshipman Richard Worsam Meade; *U.S. Naval Institute Proceedings*, Vol. 53, No. 289.

[50] M. E. Curti, *Austria and the United States, 1848–52* (Smith College Studies of History, 1926, Vol. IX, No. 3), p. 142.

[51] Letter by W. H. Seward, 1849 (no specific date); C. R. Fish, *The Rise of the Common Man* (N.Y., 1927), p. 74.

[52] Quoted in *New York Weekly Tribune*, September 20, 1849.

[53] Mr. Mann to Secretary of State Clayton, Paris, October 11, 1849.

[54] Mr. Hülsemann to Secretary of State Webster, October 1, 1850.

[55] Secretary of State Webster to Mr. Hülsemann, December 21, 1850.

[56] *Senate Journal*, 31st Cong., 1st Sess., pp. 260–61.

[57] *House Misc. Docs.*, 31st Cong., 1st Sess., No. 39.

[58] *Senate Misc. Docs.*, 31st Cong., 1st Sess., No. 35.

[59] *Senate Journal*, 31st Cong., 1st Sess., pp. 59–64.

[60] Justin McCarthy, *A History of Our Own Times* (London, 1879), II, 110.

[61] Common Council of New York, *Report of the Special Committee* (N.Y., 1852), p. 574.

[62] *Senate Ex. Doc. 9*, 31st Cong., 2nd Sess., pp. 7–8.

[63] Daniel Webster, *Writings and Speeches* (Boston, 1903), XVI, 586.

[64] Mr. Buchanan to Mr. Johnson, May 3, 1853, in *Buchanan's Works*, VIII, 508.

[65] E. L. Pierce, *Memoirs and Letters of Charles Sumner* (Boston, 1877–93), III, 334.

[66] Secretary of State Marcy to Mr. Whetmore, August 17, 1853.

[67] G. T. Curtis, *The Life of James Buchanan* (N.Y., 1883), II, 80.

[68] E. Plischke, *Conduct of American Diplomacy* (N.Y., 1950), p. 91.

[69] *Century Magazine*, Vol. 35 (1898–99), p. 604.

[70] *Littel's Living Age*, October–December, 1853.

[71] *New York Weekly Tribune*, September 10, 1853.

[72] *New York Weekly Tribune*, October 8, 1853.

[73] Williams v. Fears, 179 U.S. 270, 274.

[74] U.S. Court of Appeals for the District of Columbia Circuit, No. 12406, Schachtman v. Dulles, June 23, 1955.

[75] Rep. Gilbert Dean (N.Y.); *Congressional Globe*, 33rd Cong. 1st Sess., Vol. XXVIII.

[76] Letter to me from the secretary of the commonwealth of Massachusetts, Boston, January 23, 1942.

[77] Sir Edward Coke, *The First Part of the Institute of the Laws of England, Or, A Commentary upon Littleton* (London, 1832), I, 129-a, 25-b.

[78] Sir William Blackstone, *Commentaries on the Laws of England* (Philadelphia, 1893), I, Secs. 369–70.

[79] James Truslow Adams, *The American* (N.Y., 1943), pp. 306–7.

[80] J. S. Hittell, *A History of the City of San Francisco* (San Francisco, 1878), pp. 185–88.

[81] *Report for 1909 of the Commissioner General of Immigration* (Washington, D.C., 1910), 112.

[82] R. W. Flournoy, Jr., "Naturalization and Expatriation," *Yale Law Journal*, XXXI, No. 7, May 1922, p. 708.

[83] Mr. Brent to Mr. Graff, June 7, 1823, *MS Notes to For. Leg.*, III, 137.

[84] Secretary of State Clay to Mr. Gallatin, June 19, 1826.

DARING DIPLOMACY

[85] Mr. Barnard to Secretary of State Marcy, September 13, 1853.
[86] Secretary of State Marcy to Mr. D'Oench, November 16, 1853.
[87] Mr. Tousig to Mr. Jackson, November 26, 1853.
[88] Mr. Jackson to Foreign Minister Count Buol-Schauenstein, December 4, 1853.
[89] Mr. Jackson to Secretary of State Marcy, December 3, 1853.
[90] Secretary of State Marcy to Mr. Jackson, January 10, 1854.
[91] Undated note in Ingraham's handwriting, in the collection of the late Mrs. George Ingraham Hutchinson, Charleston, S.C.
[92] Secretary of State Marcy to Mr. Jackson, September 14, 1854.
[93] Secretary of State Marcy to Baron de Kalb, July 20, 1855.
[94] Secretary of State Marcy to Mr. Vroom, July 7, 1854.
[95] Secretary of State Cass to Lord Napier, April 10, 1857.
[96] Secretary of State Cass to Mr. Fay, November 12, 1860.
[97] Assistant Secretary of State Davis to Mr. Fox, May 12, 1869.
[98] *Congressional Globe*, 40th Cong., 2nd Sess., I, 1867–68.
[99] 33 Vict. Ch. 14.
[100] U.S. For. Rel., 1881, p. 758.
[101] Secretary of State Olney to Mr. Denby, January 15, 1897.
[102] *U.S. Rpts.*, Vol. 135, p. 64.
[103] John Bassett Moore, *A Digest of International Law* (Washington, D.C., 1906), III, 813.
[104] Price v. Price, 156 Pa. St. 617, 27 Atl. 291; Cooper v. Beers, 43 Ill. 25, 33 N.E. 61; Cobb v. Rice, 130 Mass. 231; Reed's appeal, 71 Pa. St. 378; Cruger v. Phelps, 47 N.Y.S. 61, 21 Misc. 252.
[105] Somerville v. Somerville, 5 Vesey 787.
[106] A. Berzeviczy, *Az absolutizmus kora Magyarországon* (The Age of Absolutism in Hungary) (Budapest, 1921), I, 297, 412–19; II, 312–20.
[107] G. Kende, *Magyarok Amerikában* (Hungarians in America) (Cleveland, 1927), I, 127, 241–42, 355.
[108] A. Ipolyi, *A Magyar Szent Korona és a koronázási jelvények története és müleirása* (History and Technical Description of the Hungarian Holy Crown and of the Coronation Insignia) (Budapest, 1886).
[109] H. Schlitter, *Kempen's Denkschrift über d. Auffindung der Stephans-Krone* (Kempen's Memorandum and the Discovery of Stephen's Crown) (Vienna, 1919).
[110] K. Tábori, *Titkosrendőrség és Kamarilla; akták és adatok a bécsi titkos udvari és rendőrségi levéltárból* (Secret Police and Camarilla; Documents and Data from the Secret Archives of the Viennese Court and Police) (Budapest, 1921), pp. 148–71.
[111] Julius Kuné, *Reminiscences of an Octogenarian Hungarian Exile* (Chicago, 1911).
[112] *Kolozsvári Közlöny* (Kolozsvár Gazette) (Kolozsvár, Hungary, 1858), No. 56.
[113] C. W. Doubleday, *Reminiscences of the "Filibuster" War in Nicaragua* (N.Y., 1886), pp. 177–201.
[114] E. W. Fornell, "Texans and Filibusters in the 1850's," *Southwestern Historical Quarterly*, LIX, No. 4, April 1956, pp. 418–19.
[115] E. Figueroa, *El Redactor de la Revolución* (The Editor of the Revolution) (Santiago, Chile, 1932), a biography of Horváth.

Index

✓ INDEX

DARING DIPLOMACY

Dean, Gilbert, 173

"Declaration of intention" documents: consular attitude toward, 32, 79, 83; Turkish attitude toward, 32–33; *1795* and *1802* laws on, 163; Clay and, 165–66; not passports, 183–85; act of *1907*, 193–94. *See also* "First paper," Naturalization, Passports, Protection

Diplomatic protection, *see* Protection

Dobbin, James C., approval of Ingraham's action, 122

D'Oench, Henry, 168–69

Doubleday, C. W., 230

Emancipation Proclamation for Adopted Americans, 190

Engels, Friedrich, 9, 118n

England, 11, 158: attitude toward Hungarian exiles, 22–23, 70; anti-Austrian feeling in, 23–24; principle of allegiance to the Crown, 160–61; naturalization under, 161–62, 191

English language, Magyar difficulty with, 30–31

Everett, Edward, on "first papers," 34–35

Expatriation, 134, 160–61, 189, 190–91. *See also* Naturalization

Farkas, Sándor Bölöni, 14

Figyelmessy, Colonel Philip, 210

Filibuster, 228

Filipucci (kidnapper of Koszta), 39

Fillmore, Millard, 111, 114

"First paper": of Koszta, 27, 32, 35, 45–46, 59, 76, 79, 134; confusion about status of persons with, 34–35, 165–68; official attitude toward, 59–60, 135; D'Oench case, 168–69; Tousig case, 169–72; not passport, 183–84; Burnato case, 191–92; ceases to exist, 211. *See also* "Declaration of intention" documents, Naturalization, Passports, Protection

Foote, Henry Stuart, 16

"Forty-Eighter," 29–30n

France, 11: attitude toward Hungarian exiles, 22, 78

Francis Joseph I, of Austria, 15, 18n, 200, 201, 209, 220n

Franklin, Benjamin, 31n

Fumagalli (Italian exile), 47, 77

Gallatin, Albert, 12, 165

Genna (exile in Smyrna), 77

Gottra (Italian exile), 47

Grillparzer, Franz, 17

Grimm, Rudolf, 202, 203

Hackelberg, Baron, 66, 69, 70, 74–75

Haraszthy, Ágoston, 29n

Haynau, Baron Julius, 23–24

Házmán, Ferenc, 202, 203

Holy Crown of Hungary, 198–206

Horthy, Miklós, 220n

Horváth, János, 231–32

Hugo, Victor, quoted, 10

Hülsemann, Chevalier Johann Georg von: and Daniel Webster, 18–19, 113–15; background of, 110–11; and Austrian protest, 130, 132–39

Hungary: relations with United States, 12–15, 16–17, 18, 111–13; Revolution of *1848–49*, 13–18; "Declaration of Independence," 15; Doctrine of the Holy Crown, 199; Compromise of *1867*, 200

Hunter, William, 131

Hussar, 36, 94

Ihász, Dániel, 22, 26, 208

In Re Neagle, 194

Ingraham, Duncan Nathaniel, 19, 74: background of, 49–51; and Offley, 55, 61–62; takes action, 60–61, 81, 89, 94–99; on Koszta, 68; and the ultimatum, 91–92; right to act, 136–37, 196; in Egypt, 155–56; congressional recognition, 173–82; after *1853*, 215–19

Ipolyi, Bishop Arnold, 203

Iredell, James, on expatriation, 160

Islam, embraced by Hungarian exiles, 24–25

Jackson, Henry Rootes, 170–71

Jones, John Paul, 31n, 90

Jovicich (kidnapper of Koszta), 35–36, 39, 77

Kempen, General, 204–6

Klapka, General György, 108n

Kmety, General (Kiamil Pasha), 25

Konduriotis (exile in Smyrna), 77

Kossuth, Lajos: in United States, 14–15, 26, 112–13; on liberty, 16; in exile, 18, 19, 24, 206; and Napoleon III,

244